THE

CLASSIC GUIDE TO
FLY ⸱ FISHING

FOR TROUT

THE
CLASSIC GUIDE TO
FLY-FISHING

FOR TROUT

CHARLES JARDINE

PHOTOGRAPHS BY PETER GATHERCOLE

RANDOM HOUSE

NEW YORK

CONTENTS

A DORLING KINDERSLEY BOOK

Project Editor Corinne Hall
Designer Michael Wood
Managing Editor Carolyn King
Managing Art Editor Nick Harris

Originally published in Great Britain
by Dorling Kindersley Limited, London
in 1991

Library of Congress Cataloging-in-
Publication Data

Jardine, Charles,
The classic guide to fly-fishing for trout:
the fly-fisher's book of quarry, tackle, and
techniques / by Charles Jardine;
photographs by Peter Gathercole.
p. cm.
Includes bibliographical references and
index.

ISBN 0-394-58719-7 : $35.00
1. Fly-fishing. 2. Trout fishing. I.
Gathercole, Peter.
II Title.
SH456.J37 1991
799.1'755--dc20

Originated by Toppan, Singapore
Printed by Mondadori, Italy

24689753 23456789 98765432
First US Edition

CONTENTS

Fishing Fresco
From Santorini, this Minoean
fresco (above) *dates back to*
the second millenium BC.

FLY-FISHING: AN INTRODUCTION

HIS BOOK IS DEDICATED primarily to the newcomer, but I hope that the seasoned fly-fisher will find the occasional fly pattern or piece of advice advantageous. Before plunging into the plethora of fly-fishing minutiae, "Fly-Fishing: An Introduction" explains something of the origins of the sport, demonstrating how little has changed from original concepts or function over the years. Following on from this, "The Quarry" analyzes the physiology of the trout and its diet. The process by which it sees, its habitat, and its lifestyle - all dramatically affect the fly-fisher's approach with a rod. Considerate fly-fishing can help protect and conserve both the trout and natural resources from damage.

"Equipment" introduces the newcomer to the bewildering array of fly-fishing tackle and accessories that cater to specific fly-fishing requirements. You can also economize in certain areas. Fly boxes are a prime example of this. They range from the foam-lined tobacco tin and the simple plastic box through to the aluminum spring-lid compartment. Each one fulfils an identical role - that is, to keep flies dry, accessible, and in reasonable order.

Keeping dry and warm, especially when fishing in such places as Alaska or Finland, is obviously important, so it is wise to be familiar with the types of clothing available. Mobility when casting is essential, so bear this in mind when selecting fly-fishing clothing. Casting is the single most important (and sometimes most difficult to learn) action in fly-fishing. Read "Casting Techniques" and take two or three hours' professional instruction and you will short-circuit weeks or even months of frustration as a beginner.

The crowning glory for any fly-fishing strategem is, however, the artificial fly patterns you choose. In "The Fly," I have categorized these according to the types of water on which they are designed to be fished. Each category describes the heavy nymph fished on the river bed, moving through to the adult fly fished on the surface. Next, "Waters and Tactics" outlines specific fly-fishing procedures, followed by "The Catch," a series of expeditions fishing for particular types of trout. "Fly-Tying" introduces the beginner to the fundamentals of tying flies, and is then complemented by the "Directory of Fly Dressings," which gives each fly's component parts.

The Classic Guide to Fly-Fishing for Trout is an introduction to a challenging and rewarding sport. May it give you as many happy hours (and as many trout) as it has given me.

THE SPORT OF FLY-FISHING is much more than just a method of enticing fish from the water. There are easier and more efficient ways of doing that with nets, traps, and electric currents, though none perhaps so intriguing as the sacred fish ceremony of Lake Masomo, a small lake on the Fijian island of Vanua Mbalavu. Ritual dictates that one hundred islanders, naked but for a liberal coating of oil, swim together for a night, whereupon the fish will give themselves up to the swimmers in the morning. And they do. There is, however, a more prosaic explanation: the commotion stirs the stagnant bottom mud and the half-asphyxiated fish wallow to the surface.

Tunisian Fishermen
The Roman mosaic (above)
*from Utica, Tunisia, dates
back to the fourth century.*

Peace Standard
Detail (above) *showing the standard carried by the Ur peace side, 2500 B.C.*

Fyshynge Wyth an Angle
Detail (above) *from the 1496 edition of Dame Juliana Berner's* Treatise of Fyshynge Wyth an Angle.

IT IS FUTILE TO ASK when man first fished, but he has always been an angler. The gorge was the forerunner of the hook. Hidden inside a bait, it is swallowed and lodges inside the fish, which is then hauled ashore. A gorge dating back at least 7000 years has been found in France, a country familiar with such ingenious fishing methods. Fish-hooks have been unearthed from the 5000-year-old city of Ur, located on a former channel of the Euphrates. Fishing rods are depicted in an Egyptian wall painting dating from around 2000 BC.

The Chinese were among the first to value the sporting nature of angling. They had been uniquely blessed with materials: the Tonkin cane, the silk line, and gut of fly-fishing's most artistic period were all native to China. In the Chou dynasty, around 400 BC, angling with rod and line was a contemplative pastime. The philosopher Chiang Tzu-Ya carried the sporting ethic so far as to dispense with a hook altogether, but this was something of a blind-alley in fishing technique. Such esoteric refinement was not a Roman trait and it is a Roman author who gives us the first glimpse we have of fishing for trout with a fly. The first unequivocal description of fly-fishing is also the first appearance of trout in angling literature. This is hardly a coincidence, since a trout rising to take a surface fly in crystal water is perhaps the easiest of fish to watch feeding. It would be more surprising if such consummate craftsmen as the Greeks had not i nitated those flies in feather, fur, and wool.

Assyrian Fishermen
Detail (above) *from a frieze housed originally in the Sennacherib's Palace, Assyria, showing fishermen and their esteemed booty.*

IN HIS BOOK *De Animalium Natura*, Claudius Aelianus described the process of fly-fishing early in the third century: "The fishermen wind red wool around their hooks and fasten to the wool two feathers that grow under a cock's wattles and which are the colour of dark wax." It is not clear whether the hackles Aelianus mentions were tied as wings or, palmer-style, down the body. Either method would serve its purpose on those "fish with speckled skins." The river was in Macedonia, between "Beroea [now Stara Zagora] and Thessalonika." There are still hill trout to be caught in the Rhodopi Mountains of southern Bulgaria.

Trout are first named in the fourth century, in the poem Ausonius wrote to his beloved River Moselle. They can still be found in the upper Moselle as it tumbles off the Vosges Mountains of northeastern France, or in tributaries such as the Kyll in the Eifel hills of Germany.

Antique Vise and Wallet
The vise (above), *dating back to 1870, is one of the earliest of its kind, and probably American. Its base is lead-filled for stability. The mayflies in the fly wallet* (above) *are cut to shape from dyed mallard feathers, and date from the same period.*

French-Reed Creel
A woven creel (above) *was, and still is, the best way of keeping the catch fresh on a bed of damp grass. This example, dating from the late 1800s, has an inch-scale along the hinge.*

An Angler's Morning
An evocative, pastoral fly-fishing scene (above).

A THOUSAND YEARS PASSED, however, before fly-fishing surfaced from the silence of the Dark Ages. In 1496, it emerges as a fully fledged sport, "fysshynge wyth an angle," from the somewhat unlikely pen of the abbess of Sopwell Priory near St Albans in Hertfordshire. A devout nun, Dame Juliana Berners shows a remarkable knowledge of all aspects of the sport. She gives the recipes for a dozen artificial flies to match the important hatches through the season. One of her dressings specifies the same "roddy wol" and "redde capons hakyll" as Aelianus' Macedonians. Dame Juliana's priory lay on the small River Ver which runs between the chalk stream rivers Gade and Lea. One hundred and fifty years later, it was to be fished by the most famous angler of them all, Izaak Walton. His book *The Compleat Angler* is, without doubt, the best-known and best-loved work in the rich literature of angling. The title is apt: Aelianus described fly-fishing as an observer; Dame Juliana provided a wealth of practical details and advice on the art of angling; but it is Walton who breathes life and soul into the sport. His reflective philosophy beguiles the reader into an enchanting flashback to idyllic pastoral England.

Antique Fly Box
Wooden drawers (above) *from a cabinet containing antique fly dressings and tying implements.*

IN TRUTH, THERE WAS little new in Walton's practical details of tackle and tactics. Rods had not changed significantly from Dame Juliana's fifteen-foot weapons. The artificial flies he recommends in the early editions are identical, but then much of Walton's fishing had been on the lower River Lea, where a minnow or a worm was a surer way to catch trout.

Walton was fifty when he left London in 1642 for Staffordshire. Over the following ten years, *The Compleat Angler* was written. On the clear limestone streams of the nearby Derbyshire Dales he was to find a different stamp of trout and a different breed of angler. The trout of the spring-fed River Dove rise freely to the aquatic flies of that stream. Fly-fishing on these waters was already well-developed, with an abundance of local flies and lore accompanying it.

It was here that Izaak Walton met Charles Cotton. A high-living scion of landed gentry, Cotton was cultured, well-educated, dissipated, and a first-rate fly-fisherman. He and Walton became firm fishing friends. The celebrated stone fishing lodge that Cotton built in 1674 beside the River Dove bears their interlocking initials on the keystone of the doorway.

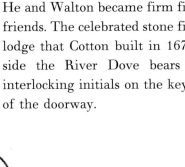

Folding Net
The net (above) is made from waxed cord. Its handle is mottled cane with a brass cap.

English Rod
Late eighteenth-century ash rod (above left) with brass winch.

Antique Fly Reels
The winch (left) from around 1765, has a bone handle. A ratchet system (left) offers some resistance to running fish. The brass winch (above) clamps around the rod handle.

Scottish Loch
Loch Leven
(right) *is home
of competitive fly-
fishing and the
silvery trout
named after it.*

Brook Fly Rod
*A two-piece Green-
heart rod* (below)
*with bone-handled
reel, circa 1830. The
line is plaited flax.*

T HE FIFTH EDITION of *The
Compleat Angler*, published
in 1676, included a new section,
"Instructions How to Angle for
Trout or Grayling in a Clear
Stream." It contained practical
advice on fly-fishing and fly-dress-
ing, and it gave details of wing construction, dubbing a
fur body and no less than 65 patterns of artificial flies
used on the local waters. The author was Charles Cotton,
the father of modern fly-fishing.

The literature of tactics was accompanied by significant changes in fly-fishing tackle. Claudius Aelianus's
Macedonian fly-fisherman used a 2m. (6ft.) rod with a

similar length of plaited horse-
hair on the end. The farthest he
could have cast his Red Spinner or
Palmer was 4m. (12ft). There is,
however, an advantage in a long
rod as the longer the rod, the further the fly can be cast. But weight
increases with length. By the end

Reels and Winches
*Early reels were simple
winches designed to
hold a reservoir of line.
Line was often made
of braided horse-hair.
Plutarch recommended
stallion's hair.*

of the fifteenth century, Dame Juliana was recommend-
ing a 5m. (15ft.) rod with   a butt of "hasyll,
wyllowe or ashe" and   a tip of blackthorn.

Blue Dun
The Blue Dun
(above) *is a
traditional
dry-fly pattern.*

LONGER RODS OF UP to 6m. (20ft.) were only made possible by the use of exotic woods such as lancewood and greenheart from the forests of Guyana. The arrival of split cane revolutionized rod-making. The technique was probably attempted first in London but it was American rod-builders of the second half of the nineteenth century who perfected the construction. This new material was ideal but expensive, and at first used only for tip sections where its properties were most cost effective. It was the invention of reels and line guides or rings that reduced the need for great length in rods. The lightness and power of split cane, combined with the nineteenth-century vogue for the dry fly, led to the creation of the two-piece, 2.5 or 3m. (8 or 9ft.) trout rod which weighed ounces rather than pounds. It is still with us today. The rod changed very little indeed until the last century, but the line changed even less: a tapered line of braided horse-hair was still in use.

Freestone Fishing
The River Wharfe (above) in North Yorkshire in England is home to both wild brown trout and grayling.

Duck Feather
Carolina lemon wood duck feathers (left) were once used in a variety of fly patterns, but are rarely tied today.

Put-and-Take Fishery
Stocked to meet a growing number of fly-fishers, the Cottington Fishery (right) in Kent, England, operates a successful Catch-and Release policy.

A NGLERS THEN, AS NOW, would boast of their ability to land large fish on fine lines. Silkworm gut was widely used for leaders in the nineteenth century. Lines of braided cotton and linen were used from mid-nineteenth century, as were lines of braided horse-hair and silk. The polished silk line was available towards the end of the century. The reel is a relative newcomer to fly-fishing. Cotton tied his line to the rod tip despite the fact that reels had been used for decades.

Gradually, tiny reels were to adorn the shafts of the most unwieldy rods. These were winches without any form of drag or check, simply a revolving drum holding

Irish Lough
A typical Irish scene (above) with a brew, boat, and a wild brown trout.

a reservoir of line. But the reel that released the fly-fisherman from the tyranny of long rods. Brook rods under 2.1m. (7ft.) in length were available in the first half of the nine-teenth century. Lighter rods demanded sophisti-cated reels. Tackle is still evolving in the quest for the ultimate equipment for all fly-fishing contingencies.

Peacock Quill
The quill (above) is used for dry-fly bodies and for wet flies such as the Alexandra.

Sawyer's Grey Goose
This nymph (above) was one of the first patterns to be weighted.

THE QUARRY

TROUT ARE MEMBERS of the large family of salmonids. They share that distinctive badge of membership, the adipose fin (see pp.20-21). Salmonids are predators, slim-built for endurance and speed; their well-muscled bodies have made them highly regarded both for the table and for their hard-fighting and sporting qualities. Most of the salmonids, including the three major species of trout, have the unusual potential to live in both saltwater (ocean and estuary) and freshwater (rivers and lakes). They can migrate between these vastly differing habitats. This has allowed the salmonids to spread throughout the cooler waters of the Northern Hemisphere, where rivers have enabled spawning fish to find an appropriate habitat of oxygen-rich, cool freshwater flowing over a bed of loose stones and gravel. Here the hen-fish can excavate a shallow trench or "redd" in which to lay eggs. However, migrating between salt- and freshwater poses some severe biochemical problems: the trout's tissues are perpetually gaining water in the river, and then losing water in the sea. The advantages of such flexibility may be enormous: the mature trout can feed in the food-rich but dangerous ocean, while the vulnerable eggs and fry start life in the shallow waters of the headstreams; food may well be scarce, but so are the predators. This migratory habit is also problematic for the fish zoologist. Rivers and lakes can be colonized by trout from the sea. A change in climate, or even a minor rock fall, can isolate a population that then continues to live and breed in freshwater, evolving to suit that habitat. Within one population of trout there may be variation in both coloring and shape as a result of different diet and background. All this has led to a vast array of subspecies, varieties, and races.

THE SALMON FAMILY: EVOLUTION & DISTRIBUTION

Trout and salmon belong to the salmonids, one of the most primitive families of the Bony Fishes (teleosts) that first made an appearance during the Cretaceous period, around 100 million years ago. About 70 million years ago, as the dinosaurs were nearing the end of their 150-million-year reign of the land, the most distant of the trout's relations, the whitefish, branched off the family tree. The whitefish (coregonids) all bear the distinguishing flag of the salmonid family, the adipose fin. They are herringlike, with large, silver scales and small, pointed mouths.

FAMILY RESEMBLANCES
The grayling (*Thymallus* species) shares some of these features. The earliest trout-like fossil, Eosalmo (dawn-salmon), turned up in present-day British Columbia in Eocene rock laid down 40 million years ago.

Large-finned Grayling
Grayling (above) *are strikingly elegant.*

THE ICE AGE
The subsequent history of both these groups seems to have followed along similar lines. The coming of the Ice Age or Pleistocene era, around 2-3 million years ago, brought successive layers of ice across northern Europe, Asia and America.

Temperature change resulted in the emergence of predominantly marine forms (various Pacific salmon and the Atlantic salmon) and predominantly freshwater forms (the New World cut-throat, the rainbow trout and the European brown).

This shift in weather patterns brought cooler conditions to the lands of the south. North Africa, southern Asia and Central America were colonized through the cooler seas.

GLOBAL CHANGE
At the edge of the retreating ice, even the species that do not normally migrate to sea (like the grayling) were able to recolonize the northern rivers. In the south, populations that had colonized the cool highlands at the height of the glaciation were cut off by the warmth of the lower reaches of the rivers.

Other populations were trapped as glaciers diverted whole drainage systems. The trout of the southern fringes have evolved into a bewildering array of varieties and subspecies: the golden trout of California and Mexico, the brown trout varieties of the Aral and Caspian Seas, and of the Atlas Mountains in North Africa.

TELEOST •

WHITEFISH

GRAYLING

70 MILLION YEARS

HUCHEN

40 MILLION YEARS

CHARS

SALMO SPECIES

10 MILLION YEARS

ONCORHYNCHUS SPECIES

Rainbow Trout
The rainbow body (above) *is generally silvery with a pinkish zone along either side of the lateral line. Both body and fins are sprinkled with black spots.*

During the next 30 million years the salmonid family tree sprouted three further side branches. The first two produced the *Brachystymax* and *Hucho* lines, which are now confined to the limitless rivers of Siberia with only one representative, the huchen, in European waters, where it fights a rear guard action in the polluted waters of the Danube basin. The third branch of the salmonid family, the chars *(Salvelinus* species*)*, have spread throughout the cooler waters of the northern hemisphere.

Approximately 10 million years ago, the shift of the continents isolated the Pacific Basin by throwing up a land bridge between America and Asia. The subsequent isolation contrived to split existing ancestral lines. The Old World salmon and trout (*Salmo* species) were separated from those of the New World (*Oncorhynchus* species).

Dolly Varden
A relative of the Arctic char (above).

Whitefish
The Coregonidae *family is a group of slender-bodied, herring-like fish with deeply forked tails and large mouths. Their small or non-existent teeth are suited to their diet of plank-tonic crustaceans and small, bottom-dwelling animals.*

Grayling
The grayling (Thymallus *species) shares some white-fish features; it diverged from the trout line some time during the next 30 million years. A grayling-like fossil,* Protothymallus, *was found in Miocene deposits in Germany.*

Huchen
The huchen is a large salmonid of the Danube basin. The back is a dark green and the coppery sides have the light spot-ting of many salmonids. It is longer and leaner than a typical trout and is a highly regarded game fish.

Char
The chars (Salvelinus *species), located in the northern hemisphere, are similar in appearance to the true trout species. The American brook trout* (S. fontinalis) *and American lake trout* (S. namaycush) *are two char species.*

Brown Trout
The brown trout (Salmo trutta) *developed as a result of the Ice Age temperature changes. Brown trout come in a variety of shapes and sizes. They can be silvery and fat with small black spots; small, thin and blackish in colour; or a distinctively spotted, heavyweight version.*

Rainbow Trout
Rainbows (Oncorhynchus mykiss) *are generally distinguished by numerous small, dark spots on the dorsal fin. These are not found in any other trout in Europe. The body is silvery with a pinkish zone along both sides of the lateral line. Body and fins are also spotted.*

WHITEFISH HABITAT
The typical whitefish habitat is large deep lakes throughout the northern hemisphere, but migratory forms can be found in rivers, brackish water and the sea. The lake popula-tions often show small variations from one lake to another that makes any classification a nightmare.

To add to the confusion, each of these local varieties is often given a local name. All whitefish, however, carry an adipose fin. Their lack of color, forked tail and small mouth distin-guish them from all but the grayling. The grayling is only rarely found in lakes. It sports an enormous and unmistakable dorsal fin, edged with brownish-red. Its small adipose fin is similar to that of the trout and salmon.

A CHANGE OF NAME
The proper classification and naming of both the rainbow trout and the cut-throat trout has recently been a subject of consider-able debate amongst zool-ogists worldwide.

The rainbow trout and the cutthroat were both included in the genus *Salmo* along with the brown trout (*Salmo trutta*) and the Atlantic salmon (*Salmo salar*).

However, it is now generally agreed that these trout of the New World are, in fact, more closely related to the various Pacific salmon (genus *Oncorhynchus*). This change of classification has meant that the rainbow trout is now designated *Oncorhynchus mykiss* and the cutthroat trout, *Oncorhynchus clarki*.

Irish Brown Trout
The Irish brown (above), scattered throughout western Ireland, is usually heavily spotted, but silvery and salmon-like.

THE TROUT'S ANATOMY

A BASIC UNDERSTANDING of the anatomy of the trout is invaluable to the fly-fisher. The trout is a predator, holding wriggling prey with its numerous small teeth. The victim is then swallowed whole and passes into the stomach. To allow for buoyancy adjustment the trout has an air-filled swim-bladder, which is connected to the outside by a narrow tube to the esophagus and the mouth. The trout is covered in skin. Small scales are embedded in the outermost layer of the skin (epidermis), which also contains glands that secrete mucus. The mucus maintains a smooth, slippery surface.

Color is provided by pigment cells (chromatophores) within the skin. There can be enormous color differences between individual trout, even those of the same species, inhabiting the same lake or stream. The trout has seven fins besides its tail. Stability is provided by the paired fins and by the dorsal and anal fins. Trout are built for rapid acceleration rather than sustained high speed. The broad tail provides great thrust over the first strokes.

Roof-of-the-Mouth Teeth
The teeth on the vomer bone located in the center of the trout's mouth are one of the distinguishing features for species and varieties of trout.

Gills
The trout's respiratory organs, well supplied with blood vessels.

Dorsal Fin
Maintains balance during locomotion.

Pectoral Fin
Both pectoral fins help to direct the fish during locomotion.

Pelvic Fin

MOUTH AND STOMACH
The teeth lining the jaw, the tongue, and the roof of the mouth are used for grasping rather than chewing, and prey are swallowed whole. The digestive juices, secreted from the muscular wall of the simple U-shaped stomach, then begin to break down the food. The semidigested food passes through a sphincter to the intestine. Numerous growths, called the pyloric caeca, increase the area of the intestine. These growths are distinguishing features. To help the fly-fisherman select the correct artificial, the recent meals of a trout can be examined by extracting food from the forward end of the stomach. This can be done without harming the fish, using a suction device or a marrow spoon (see p.68).

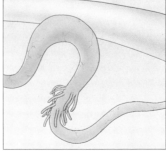

Pyloric Caeca
The pyloric caeca increase the intestinal digesting area.

SWIM-BLADDER
The swim-bladder inflates or deflates, allowing the trout to adjust rapidly to changes in salinity and depth. Salinity alters when the trout leaves the river for the sea; depth can change dramatically when, for example, the fish is hooked deep on a fast-sinking line. The position of the swim-bladder is rather awkward:

FINS

Many fish have a second dorsal fin. In salmonids this fin is reduced to a short stump known as the adipose fin. It is curious that it has been retained in all members of the family as it seems to have no function, and yet it must cause a small amount of disadvantageous drag. The trout uses the dorsal and anal fins to control turning and to swim straight. If they are removed, speed is unaffected but there is considerable rolling and pitching.

Adipose Fin
The posterior dorsal fin occurs in trout, salmon, and related species.

Anal Fin
A median ventral unpaired fin that helps maintain the trout's equilibrium.

the upward thrust of the buoyant bladder is centered just below the trout's center of gravity, threatening to flip the fish upside-down. This tendency is counteracted by making constant adjustments with the paired fins. In practice, this instability can be useful, since it allows the trout to perform a sudden "banking turn" and so make rapid maneuvers at speed.

PAIRED FINS

The paired fins of a trout constantly maintain the stability of the fish with small balancing movements. Without the paired fins, the fish would be unable to balance and would turn upside-down. These paired fins also act as brakes and, used singly, as rudders in turning and changing direction at speed. Young fry rest on the bottom using their pelvic fins as supports.

Caudal Fin
The caudal fin, or tail, is used for propulsion during locomotion.

TAIL FIN

From a standing start the thrust of the tail fin can produce, for an instant, a force six times that of gravity – hence the need to keep the rod tip up, allowing the bend to absorb this first shock. Once at cruising speed, the tail creates as much drag as thrust. For sustained speed, a tail the shape of a tuna's, or a swift's wing, is necessary.

SCALES

Newly hatched trout have no scales. Scales develop in fry, growing in proportion to the rest of the fish. The growth takes place around the edge of the scale, forming "growth rings" that record annual cycles of rapid growth and leaner periods of spawning. Light reflecting from minute guanine crystals in the scales gives the silvery effect. Although the crystals are arranged in different ways

Scale Structure
The "growth rings" on the scales are shown in the bird's-eye view (below).

Exposed part of scale   *Narrowly spaced rings*   *Widely spaced rings*

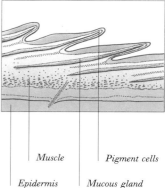

Trout Scales
The attractive silvering of the trout's scales (left) is caused by light reflecting from minute guanine crystals in the fish's dermis.

COLOR

Most trout are spotted, with dark backs shading to pale undersides. This dark-over-light pattern is common in many animals. It is good camouflage, as it reduces the telltale shadows caused by overhead lighting. The variation in the color of trout of the same species is either caused by differences in the concentration of the pigments in

on different scales, in general they are stacked with their reflecting faces vertical. Light from the side is reflected, allowing the fish to blend into its surroundings. Vertical light passes between the crystals so the trout appears dark when viewed from above with little of the light reflected. When the trout twists, the side of the reflecting flank is uppermost and a silver flash is seen deep in the water.

Skin Section
The cross-section view (below) shows scales in the pockets of the dermis.

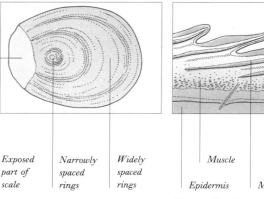

Muscle   *Pigment cells*

Epidermis   *Mucous gland*

their diet, or it is the trout's response to its environment. By contracting or expanding the different chromatophores, the trout is able to alter its color to match the background – trout over a bottom of light sand are pale. Blind fish are always dark in color. Many of the salmonids become particularly vivid while spawning.

THE TROUT'S SENSES

THE TROUT HUNTS by sight. Its view of the world is very different from man's, partly because the trout has specially adapted eyes and partly because it lives in water, which has its own peculiar optical properties.

VISION IN WATER

When a trout – or a human – underwater looks directly up at the calm surface he sees the outside world through a large round window with a diameter of a little over twice his depth in the water. Although almost all of the world above the surface is visible through this window, objects nearing its edge (that is, objects low down, close to the water level) become increasingly dim and distorted; very low objects are invisible. The surface surrounding the window appears as a mirror reflecting the underwater world.

It is often stated that a trout lower in the water has a "bigger" window and thus can see more of the outside world. This is misleading: as the trout doubles its depth it doubles the window's diameter – but it is twice as far away from that window. Yet the

picture through the window does change a little as it sinks. All outside objects get smaller but objects closer to the surface level come into view. The whole window becomes dimmer as more light is absorbed by the water. Trout *are* sometimes easier to approach when feeding close to the surface, but this is more likely to be because the angler is out of focus.

When the surface is rippled, the window and the mirror shatter into confusion, making detection by the fish much more difficult – but not impossible. It is easy to pick out a trout beneath a rippled surface, and presumably the trout can discern us: we are, after all, less well-camouflaged. In practice, keep low and avoid fishing over flat, calm water.

THE RETINA

The trout's retina, like a human's, contains two types of light-sensitive structure: rods and cones.

The rods are extremely sensitive to changes and low levels of light. The trout's eye contains more rods than a human's and they are spread more evenly over the retina. The trout's

eye is extremely good at detecting movement over its whole 180° field of vision, and it retains this ability as darkness falls. In practice, when close to a fish, avoid movement where possible. When it is necessary, when casting, for example, keep the movement low down by side-casting.

The cones are less sensitive than the rods but they can distinguish between colors. The trout's retina is most sensitive to red and orange, least sensitive to blues. In the human eye the cones are packed into one tiny spot on the retina. In trout they are more diffuse but positioned for the optimum viewing of objects located directly ahead and slightly above.

Even when hunting underwater, trout prefer to attack from below. In practice, flies, particularly wet flies, will be most visible to the trout when the color red features in the artificial fly dressing.

The Trout's Vision
Outside the angle of vision of 97.6°, the fish (below) sees nothing more than a black surround or, in well-lit water, a reflection of the bottom.

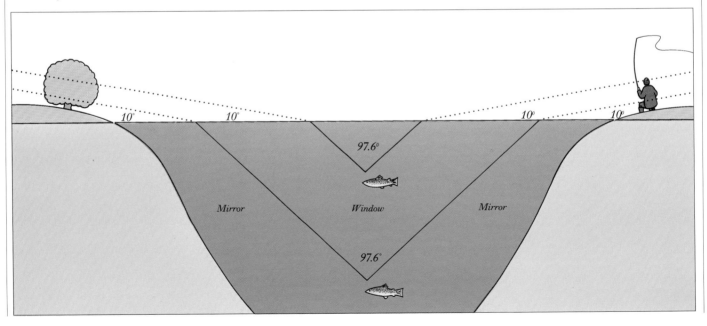

THE LENS

The trout's eye has a lens with a 180° field of vision. A retina with rods spread across the surface enables the trout to focus objects across a vast field. The short focal length of the lens gives a great depth of field. Objects anywhere from infinity to 60cm. (2ft.) away can be in focus at the same time. When the trout focuses on an object very close by, distant objects are out of focus and less discernible. In practice, a downstream cast is less likely to be noticed if the trout is feeding very close to the surface.

EYE STRUCTURE

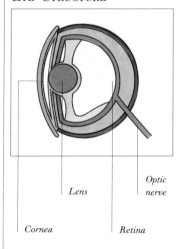

Lens

Optic nerve

Cornea   *Retina*

Binocular vision with depth perspective

Monocular vision   *Monocular vision*

Blind region

TASTE AND SMELL

Salmon, and presumably trout, are guided to the waters of their birth largely by the chemical senses of taste and smell. Neither of these senses is of great concern to the fly-fisherman – apart from the common observation that, when several different flies are on the water, trout often seem to select just one species and ignore the others. Perhaps some actually do taste better than others.

THE LATERAL LINE

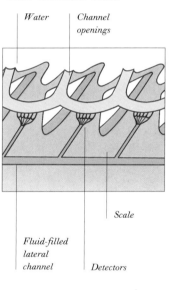

Water   *Channel openings*

Scale

Fluid-filled lateral channel   *Detectors*

EYE POSITION

A prey species needs as wide a field of vision as possible in order to stay alive – it has eyes at the side of its head. A predator needs binocularity, with overlapping fields of vision, for accurate depth judgment – it has forward-facing eyes. As both predator and potential prey of other predators, the trout has settled on a compromise eye-position. The fields of vision overlap about 30° in front and above the fish. This is its preferred zone of attack, with the greatest concentration of cones on the retina. The price the trout pays for this is a 30° blind zone immediately behind it.

In practice, trout can be approached very closely, with careful wading, from directly behind. In casting the fly into the attack zone, it can be difficult to prevent the line falling across the fish, thus spooking it and making it aware of your presence.

HEARING

Trout detect vibrations in two different ways. Low-frequency vibrations, from heavy footfalls or a swimming fish, are detected by the lateral line that runs down either side of the body and across the head. Vibration in the water causes movement in a fluid running in a channel beneath the skin. The fluid movement is detected by receptors set along the channel. In practice, avoid heavy movements and footfalls, particularly when wading. Scraping studs and loose stones scare trout.

High-frequency vibrations are picked up by ears deep within the fish. In the carp family, the swim-bladder is used as an eardrum and the hearing is excellent. Happily, trout do not have this arrangement. Under-water sounds are heard to some extent; airborne sounds (a conversation between anglers, for example) not at all. In practice, chat as much as you like.

THE TROUT'S ENVIRONMENT

MOST FRESH WATER begins as rain. It contains oxygen and carbon dioxide in the form of dilute carbonic acid. In a rain-fed river, the water quickly feeds into streams and rivers. In spring-fed rivers, the water may have been underground for many centuries before emerging at a spring. Both types of river may be interrupted on their way to the sea by natural or man-made lakes. All these variations will have some sort of impact on a trout population.

SOURCE AND TEMPERATURE

The water source determines temperature. The temperature of rain-fed streams varies with air temperature. In hot, dry weather the flow slows, allowing the water to heat up considerably. Underground spring water is usually cool and varies very little in flow or temperature. Large lakes and their outflows are resistant to the fluctuations in temperature and flow that harm invertebrate life in the water.

TEMPERATURE AND OXYGEN

As the water temperature rises, so does the trout's demand for oxygen. Water, however, holds less dissolved oxygen as the temperature rises. At 5°C (41°F) water holds around 13ppm (parts per million) – half as much again as it contains at 25°C (77°F).

Oxygen dissolves at the water surface, particularly where there is turbulence or high air pressure. Oxygen is also produced by aquatic plants as a by-product of photosynthesis which occurs only in sunlight. However, the breathing of these aquatic

Flora and Fauna
Waterside flowers such as these (right) flourish only in a pollution-free environment. Vigorous plant life is vital if an adequate food supply is to be provided.

Environmental Factors
The diagram (below) shows how the components of the trout's environment must inter-relate to ensure a healthy trout habitat.

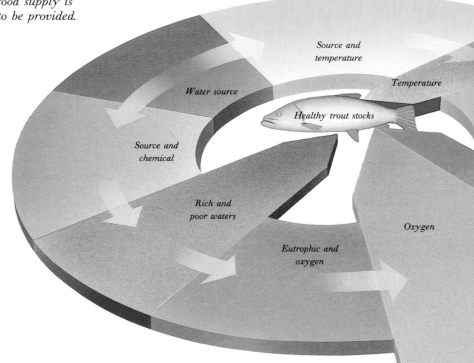

Source and temperature

Water source

Temperature

Healthy trout stocks

Source and chemical

Rich and poor waters

Oxygen

Eutrophic and oxygen

plants and the decaying process of any organic material uses oxygen and produces carbon dioxide. This gas is very soluble in water. The lethal limit of oxygen is compounded by dissolved carbon dioxide and temperature.

Trout can survive in low oxygen levels (below 4ppm) only at low temperatures when there is little carbon dioxide. They can survive in temperatures above 20°C (68°F), if the water is oxygen-saturated.

The trout is cold-blooded: the temperature of the water in which it swims determines its body temperature. This, in turn, determines its metabolism, appetite, energy demands and expenditure – its body chemistry.

Trout are cold-water creatures. They can survive in the range 0-25°C (32-77°F) but growth is very slow outside the range 7-19°C (45-66°F). Such waters are common in the northern half of the

Northern Hemisphere (the natural range of the trout species), but farther south they are found only at high altitudes; in the Rockies and the high sierras of Mexico, the Atlas Mountains of Morocco and the mountains of the Himalayan range. South of the equator, trout have been successfully introduced in the cooler waters of South America, New Zealand, and Australia.

WATER CHEMISTRY

Water running over or through the land takes up the chemicals and nutrients that form the first links in the food chain that will support fly life and, eventually, trout. These chemicals determine the alkalinity (or hardness) of the water. Most spring-fed streams originate in porous chalk or limestone rocks, which dissolve easily to provide nutrient-rich alkaline water – the home of fast-growing food supplies and fish.

Water-resistant granite rock provides very few nutrients, as the water supports little weed growth and insect life.

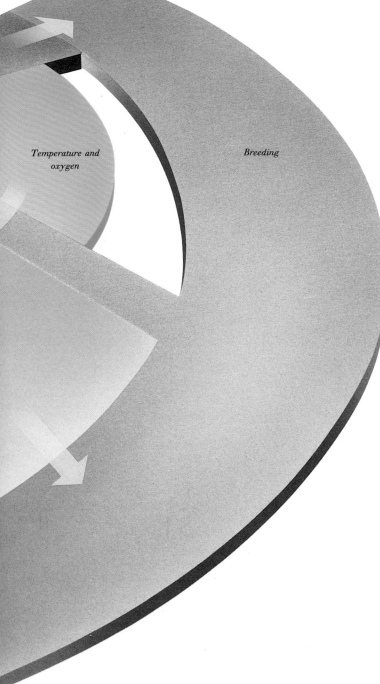

Temperature and oxygen

Breeding

RICH AND POOR WATERS

Oligotrophic waters are those poor in dissolved nutrients. These are waters close to the source in hard rock areas that can provide ideal conditions for spawning. Oligotrophic lakes can be improved further by artificial fertilization to become mesotrophic (of average fertility).

Eutrophic waters are those nutrient-rich rivers and lakes that support large populations of plant and animal life. Paradoxically, the very richness of the water, with its lush growth of oxygenating plants, can result in disastrous fish-kills through oxygen depletion.

BREEDING

Most trout spawn in running water. A few spawn in stillwaters, but this is usually because they do not have convenient access to suitable streams.

The size of the river or stream is unimportant. What is vital is the quality of the substrate, the bottom, which is usually a mixture of stones and gravel. It must be loose enough for the female to dig a channel or "redd" using the thrust of water from her flank and tail. A strongish current helps displace any stones she disturbs.

Environmental Hazards

Pollution (above) *is a major concern in trout habitats.*

INCUBATION TIME

After egg-laying and fertilization the eggs are buried by the female. The incubation time depends on the water temperature, but mortality is high outside the range 5-13°C (41-55°F). Newly hatched fry are sometimes eaten by adult relatives, so an oligotrophic stream supporting few adults may provide a more successful hatchery than a rich chalk stream.

EUTROPHIC WATERS

Photosynthesis takes in dissolved carbon dioxide from the water and releases oxygen as a by-product. In darkness the process is reversed. Winter fish-kills can occur in lakes when the richly weeded water, with a covering of ice and snow excluding the light, depletes the oxygen and increases the carbon dioxide above the lethal limit.

Eutrophic waters can also suffer explosive weed growth in very hot weather when the oxygen capacity of the water is low. Rapid decay of this mass of vegetation then robs the water of its oxygen and results in a fish-kill.

CONSERVATION

IT IS NOT NECESSARY to kill trout or prevent them breeding to dislodge a population. Merely tilting the balance in favor of competing species may be enough to cause havoc.

Agriculture, modern man's oldest occupation, has had a profound effect on the natural flora and fauna of the planet, not least on trout. Industrial pollution, mining waste, toxic chemicals and acid rain proliferate. One of the most problematic, however, is fishing: a fish for the pan means one less fish in the river. To compensate for this, two regimes have evolved: put-and-take, when trout caught and kept by the angler are replaced with regular stocking of hatchery-bred fish; and catch-and-release, which simply means that all fish that are caught are released again to the water without damage.

AGRICULTURE
Digging increases both drainage and the amount of silt in the run-off. Excessive silt clogs up the gravel redds, essential for successful breeding since this is where eggs are laid. Deforestation also produces vast quantities of silt that threaten migratory trout and salmon runs in the US, Canada, and Britain. Silting of the bottom will also change the plant and food species in the water.

Logging and the draining of uplands for agricultural purposes increase the run-off after rain. This creates greater fluctuations between flood and drought that strain the carefully balanced ecosystems of the river. Fertilizers sometimes leak into the water, increasing plant and invertebrate life – and trout growth. In eutrophic waters any increase in fertility can produce an explosion of growth that can be disastrous for a fishery.

Preservation
Put-and-Take and Catch-and-Release (above) *ensure trout survival.*

Urbanization
Population expansion (left) *encroaches on the countryside.*

CITIES AND INDUSTRY
Extraction of water for industrial and domestic use is sometimes called "borrowing" – and so it is. The water is returned having passed through the factory, power station, or human digestive system. The result is water that is richer in nutrients or much warmer, or both – and much better suited to the species of the warmer lowlands.

Frequently the water is extracted from the upland areas of trout habitat to be used and returned elsewhere: water taken from Ullswater in England's Lake District is consumed and discharged in the troutless wastes of Manchester. The effect of this extraction is to exacerbate any other problems of the source water. Pollutants and other discharges are concentrated, droughts exaggerated and the slower flows become warmer, holding considerably less oxygen.

Reservoirs for extraction or hydropower are usually constructed in the well-watered uplands – trout country. Here it is the migratory fish, the sea trout and steelhead, that suffer when dams are thrown across the valleys, blocking their route from the sea to the spawning beds.

But even extraction can benefit the trout population. Reservoirs formed along rivers with no natural trout are stocked and maintained as trout fisheries: the English Midlands have far more trout now than a century ago. In the US, superb river fisheries have been created in the cool tailwaters from reservoirs the warm states of Tennessee and New Mexico and in the Ozark Mountains.

PUT-AND-TAKE

The appeal of this policy is that any fish hooked has never been caught before – to that extent the fish is "natural." Some anglers dislike the idea of inflicting on the trout the gratuitous distress of being hooked and landed to no other end than the angler's pleasure.

The policy is best suited to large stillwaters with no natural head of trout.

CATCH-AND-RELEASE

The advantage of this method is that fish remain in the water for a long time. Ideally, they are an indigenous, self-supporting population – wild fish.

The disadvantage is that the fish may be caught many times, and to that extent are not wild. The success of catch-and-release depends on the released fish surviving the ordeal. Without due consideration and the most careful handling, these trout can die needlessly.

The catch-and-release policy is generally best suited to rivers with a natural head of trout and good spawning prospects.

RELEASING TROUT

When fish are to be returned, all flies should be tied on barbless hooks.

Trout can fight to exhaustion and beyond. Keep this to a minimum by using tackle that can exert firm pressure on the trout. Having brought the fish to the net, land it quickly and gently. Without a net, a wriggling fish must be held firmly, otherwise you may cause internal damage. A wriggling fish can also be dropped, so hold tightly. Removing the fly is easy with a barbless hook, but always carry surgical forceps to remove a hook in some inaccessible spot deep in the throat or gill.

Never throw or dump a trout back into the water. Cradle it in your net or hands, head to current in a river, until it swims away of its own accord. In a stillwater it may be necessary to move the fish through the water to revive it; check that the gills are moving regularly before you release the fish. Be ready to spend as much time restoring the fish as you took to land it.

TROUT MANAGEMENT

Where there is a natural population and fishing pressure is slight, stocking may be unnecessary. Stocking trout can be unhelpful, even disastrous, for an

Grayling Released
A perfect specimen (above) is returned undamaged.

Fishing for All
A fly-rod can be set up almost anywhere (left).

indigenous trout population. Stocked adult fish can sometimes drive younger natives from their feeding lies and spawning redds. Where they are of the same species, the indigenous population that has evolved over the millennia to suit the conditions of that water is sometimes ousted by or absorbed into a population that man has shaped to suit the needs of the hatchery.

THE LIFE CYCLE OF THE TROUT

THE FERTILIZED EGG, snug in the gravel bed of the river, hatches after 30-50 days into an alevin, an embryonic trout with a large yolk sac. When this food supply is nearly finished, the tiny fish struggles up through the gravel toward the light, emerging as a miniature trout, a fry.

The fry rests on the bottom, swimming up to intercept any suitable food organisms. Soon, it takes to mid-water, occupying a small feeding territory. As the fry develops, the characteristic parr-marks will appear down each flank, and the young fish will become a parr.

Growth rates, even in the same water, vary enormously. The larger parr occupy the lies that have a better food supply and so increase any size difference. The young trout remains a parr in river or lake for one to three years. During this time, it is not possible to distinguish trout that will remain in the river from those that will spend most of their adult life at sea. At this stage, the young trout begin to lose their distinguishing parr marks, some taking on the coloration of the freshwater adults. In others the colors fade beneath a silver coat and they move downstream. They have become smolts.

THE SEA GOING HABIT

All trout have the potential to leave the freshwaters of their birth and take to the rich feeding grounds of the sea. Whether or not this sea going potential is realized during the trout's lifetime depends on several factors.

One factor seems to be inherited, but not genetically. Sea-trout eggs, stripped from migrating adults, fertilized, and raised in a hatchery, develop the silver garb of migrating smolts. If these fish are prevented from migrating, their offspring lose this inheritance. They do not develop into smolts, and yet their genetic material is the same as that of their migrating parents and grandparents.

Similarly, river-trout eggs reared in a hatchery develop into adults without the smolt stage. When they are stocked into the troutless rivers of the Southern Hemisphere, a run of sea trout usually develops, colonizing the neighboring rivers.

Hatching Rainbow Trout
Alevin (above) are most vulnerable to predators.

Rainbow Trout Fry
Fry at three months (right) can rest on their dorsal fin.

SURVIVAL INSTINCT

Some trout spend their adult life in brackish estuaries; others swim to the ocean in silver hordes of steelhead or sea trout.

Exactly what triggers the sea going habit in one trout and not another is unclear. Hunger may be part of the answer. Whatever it is provides the trout with a superb strategy against natural calamity, since any part of their habitat can be quickly recolonized from the sea or the headstream when the disaster is over.

Sea-Running Trout
Sea trout (left) sometimes become silver in saltwater.

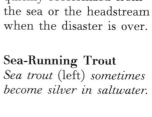

NORTHERN EUROPEAN BROWN TROUT

THE BROWN TROUT (*Salmo trutta*) is the native trout of Europe and western Asia. Almost any description of the "typical brownie" is doomed to exception; they are incredibly variable in color and patterning, even when from the same water.

As its name suggests, the back is usually a greenish-brown and can be heavily marked with large spots of black, dark brown, or red. The dark spots are usually surrounded by a pale ring, which increases their prominence, and any red spots are commonly on the flanks. The spots also cover the dorsal fin but never, or at least rarely, carry onto the shallow-forked tail fin. The belly is pale, from white to a rich butter-yellow. The fins can vary from near-black to orange-red, but a red adipose fin, if present, is a brown-trout hallmark.

Salmo trutta is indigenous to all the seas and watersheds of Europe, from Iceland in the northwest, to Spain in the southwest, and the Arctic coast of the Soviet Union as far east as the White Sea. There must once have been sea trout in the Mediterranean, at a time when it was still connected to the Caspian and Aral seas, for there are brown trout in waters draining into those inland seas.

DISTRIBUTION OF THE BROWN TROUT

Brown Trout Range
The map (above) *indicates the natural range of the brown trout throughout the waters of Northern Europe.*

Reservoir Brown Trout
A healthy specimen (below) *shows all the characteristics of the reservoir brown.*

SEA-TROUT MIGRATION

There are no sea trout in the warm waters of the Mediterranean now, but there are populations of native brown trout in the Atlas Mountains of Morocco and in Corsica and Sardinia. Where there is no sea-trout migration, these isolated populations have evolved distinct subspecies.

Many brown trout thrive where no native sea trout ever swam. The first successful transportation of eggs from the Itchen, Hampshire, to the Antipodes reached Tasmania in 1864. The progeny of this first transportation were later used to stock waters in Australia and New Zealand. Loch Leven (Scotland) fish were stocked in southern India in 1868;

Capetown and the Drakensberg Mountains of Natal (South Africa) had a thriving population after 1892; and some rivers in Kenya and Tanganyika followed early in this century.

The first brown trout to cross the Atlantic, in 1883, were from Germany. These were joined by fish from the Itchen and Loch Leven the following year. They were stocked in the eastern rivers of Pennsylvania and New York State and have since been successfully introduced into 44 other American states and many Canadian waters.

In the first decade of this century, brown trout were introduced into Argentina, the Falkland Islands, and Chile, where they now reach world-record weights.

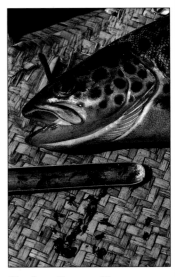

Perfect Brown Trout
Brown trout (above) *are readily distinguishable from rainbow trout because of their lack of spots on the tail fin and the pronounced spots, which are sometimes red, on the body.*

Distinguishing brown trout coloration.

BROWN TROUT IN RIVERS & LAKES

BROWN TROUT SPAWN in November and December, the fry emerging to feed from March to May. Their rate of growth depends on temperature and food supply, although some strains are faster-growing than others.

In the food-rich waters of a chalk stream or limestone lake, the average length of a three-year-old brown trout is around 30cm. (12in.). In the oligotrophic waters of a spate stream or hill tarn a three-year-old fish is likely to be around 15cm. (6in.) — and about *one-eighth* the weight of its chalk stream cousin. Brown trout in rivers are rather sedentary. They may inhabit one feeding lie for months or years, the larger fish occupying the better lies until removed by old age or the angler. The trout in these permanent lies will change color to blend in with the background. Diet will also affect color. The trout's red spots are the result of the pigment carotene. Where the trout's diet is high in crustaceans containing this pigment the trout will, in general, have bright pink flesh and the flanks will have vivid red spots. The trout of Loch Leven are the exception to the rule, however: famous for their sporting fight and their firm pink flesh, they have no red spots at all.

VARIATIONS ON THE THEME

When brown trout specialize in their feeding they can develop or preserve quite distinct varieties within a single lake. Lough Melvin, close to the northwest coast of Ireland, holds at least three: sonaghen trout are small, dark fish with striking black fins and a largish tail. They spend all their lives in deep water, feeding on shoals of tiny zooplankton.

Gillaroo trout, in contrast, are emblazoned with intense spots of red and black. They have stomach walls of thick muscle to suit their tough diet of snails and crustaceans browsed from the rocks of the shallow margins. The feeding habits of these two

varieties ensure that they rarely meet. They even choose to spawn in separate streams, ensuring that the two races are genetically and structurally distinct.

The third variety found in Lough Melvin (and elsewhere) is *Salmo ferox*. These are the large trout, with large heads and jaws, that are primarily fish-eaters. Their status as a distinct variety is debatable. They are very long-lived (a characteristic of brown trout compared to rainbows) and many of their features might be simply a product of age and size.

Brown Trout Catch

It is important to imitate the trout's preferred food supply (left) *with the appropriate artificial fly.*

LAKE BROWN TROUT

Lake brown trout migrate to the feeder streams to spawn. They gather at the outflows as the days shorten in mid-autumn. The croneen of Lough Derg on Ireland's River Shannon (and brown trout in other large lakes) behave more like sea trout. These large silvery fish enter the tributaries in a "run" during mid-summer, mimicking the spawning runs of the true sea trout.

Irish Brown

Fine lake brownie (below).

BROWN TROUT FROM THE SEA

THE SMALL SILVER smolts drift down from the headstreams in loose shoals and swim out into the sea. Usually they do not go far out, preferring to gorge on the concentrations of sand eels, sprats, crabs, and shrimps, and their larvae and young, of the North Sea and the Atlantic coasts of Europe. The young sea trout grow rapidly. Some will return to freshwater after just a few months at sea. These small sea trout occasionally spawn, but most will return to sea after just a month or so.

Why some sea trout stay at sea so much longer than others is not known. Eventually all must return to spawn. The returning fish form loose shoals along the coast before turning into the once-familiar waters of their youth: sea trout, like salmon, rely on smell and taste to return to their natal stream. Unlike salmon, they do not need flood water to run the river. On dark summer nights sea trout can be heard "whirring" through shallow riffles between pools on their way upstream, but a spate undoubtedly brings in the larger runs of fish. These arrive in early summer and continue throughout the summer, but some fresh-run fish can be taken as early as mid-spring.

SEA-TROUT TRAITS
Straight from the ocean, sea trout are silver-bright with dark spots. Gradually they gain tints of copper, darkening into the dull brown-red of the spawning adult fish.

Unlike the steelhead, the Atlantic sea trout does not regain the complete coloring of its non-migratory sibling, the freshwater brown trout.

EUROPEAN SUBSPECIES
Wherever a population of brown trout has become isolated, particularly for many millennia, there is a chance that it will have diverged sufficiently to be considered a subspecies, but this is largely a matter of scientific opinion. What is of significance to the angler, however, is the rich diversity of forms the brown trout can assume throughout its range.

Each of the inland seas, the Aral Sea, the Caspian Sea, the Black Sea, and the Mediterranean, has developed its own form of brown trout. In the Mediterranean, the lack of sea trout has further isolated many watersheds: the rivers of Yugoslavia can boast several unique varieties. Two of these varieties, the marbled trout (*Salmo marmoratus*) of the north and the trout of Lake Ohrid in the south (*Salmothymus ohridius*), are species distinct from the brown trout of the Mediterranean basin (*Salmo trutta macrostigmata*).

These Mediterranean trout are still to be found in the Atlas Mountains, in Corsica and Sardinia and, in an enticing echo of the very earliest Macedonian fly-fishers mentioned by Claudius Aelianus, in the high mountains of Greece.

Alpine Trout
This freshly caught trout (above) *is a typical alpine-stream specimen in the peak of health.*

PLIGHT OF THE TROUT
The case of the small Greek trout illustrates the threat to many varieties of brown trout. Greece in summer is a dry country with a massive tourist population on the coast. The water taken from mountain rivers to meet the needs of tourism has severely deprived the native brown trout. Fish farming of the quicker-growing rainbows in the reservoirs and streams has all but sealed their fate.

Caught and Landed
A highly prized reservoir brown trout (left).

THE TROUT OF THE NEW WORLD

NORTH AMERICA HAS four species commonly called trout. Two of these, the brook trout and the lake trout, are in fact chars, close relations of the true trout species. The other two species are natives of the Pacific Coast and the Rocky Mountains of the west. Both share their ancestry with the Pacific salmons (*Oncorhynchus* species) and are now recognized as belonging to that group rather than to the *Salmo* species of Europe. The rainbow trout (*Oncorhynchus mykiss*, formerly *Salmo gairdnerii*) is named for its iridescent colors, shading from an olive green on the back through a roseate or violet band running the length of its flank to a paler underside. The colors deepen toward the winter spawning. The spots that freckle the back and flanks are smaller than those of the brown trout and lack the pale rings. Unlike the brown's, the rainbow's spots are carried through to the tail fin. The rainbow trout is native to the brawling rivers of the West Coast, and of rivers from the Bering Strait in the north down to the Mexican rivers of the Gulf of California. Across the Bering Strait the same species runs the rivers of the Soviet Union as far south as the Chinese border.

DISTRIBUTION

Rainbow Trout Range
The map (left) shows golden and rainbow trout range.

TRAVELING TROUT
The rainbow can be caught almost anywhere in the world. It is simple to raise in hatcheries and tolerant of a wide range of waters, temperatures and conditions. It is the ubiquitous pond trout and yet retains the superb fighting qualities evolved in the swift rivers of its home. Many of the now-famous rainbow fisheries of the Rockies (and all of the easterly flowing rivers) had no native rainbows: these and the eastern and midwestern states were the first to be stocked with the newcomers (they were christened "rainbows" by the first of the eastern importers).

In many waters these vigorous visitors supplanted the native trout. Where there is no competition from native trout their speed of growth can be astounding, producing world-famous rainbow fisheries in New Zealand and in the mighty waters of Chile and Argentina. Paradoxically, it is here that the "purest" original stock varieties are to be found, such has been the indiscriminate stocking in their native waters. In Europe the rainbows breed in the wild only rarely; it is the "stockie" rainbow that has fueled the boom in stillwater fly-fishing and commercial fisheries.

Rainbow Trout
A rainbow trout (left) with a healthy bloom.

Brook Trout
*The American brook trout (*Salvelinus fontinalis*) was first introduced into New Zealand (right) in 1877. The type continues to live and breed successfully.*

RAINBOW TROUT IN FRESHWATER

RAINBOW TROUT ARE great travelers. There are non-migratory strains (like the famous shasta variety of the McCloud River in northern California and the kamloops variety from the lakes on the Thompson River in British Columbia), but these are usually the result of barriers preventing migration. Where possible most rainbows run to the sea, returning as steelhead, the sea trout of the Pacific. When young, the fish that will migrate are indistinguishable from those that will spend their lives in the river. Young rainbows grow faster than browns, and their more rapid growth rate is reflected in a larger appetite.

The rainbow is a voracious feeder. Where the river brown trout is content to occupy a lie and take any food carried by the current, the rainbow will go off in search of food. As you would expect of such an appetite, rainbow trout are less discriminating in their diet than brown trout. They will also accept a far wider range of food. As far as the fly-fisherman is concerned, matching the hatch is more important with wary and choosy browns, but is becoming increasingly necessary on many of the hard-fished rainbow waters of the West.

STEELHEAD LIFESTYLE

Migratory rainbows become smolts in their second or third year, dropping quickly down the rivers into the Pacific waters off North America and, more recently, New Zealand. At sea they can range far out into the ocean or, more usually, along the coasts, gorging on the rich shoals of baitfish and crustacea from Mexico to Alaska. This behavior may be the result of natural selection in these mighty tumbling rivers: only the larger fish are able to return and spawn successfully. Steelhead and rainbows spawn in the late winter and spring when the first snowmelt produces copious cool water.

The runs of large steelhead enter the river in autumn and winter, making steelhead fishing a different prospect from the warm summer nights of the Atlantic sea trout. As the steelhead enter the river, they begin to take on the colors of the river rainbows. Returning steelhead are indistinguishable from the resident rainbows — except for their size.

Adult Rainbow
This rainbow trout (below) was caught in New Jersey. The rainbow has an average life expectancy of six years.

Rainbow Size
A two-season rainbow (above) can reach 15-19cm. (7-9in.), growing to 32cm. (15in.) in food-rich waters.

Catching a rainbow
Anyone hooking and playing rainbow trout (above) in a wild river will testify to their athleticism and lust for life. They usually die younger than their brown counterparts, perhaps burned out by their exuberant lifestyle.

THE CUTTHROAT

THE CUTTHROAT (*Oncorhynchus clarki*, formerly known as *Salmo clarki*) is the second trout of the American West. Its name derives, as is immediately obvious, from the two distinguishing red throat slashes under its lower jaw. These become more apparent in the spawning season, and are shared by all the varieties. It is fortunate that they have this feature in common, for the cutthroats are very variable in size, patterning, and color. In general they are not large trout, although one subspecies in Pyramid Lake (now, sadly, either extinct or lost through interbreeding) produced the heaviest average recorded weight of all freshwater trout – around 12kg. (20lb.).

As with the lake trout, this species has been used occasionally in Europe as an introduction fish to stock waters, and hybrids between this species and the rainbow have occasionally been reported. The back and sides of the cutthroat trout are typically an olive green, shading into an ocher-yellow belly, becoming paler or white between the paired fins.

Characteristically, cutthroats are often heavily spotted toward the tail and back, carrying these spots through to the dorsal, tail, and the adipose fin.

DISTRIBUTION

Cutthroat Range
The original range of cutthroat (above). Some protection is afforded by national parks.

CUTTHROAT LOCATION
The cutthroat is a trout of the West-Coast rivers and of the high, cold waters of the mountains. It is the indigenous trout of the Rocky Mountains, native to rivers flowing east and west of the Continental Divide. To the west, it is found in the same rivers as the rainbow, but its stronghold is in the cold headwaters above the rainbow range, and ideally with an impassable barrier between itself and its ebullient cousin.

As stream temperatures and pollution have risen with the coming of man, the cutthroat habitat has been under pressure, and the short-term solution to falling populations – stocking with the hardier rainbow – has only hastened its decline. The distribution map shows its native range, but in many places the native strains are under threat, lost or hopelessly diluted through hybridization with its close relative, the ubiquitous rainbow.

MOUNTAIN HABITAT
Cutthroat populations have often become isolated in their mountain fastnesses, and this isolation has produced the myriad local varieties and strains that are the delight of angling for these sometimes small but always strikingly beautiful trout.

Albino Cutthroat
An unusual specimen (above) *from Pyramid Lake.*

Small Cutthroats
Cutthroat color variety (left) *is considerable.*

The cutthroats of Yellowstone are under no such threat. They are protected from introduced species and overfishing in this national park. Farther south, and on the other side of the Continental Divide, a cutthroat variety (*O. lewisi*) has its stronghold in the waters of the Snake and its tributaries within Wyoming's Grand Teton National Park.

COLORADO CUTTHROAT
The Colorado cutthroat (*O. pleuriticus*) was once to be found throughout the northern watershed of the Colorado River, but now it is only found in the headstreams and a few high lakes.

It is a similar story with the cutthroats of the Rio Grande (*O. virginalis*) and Gila rivers. The cutthroats of the Lahontan basin (around Reno in the Nevada deserts) are another isolated variety (*O. henshawi*). This fish-eating subspecies once produced the enormous fish of Pyramid Lake, now lost for ever, but vestigial populations in remote Lahontan waters are being used to restock and replenish Lahontan lakes, such as Tahoe and Pyramid.

COASTAL CUTTHROATS

THE RIVERS ALONG the western seaboard of North America, from Alaska to northern California, have cutthroats that run down to the sea. These can be large fish in the north of their range but, unlike the Atlantic sea trout and the steelhead, they are rarely larger than the cutthroats that never leave fresh water. These sea-run cutthroats do not disperse along the coast like the wandering steelhead:

they stay close to the estuary in large shoals and return to the tideway after only a few months in saltwater.

The large shoals of silvery cutthroat with their distinctive spotting move into the rivers in late summer. These are the harvest trout of the West Coast. The strong migratory urge of the majority of rainbows has prevented the isolation and variation that is characteristic of the cutthroats.

In northern Mexico and the southwest of the US the warmth of the lower reaches and frequent seismic movements have trapped several populations in the headwaters and mountain lakes of the high sierras. At this considerable height the water is cool and supports several varieties of small trout, whose coloring of iridescent gold makes them perhaps the most beautiful of all salmonids.

GOLDEN TROUT ORIGINS
Golden trout are classified as a variety of rainbow and are similar to the rainbows of the Kern River of the Sierra Nevada. Golden trout (*Salmo aguabonita*), native to the south fork of the Kern, stock mountain waters where no trout exist or where indigenous goldens have been lost through the introduction of stocked rainbows and other species.

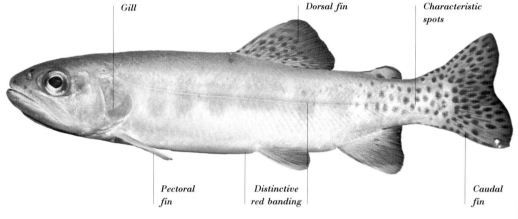

Gill — Dorsal fin — Characteristic spots — Pectoral fin — Distinctive red banding — Caudal fin

Perfect Specimen
This cutthroat (above) is typically small and delicate.

PURE VARIETIES
Pure populations of golden strains are now to be found only in waters upstream of impassable barriers.

There are golden trout native to all the lands of the high and dry southwest. The southernmost salmonids of all are the rare Mexican golden trout, found in the high mountains of Chihuahua.

GOLDEN VARIETIES
The Mexican golden trout is the most divergent of all trout subspecies, but most closely related to the Apache goldens of Arizona, still found in the Little Colorado River and, across the watershed, in the Black and White rivers, tributaries of the Gila. The headwaters of the Gila itself lie in New Mexico and have their own golden trout (*S. gilae*), a cutthroat-like variety that is strikingly similar to the Rio Grande cutthroats found in the headwaters of that river.

One suggestion is that these ancient and beautiful golden trout may be the last trace of the ancestral genetic bridge between the rainbow and cutthroat trout of the New World.

Golden Trout
This exquisite golden trout (above) native fish of the Kern River, was hooked and landed in California.

Exquisite Orientals
These vividly colored Japanese golden trout (below) may have ancestral links with the trout of North America.

Brook Trout, Arctic Char, & Dolly Varden

THE CHARS (*Salvelinus* species) are close relatives of the trout and can interbreed with them to produce beautiful, but sterile, offspring. They can be colorful toward spawning time: characteristically, they have light markings on a darker background (trout are the reverse).

The brook trout is the native "trout" of the Northeast and Mid-West of the United States. The back is gray-green with a lighter mottled, twisting pattern that carries into the dorsal fin. The sides are paler and the belly is white tinged with orange-yellow that darkens to a brighter orange-red as spawning approaches.

The body shape is thickset, accentuated by the square tail fin. The lower fins are a bright orange-red with edges of white bordered with a black stripe. Native to arctic watersheds and cold lakes in the more temperate latitudes, these fish are bright silver until spawning, when the back is suffused with red and the pale belly and spots become a gaudy orange-red.

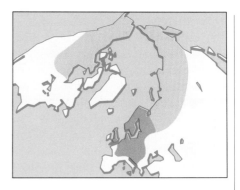

Arctic and Pacific Char Distribution
The map (above) *shows the extensive natural range of both these trout.*

BROOK TROUT RANGE
The brook trout is native to the cold waters of eastern North America. As the impact of man has warmed these waters, so the brook trout has retreated north. As a result, the finest native fisheries are now in Canada.

The brook trout has traveled successfully to New Zealand, Argentina, and Chile. In these locations, it can reach up to 5kg. (10lb.) in weight in its short 4-5-year lifespan.

In Europe the brook trout is used extensively as a fine put-and-take fish. It is less sophisticated than the native browns and a large percentage is caught soon after stocking.

Brook Trout Distribution
Brookies (above) *thrive in eastern North America.*

Arctic Char
This char (left) *swims in Umiakovik Lake, Labrador.*

CHAR & DOLLY VARDEN
Sea-run Arctic char (*Salvelinus alpinus*) are confined to the rivers of the north, but there are many populations in the post-glacial regions of Europe, Asia and North America. The English Lake District has thriving populations, as do some Irish and Alpine

Dolly Varden
A sea-running char (left).

lakes. A subspecies of the Arctic char, the Dolly Varden or Pacific char, runs into the coastal rivers of the Pacific from northern California to Alaska.

The lake trout (*S. namaycush*) is a native of the Canadian lakes, from the Great Lakes northward. It has been successfully introduced into Switzerland and is rarely fished with an artificial fly.

GRAYLING

THE GRAYLING (*Thymallus thymallus*) is the least troutlike of all the salmonids that are commonly caught on a fly. It is closest in appearance to the whitefish, those silver, herring-like fish that were the first to diverge from the trout family; the grayling was second.

The grayling is a silver-scaled fish with none of the color variation so marked in the trout and char. The back is dark and the silvered flanks have a haunting iridescence that fades in death. The scales are much larger than the trout's and lie in rows running the length of the fish. The grayling's obvious diagnostic feature is the huge dorsal fin, which is at its most dramatic during the spring spawning season. It is probable that this enormous flag, tinged purple with dark spots, is a signaling device with the same function as the char's lurid mating colors. Behind the dorsal fin is the small adipose fin and the forked tail. The grayling's mouth is small and slightly behind the nose, as befits a bottom-feeding fish.

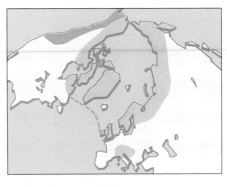

Native Range of Grayling
The map (above) *indicates the areas populated by the two grayling species.*

DISTRIBUTION
The two species of grayling of interest to anglers are the most widespread of all the salmon family. The native range of the European grayling is similar to the brown trout's with the exception of the warmer south − grayling need colder waters − and offshore lands where the freshwater grayling has been unable to colonize.

ARCTIC GRAYLING
This range is all the more remarkable for a fish that is not truly anadromous (it can tolerate brackish water) nor a great leaper of waterfalls: even a small barrier can prevent its spread. The Arctic grayling (*T. arcticus*) is even more widespread than the European, and ranges as far south as Siberia and into Canada's lakelands.

Feeding Habits
Grayling (above left) *will rise through several feet of water to take a dry fly.*

European Grayling
The species (above) *is thriving in European rivers.*

Seasonal Variation
When trout are inedible, grayling (left) *are perfect.*

MAYFLIES
ORDER EPHEMEROPTERA

O F ALL THE foodstuffs imitated by fly-fishers, the upwinged dayflies are perhaps the most loved. They start life as an egg, which after several weeks changes into the fledgling nymph. They then grow to maturity over the following 12 months. The different species (agile darters, bottom burrowers, labored swimmers, silt crawlers, stone clingers, and moss creepers) then go on to develop lifestyles appropriate to their various habitats.

When the dun (sub imago) emerges, there is little to differentiate the species apart from size. Some sport different-colored bodies and wings; some *Ephemera* and *Ephemerella* species have three tails, others two. Their lives are short: within some 12 to 20 hours the imperfect fly will have miraculously changed into the imago or perfect fly (the "spinner"), and at this stage it will mate.

The female then returns to the place she has selected for hatching. There she will lay her eggs and die (becoming "spent"), which explains this order's Latin name, *Ephemeroptera*, meaning "short-lived on the wing."

Agile Darter
This Baetid nymph (above) *is of the* Ephemeroptera *order. It lives among weeds and is easy prey for trout because it relies on its speed to escape predators.*

Stone Clinger
The Autumn or Brook dun (Ecdyonurus) (left). *Other stone clingers are* Rhithrogena *sp. and* Heptageniidae.

Hexagenia
Hexagenia *spinners* (left) *engage in their mating dance. Ovipositing, which occurs soon afterward, is followed by death. The "spinners" become "spent."*

Silt Burrower
The Ephemera danica *nymph* (above) *can burrow into gravel or silt, as can other* Ephemera *sp.,* E. vulgata, Hexagenia, *and* Ephemerella *sp.*

March Brown
Rhithrogena germanica (above) *has distinctive, heavily veined wings, a dark brown body, two tails, and six legs. It is comparatively large but still conforms to the uniform upwing dun shape.*

Blue-Winged Olive
Photographed at the point of transformation (right), *when the dowdy dun (sub imago) changes miraculously into the pristine spinner (imago) form. In this case, a blue-winged olive (Ephemerella ignita) is emerging.*

Ephemera danica
The E. danica *spinner, in fully spent position* (left), *has laid its eggs on the water's surface.*

Blue-Winged Olive Imago
Spinner stage of the blue-winged olive imago (below). *It drops eggs aerially.*

Blue-Winged Olive Dun
Before the transformation process begins, Ephemerella ignita (above) *displays its characteristic three tails and small hind wing. The dun often hatches in the evening, one of the few to do so.*

Baetis Spinners
Baetis *spinners* (below) *seek out objects on the water's surface under which to crawl and oviposit. Here they are using a pair of fly-fisher's thigh-waders! Ovipositing occurs mainly during the warmer months and toward nightfall.*

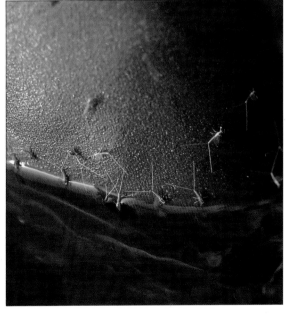

CADDIS FLIES
ORDER TRICHOPTERA

THESE AQUATIC INSECTS, also known as sedges, whose Latin name literally means "hair-winged," are most noticeable in their adult form when they are roof-winged in shape. The stages of development are egg, larva, pupa, and adult.

The larva stage differs from most other insect forms in that many species of the *Trichoptera* order build their own homes from fragments carried on the water's surface. Each species chooses different materials: for example, grannom make use of reed stems; great red sedges salvage plant fragments. *Rhyacophila* and *Hydropsyche*, however, do not build

homes as such. *Hydropsyche* builds a purse, a web for collecting prey, behind which there is a cocoon-like home. Pupation occurs in this chamber, and thereafter the pupa slowly swims up to or along the surface to eclode into adulthood.

Both larva and pupa are important food forms for trout. The pupa is the more important of the two simply because it is more noticeable. The adult caddis generally hatches from midday until evening and lives for up to one week.

OVIPOSITING

After mating, the female caddis returns to the water from her sanctuary of bankside foliage in order to lay her eggs. The ovipositing stage is also important to the fly-fisher. The female caddis lays her eggs in two ways: by

dipping her abdomen under the water and ejecting a stream of eggs, or by diving under the surface. Having accomplished this task she dies, providing yet another imitative stage for the fly-fisher – the "spent" adult.

In fishing terms, the caddis enjoys wide distribution in all water types, whether running or still. In some areas such as Germany, Austria, and many parts of the US, they are a vital source of food for the trout. The caddis should therefore never be overlooked in any capacity and on most waters. All stages are of interest to the trout and imitable in a wide variety of fly patterns.

Mystacides
Mystacides *sp. (below) are case-builders. These caddis include longhorns, silverhorns, and grousewings and are widespread on stillwaters and rivers.*

Grannom
Most species can be identified by their choice of case material. The grannom (Brachycentrus) *case (below) is consumed by trout that will also happily ingest stones, twigs, and larvae in the same mouthful.*

Rhyacophila
Trout consider free-swimming larvae (below) a delicacy, so they are important to the fly-fisher. They are found all over North America and even as far north as Finland. This larval species can make 4cm. (2in.) in length.

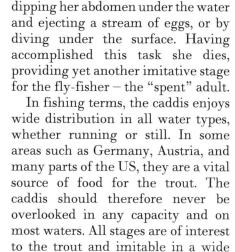

Great Red Sedge
An emerging pupa
(left), *with antennae*
and roof wing. The
adult (above), *a weak*
swimmer, is also a
favored food form.

Gray Flag
In its larval form,
a river caddis (below)
is both free-swimming
and purse-making.
It emerges during
the summer period.

Brown Silverhorn
A brown silverhorn
(left) *displaying its*
extremely long antennae.
The Anthripsodes *sp.*
is widespread in rivers
and streams. It hatches
between early summer
and early fall.

Caperer
The caperer (Halesus *sp.*)
(below) *is common on*
alkaline water, especially
chalkstreams. A late
summer to early fall
emerger, it hatches between
afternoon and early evening.

FLAT-WINGED FLIES

ORDER DIPTERA

O F ALL THE food forms available to the trout, the order *Diptera* is the most diverse and numerous. In the aquatic form it embraces chironomids and mosquitoes; in the terrestrial form, craneflies, drones, hawthorn flies, heathflies, and black gnats – the list is almost endless and of worldwide significance.

For the fly-fisher one of the most important is the family of non-biting midges, chironomids. For years, this mosquito-like fly was seen as the preserve of the stillwater angler. Only recently has its importance to the river fly-fisher been realized. Within the *Diptera* family, hundreds

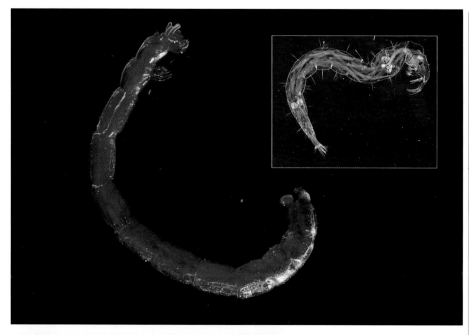

Red Midge
The midge (below) *demonstrates color variation within the pupal and adult stages. This should be echoed in the artificial. A Red Suspender imitation* (inset) *shows the effectiveness of modern materials in parodying the natural insect. This pattern imitates a pupa struggling to break through the surface film. The Ethafoam ball buoys it in the meniscus.*

Bloodworm
The color is created by haemoglobin which allows the bloodworm (above), *to function despite being incarcerated in tubes. It can dwell in depths of 5.5m.(18 ft.) in lakes and on slow-moving rivers. Very important in the diet of the trout, the bloodworm also exists in shades of green and brown. The almost transparent phantom larva* (inset) *is also an important food item.*

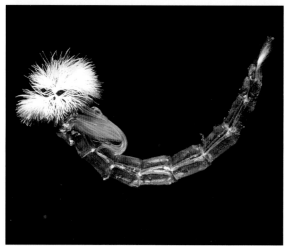

Midge Pupa
This black midge (above) *displays the distinct red banding of the larval stage. The white threads to the head and tail are breathing filaments. The midge pupa is so widespread it is indispensable to the fly-fisher.*

Phantom Pupa
The phantom pupa (Chaoborus *sp.*) (right) *is often overlooked by stillwater and river fly-fishers, yet trout occasionally feed heavily on this important form, so it is wise to carry an appropriate imitation.*

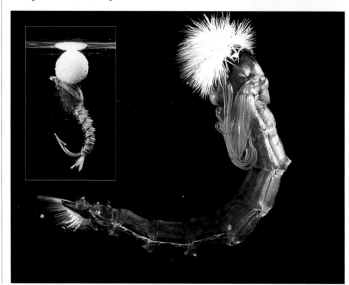

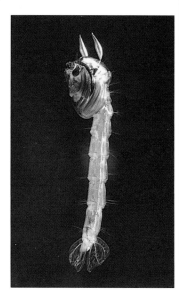

of permutations exist. Their various lifestyles, colorations, and sizes have made a significant impact on fly-fishing tactics. The midge's cycle runs from egg to larva. Often referred to as a bloodworm, the larva thrives in low-oxygen levels, making stillwaters and slow-moving areas of rivers particularly attractive to it.

PUPA AND ADULT FORMS

Next is the pupa stage, which is the most useful to the fly-fisher, then the adult. Rising trout were once considered the preserve of pupa patterns. However, success with dry midge patterns has brought about a rebirth of dry-fly-fishing on reservoirs. Trout once thought to be feeding on the pupa can, it seems, be caught

Adult Midge
A collection of adult midges (below), the largest of which is Ireland's famous duck fly. When hatching in numbers during early spring, the duck fly can incite almost epidemic rises in trout. Note the length of legs and abdomen when compared to the hyaline wings – even the smallest of the adult midges conforms to this shape. This is an important stage for both river and stillwater anglers.

with dry flies. Other important *Diptera* are the smuts and black gnats which can awaken the palate of the most sated or mayfly-preoccupied trout. The hawthorn fly, so much a feature of springtime European rivers and stillwater trout fishing, is increasingly significant, as are the oak flies and bluebottles which fall into this category. Without question, however, the piscatorial sovereign is the chironomid, the non-biting midge.

Emerging Midge
Splitting free from its pupal case (right), *this emerging midge is positioned in the surface film. The importance of fishing in the surface film cannot be underestimated, especially on calm days when the meniscus is at its thickest. Vital for stillwater fly-fishers.*

Heather Fly
The heather fly (left) *is found on acidic, high-lying lakes that are flanked by gorse, bracken, and heather. The imitation dry fly is fished in rather than on the surface.*

Cranefly
The cranefly or daddy-longlegs (Tippula *sp.*) (below) *is primarily terrestrial and can be of significance to the fly-fisher in stillwater during late summer and early autumn. Its gangling legs are a particular feature and often its downfall if they become enmeshed in the surface film and bring the struggling creature to the attention of marauding trout.*

STONEFLIES & DAMSELFLIES

PLECOPTERA & ODONATA

THESE TWO VERY different orders represent opposite ends of the fly-fishing spectrum. Stoneflies inhabit boisterous freestone rivers (though some occur on high-lying acidic lakes, along the windward shore), whereas damselflies and dragonflies, primarily lake-fisher's flies, inhabit the slower-moving stretches of river.

Both orders follow the egg, nymph, and adult cycle. The stonefly nymph (*Pteronarcys* sp.), beloved of freestone anglers, can, in some species, attain a size of 5cm. (2in.) and go through a number of instars (changes of outer skin), creating an albino nymph. The adult has flat wings which are quite hard to the touch and crisscrossed with pronounced veining. In fly-fishing terms, the adult is of secondary importance to the nymph. The adult

Yellow Sally Nymph
This specimen (above) *displays the two tails and long antennae characteristic of stonefly nymphs. The strong body and flattened wing-cases are able to withstand the rigors of fast-flowing* water and life among rocks. The medium stonefly (inset) is often referred to as a creeper in the North of England. It demonstrates the characteristics of the slimmer, "needle" type of the Plecoptera.

Large Adult Stonefly
This large dark adult (Perla microcephela) (above) *is similar to the American salmon fly.*

Little Dark Olive Stonefly
This Isogenus tostamus (right) *shows the flat, folded wings with their intricate crisscross veining.*

is of value only when the female returns to lay her eggs, or when she is accidentally blown onto the water. However, because the nymph dwells among the rocks, stones, and boulders of well-oxygenated rivers, it is constantly available to the trout. Fishing an artificial along the bottom can yield some exciting results.

DAMSELFLIES & DRAGONFLIES

The large insects of the *Odonata* order, often extremely colorful in the adult stage, also go through the egg, nymph, and adult cycle. It is generally the nymph rather than the adult that is important for the fly-fisher to imitate. There can be a great deal of color variation in the nymph of the damselfly and dragonfly (they range from light olive to dark brown), and this should be echoed in the angler's range of imitations.

The slender damsel is considered the more important of the two to the stillwater fly-fisher. When the fly is for use in stillwater, the shape, color, and appendages may need to be copied more fastidiously than usual for particularly selective trout.

Damsel Nymph
Damsel nymphs (above) *range from light green to dark brown. Streamlined, with three spiky tails, they are fast swimmers. The undulating movement attracts trout.*

Adult Damselfly
The common blue damsel (Enallagma cyathigarum) (above) *displays her adult finery. Trout feed only occasionally on ovipositing females.*

Dragonfly Nymph
The tubbier dragonfly nymph (left) *is less significant than the damsel, primarily because it spends the majority of its life lurking secretively among the weeds and is therefore less likely to be preyed upon by trout. Some species attain 5cm. (2in.) in length and in some areas are worth imitating. These can be quite aggressive, sometimes preying on small fish and nymphs.*

Eclosion
Like damselflies, dragonflies change appearance above water. The skin of the ecloding dragonfly (left) *has split along the thorax. This generally takes place near water on the stems of reed grass.*

Adult Chaser
The adult chaser (Libellula sp.) (right) *waiting for its wings to unfold and dry before taking flight. Despite some admirably close imitations, an adult chaser fly pattern is rarely used.*

AQUATIC FORMS

APART FROM THE mainstream food items such as mayflies, stoneflies, caddis, and other familiar types, there are hosts of aquatic creatures that determine the trout's lifestyle and favored position in the water. Indeed, the Irish Gillaroo trout's entire existence revolves around its predilection for snails.

Food forms such as snails, shrimps, and hoglice are the basis of the trout's everyday sustenance, and all are essential for its survival.

There exists a very definite affinity between the various river and stillwater creatures. Color and shape may alter, but the basic form appears in both types of habitat.

Carrying a selection of artificials of these creatures can form a very solid foundation to a fly box. These are patterns you should try either when all else fails or when you are unsure which pattern you ought to fish next. They are also particularly useful during the early season period just before insects begin hatching in significant quantities.

Freshwater Shrimp
The ubiquitous freshwater shrimp (below) *is an ideal food form to imitate. Its colors vary from fawn and pink to greenish-gray and golden orangy-olives. Found in most water types, this crustacean is much loved by trout.*

Great Diving Beetle
The great diving beetle (Dytiscus *sp.*) (above) *is noteworthy in its stillwater role. A ferocious predator of small fish and insects, it is relished in the nymphal form by bottom-feeding, early season trout.*

Hoglouse
The hoglouse (Asellus *sp.*) (right) *lurks in dark places amid rotting vegetation. Primarily a lake-dweller, it can also be found in slow areas on rivers. A particular delicacy for trout.*

Water Flea
Daphnia (left) *is very much the reservoir fly-fisher's friend. Vast blooms (groups of individuals) often goad the trout into a feeding frenzy. At such times, orange or bright green are the most deadly colors, and best suggested by nymphs such as Pheasant Tails with orange or green thoraxes, or by lures such as the Whisky Fly or Leprechaun.*

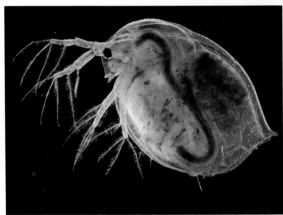

Water Boatmen

Water boatmen or back-swimmers (Corixae sp.) (left) occur on some rivers. Primarily aquatic, they can fly short distances. During the autumn, many shed their skin and become creamy-fawn. They are important to the fly-fisher because reservoir and lake trout feed heavily on this instar stage, as well as on the ever-present familiar form.

Wandering Snail

Common to still or slow-running waters, the snail (Lymnaea sp.) is an important food form when migrating from one area of a lake to another.

Ramshorn

Found in abundance on the slower areas of lime and chalk streams, the ramshorn (Planobarius cornerus) (left) is a reliable food source for trout.

Alder Larva

The alder larva (Sialis lutaria) (right) is a tyrant of stillwater and slow-moving river areas. Imitations are effective on reservoirs during mid-spring. The dobson fly and hell-grammite (larval state) are equally popular with American fly-fishers, as is the alder with the early-season British reservoir fly-fisher. The alder adult (inset) is rarely taken by trout, though its distribution is widespread.

Tadpoles

Tadpoles (below) occasionally offer exciting fishing on stillwater during spring and early summer. Frogs are imitated mostly by bass fly-fishers.

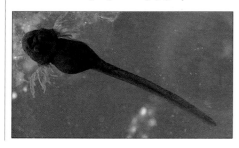

Terrestrials & Bait-Fish

Terrestrials, or land-based insects, like their aquatic counterparts, form part of the staple diet of trout. The scarcity of insects on many acidic waters renders these wind-blown tidbits an eagerly awaited repast. Even on more richly endowed waters, the ever-present terrestrial should not be overlooked, especially where trees, bushes, and tall grasses are close to the water or provide a canopy over the water from which the hapless terrestrial may fall.

Bait-fish represent that single meal of substance that is substantial enough to sustain the trout for long periods. There are certain periods, particularly on stillwaters during the autumn and winter, when there can be an explosion of fry-feeding activity by trout. At these times, the larger trout in particular can become totally preoccupied by small fish, shunning all other foodstuffs.

Ants
Ants (Hymenoptera sp.) are as important and more widespread than beetles. Although the wingless version (right) does take to the water, it is the winged version that gives rise to quite astonishing feeding from the trout during the ant's mating period (mid to late summer). To omit ant patterns, winged or otherwise, from your fly box can result in missed trout-catching opportunities.

Beetles
Beetles like this coch-y-bondhu (left) (Phyllope-tiltum horticola) live on vegetation near the bank and inadvertently fall or are blown onto the surface. Very important, especially for stream fishers, although the stillwater fly box should certainly contain some examples. An artificial with peacock-herl body will generally suffice, although specific imitations, such as the Coch-Y-Bondhu, exist.

Grasshoppers
The cricket and the grasshopper (far left) are primarily of interest to the river fly-fisher and can frequently be found hopping rashly from bankside grasses onto the stream. Trout accept even the larger 5cm. (2in.) grasshoppers, which are particularly important in the US.

Ghost Swift Moth
Although moths are not part of a trout's regular diet, during high summer the air can reverberate with the sound of enormous rises to adult moths, such as the ghost swift (left). Watch for trees that overhang water and from which the occasional caterpillar − a trout delicacy − may fall.

Roach Fly

Shiners (above) *and other bright fish are a favorite with trout. Roach are especially important to the stillwater fly-fisher. Explosive rises and tiny fleeing fish, hotly pursued by large, hungry rainbows, are a frequent occurrence. Often fry patterns have to mirror the sizable 8-10cm. (4-5in.) prey.*

Bullhead

Relying on their stone-like coloration for camouflage, the bullhead (above) *and the sculpin are chief among the bottom-dwelling fish favored by trout. Big trout, especially browns, are very partial to them, often hunting them during the hours of darkness. Important for stream-fishers, bullheads, and sculpins were first imitated by the Muddler Minnow, a pattern based on a concept originating with the North American Indians.*

Small Fish

Minnows, sticklebacks, and other small fish, especially pinhead fry (right), *can be a chosen delicacy at any time on either still or running water. When feeding on fry, trout can become preoccupied by a specific size of victim, to which your artificials must conform. Autumn fly-fishing on reservoirs often revolves around bait-fish imitations.*

EQUIPMENT

ERY LITTLE EQUIPMENT is actually needed for a fly-fishing expedition. Anglers habitually carry more tackle than is required. All that is really necessary is a rod, reel, fly-line, a few leaders, some spare nylon (to renew broken tippet sections), a few flies with the usual accessories (nylon snippers, fly flotant), and suitable clothing. Even a net can, on occasion, be dispensed with.

Your fly-fishing system must, of course, be appropriate to the waters you intend to fish, as water types vary considerably. A small stream and a large, wind-blown reservoir make very different demands.

The rod has two primary functions: casting the fly and landing the quarry. Each rod should be selected on action and application. When you are fishing a small

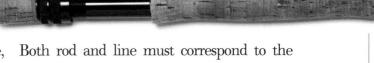

stream using small flies and fine tippets, you require a short, delicate rod with light lines. Larger lakes and big rivers call for a faster-action rod that can cast into winds and turn over big flies. Rod action can often determine presentation capabilities. To operate properly, a fly rod must be loaded with the appropriate weight of line (measured in grains).

Both rod and line must correspond to the correct AFTM standard. Thus, a #6 AFTM-rated rod should be matched to a #6 AFTM-rated line.

If possible, always try out a system before purchasing it, to make sure that the tackle is balanced and able to fulfill the function for which you intend it. The reel you select should be capable of accommodating the fly-line and at the very least 18m. (20yd.) of backing. Personal safety is an important factor. Polarized glasses not only shield eyes from glare and aid underwater vision; they also protect the wearer from a mis-timed cast. Clothing should always be comfortable and functional, warm and waterproofed if necessary, allowing for unrestricted movement when casting.

FLY REELS

THE FLY REEL acts as a reservoir for line, which can be stripped off in preparation for casting, paid out under tension when playing fish, and retrieved while fishing. The lightest reels are made from magnesium, which tends to be expensive, or from carbon fiber, plastic or metal alloy, which are also light, but often cheaper.

They must be well-engineered yet have a durable construction. When choosing a reel it is important to achieve balance with the other tackle in the system. Opt for a spool size that can accommodate the chosen fly-line comfortably. Most fly-fishers prefer a single-action reel, which for each turn of the handle winds one turn of the spool. These are available either with the spool enclosed or with its rim exposed. A checking mechanism controls the passage of line from the

reel. This gives some control over a running fish, preventing the spool from offering line too fast, creating over-runs. Most reels are fitted with an audible ratchet system. More expensive reels may have a silent disc-brake as well, which is adjustable to give greater control. A multiplying reel is geared to retrieve line faster, working on a two-to-one ratio, but its internal workings require more maintenance. Automatic reels are available but seldom used.

Front View
(right)

Holes in reel face

Check adjustment

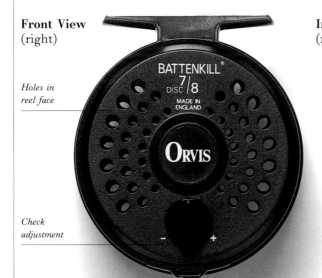

Internal Workings
(right)

Checking mechanism (Ratchet system)

Checking mechanism (Disc-brake system)

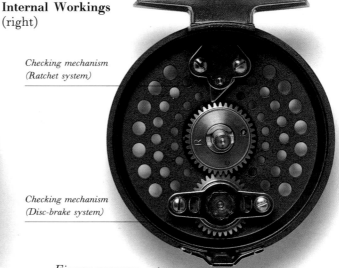

Side Elevation
(below)

Handle

Arbor

Exposed rim

Counterbalance

Holes in Reel Face
Holes cut in the face of the reel reduce weight and allow the line and backing to dry quickly. Backing line comes into use when fish strip off the fly-line, and it also pads out the spindle of a reel, helping to prevent the line from developing stiff coils.

Checking Mechanism
This reel is used for large fish, such as steelhead and other hard-fighting fish. It has a pawl-and-ratchet system and a disc-brake mechanism. To keep the reel running smoothly and the check system trouble-free, wash the reel periodically in warm, soapy water and oil it regularly. Grit or sand can ruin a mechanism in just a few revolutions.

Check Adjustment
The drag dial on the front of the reel is used to either increase or decrease the check on the spool. The dial should be pre-set to balance the spool and tippet strength. Running fish will tire under the resulting pressure and fine tip nylon will then be protected from sudden shocks and breakage.

Side Elevation
The spool must be able to accommodate the appropriate fly-line plus 46m. (50yd.) of backing. For sea trout, heavy-duty reservoir and steelhead fishing you will need 91-137m. (100-150yd.) of backing. The exposed rim on this reel allows you to apply variable pressure, with caution, with your fingers.

Finger pressure acts as a brake on the revolving spool, so controlling the speed at which line is stripped off the reel. This allows fish to be played more sensitively. There is less control when the spool is enclosed within a cage, as it is more difficult to apply pressure.

Counterbalance
A counterbalance aids the smooth delivery of line by minimizing the vibration that is caused by the revolving spool.

FLY RODS

IRRESPECTIVE OF modern materials, length and action, the fly rod of today fulfills the same role as the cane and greenheart rods of the past. Cane rods, which are still used today, are, length for length, the heaviest. They can deliver a fly accurately and delicately. Tubular fiber glass was the first material to revolutionize fly rods with its lightness. It has subsequently been superceded by carbon fiber. Rods made from these materials are lighter, thinner, and stronger. It is now possible to use a 3m. (10ft.) all day long and cast into the wind with ease. When choosing a rod you should look at the line rating, length and action. It is imperative that the rod and line are balanced and that the line can load the rod. The rod is marked with a weight of line that is suitable to use. This AFTM rating assumes that 9.1m. (30ft.) of line is aerialized outside the tip ring of the rod. If casting short distances, opt for a line size higher than that designated, but when operating with more than 13m. (40ft.) outside the tip ring, choose a line size lighter. Water type and fishing styles also dictate choice, as will the rod action. The action describes the area of the rod's length where it loads with the line and casting action. Always try out a rod with a variety of lines before buying.

1 Fast-Action/Tip-Action
This rod (top) is suited to shooting heads and severe weight-forward lines for distance fishing on reservoirs, heavy-duty river nymphing, and steelhead fishing. It is also useful for long-range dry-fly and nymph fishing on stillwaters and big rivers where both accuracy and distance are important.

2 Middle- to Tip-Action
A useful all-round rod (center), especially for the newcomer to fly-fishing. Managed properly, it can cast up to 27m. (90ft.), but the action is both delicate and accurate. The soft tip section acts as a shock absorber.

3 Middle- to Butt-Action
This highly specialized action (above) bends in the center, giving a long flexing area and creating wide loops. It is good for short-line or loch-style tactics and for the delicate presentation of dry fly or nymph on streams. It has a slow, soft action reminiscent of cane.

1

2

3

AFTM RATING
AFTM numbers describe the weight of a line, calculated in grains over the first 9.1m. (30ft.) of line, and are given either as AFTM followed by a number or # followed by a number. A rod must always be correctly matched to any line with which it is used. This information is shown on the rod handle along with other manufacturer's details. If too light a line is used for a rod, it will not have the weight to flex and load the rod. Line that is too heavy for a rod will overload it, causing it to flex too much, making casting difficult.

SHORT RODS

FOR SMALL RIVERS AND STREAMS

Partridge of Redditch Greenheart
Made from greenheart, a tropical American hardwood used for rod-building in the past, this rod (right) has a softer action than cane. It is cheaper than a cane rod and long-lasting. #6, length: 2.3m. (7ft. 6in.).

Partridge of Redditch Split-Cane/Bamboo
Split-cane or bamboo fly rods have always been revered (right). However, they have been superseded mainly by lighter manmade materials such as carbon fiber. Cane rods are still viable in short lengths but they are very expensive and are mainly for the connoisseur river fly-fisher. #5, length: 2.4m. (8ft.).

Orvis One Weight
This rod (right) is used with #1 line, which is tantamount to casting with backing. It needs accurate timing, increased line speed technique, and an effective and controlled back cast. #1, length: 2.2m. (7ft. 5in.).

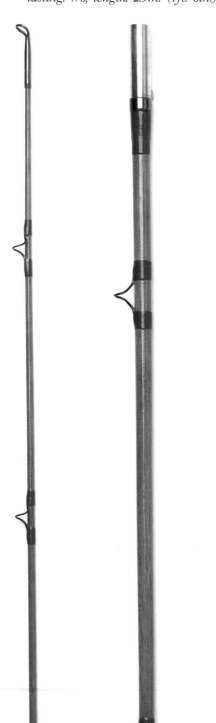

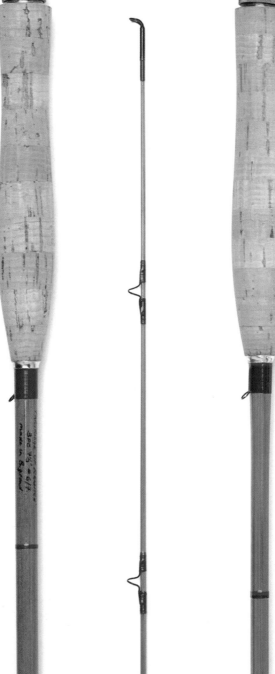

Hardy Bros. Sovereign

A popular length for river fishing, this rod (right) is used with #5 or #6 line. It is a light rod that can cast long distances, present flies delicately, and cast narrow loops to overcome wind. #6, length: 2.6m. (8ft. 6in.).

Loomis IM6

Made from carbon fiber (the rocket fuel byproduct IM6), which is a high-modulus material, this rod (right) has an increased power-to-weight ratio. It takes a #4 line and so allows delicate presentation of the fly at short range while handling fish up to 2.25kg. (5lb.). #4, length: 2.4m. (8 ft.).

Shakespeare Worcestershire Boron

This fly rod (right) is ideally suited to a variety of river fishing applications, such as fast-water nymphing at range and oval loop styles. Boron tends to soften the comparative stiffness of the carbon. #1, length: 2.6m. (8ft. 6in.).

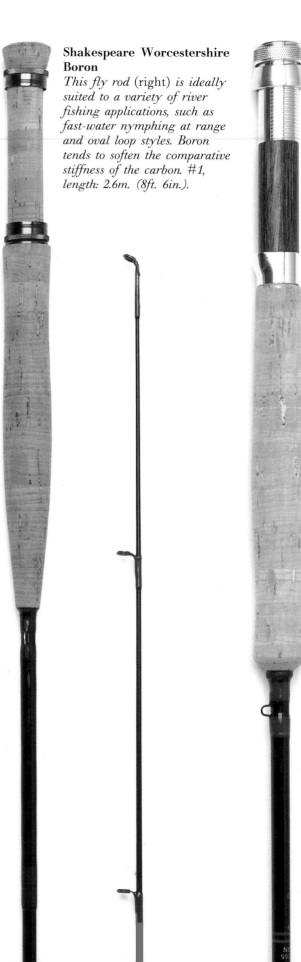

MEDIUM RODS

FOR, MEDIUM TO LARGE RIVERS AND SMALL TO LARGE STILLWATERS

L.L. Bean LL IM6
Representative of a middle-tip all-round action rod (below). *The up-locking reel seat allows for good balance.* #6, *length: 2.7m. (9ft.).*

Bob Church – Peter Cockwill Small Fishery
A carbon-fiber rod (right) *that can be used for large trout, stillwater and steelhead fly-fishing. It is a little heavy for dry-fly and nymphing techniques.* #6-8, *length: 3m. (9ft. 6in.).*

Sage Graphite II
This is a good example of an all-round rod (right). *It can cast tiny dry flies to specific fish or pitch a nymph some 25m. (27yd.) on a reservoir.* #5, *length: 2.9m. (9ft. 6in.).*

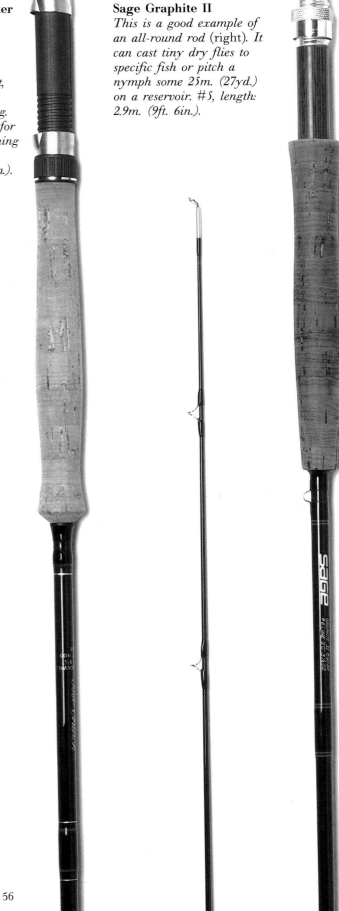

Kennedy/Fisher blank, Jardine adapted

A delicate rod with a speeded-up action (right), which is ideal for nymphs, tiny dry flies, and light tippets. #4, length: 2.8m. (9ft. 2in.).

Sage Graphite III

Graphite is a high-modulus material, which gives faster line speeds and tighter loops. This allows for better presentation of the fly at range. The Sage Graphite III (right) is best suited to long-range nymph and dry-fly fishing on stillwaters and rivers. #6, length: 2.9m. (9ft. 6in.).

Hardy Bros.

A middle-action rod (right), which is most suitable for river work, especially chalk streams. It is too soft for long-range and stillwater use and not quite powerful enough for heavy nymph fishing. #6, length: 2.7m. (9ft.).

LONG RODS

FOR LOCH-STYLE, HEAVY-DUTY RESERVOIR, AND STEELHEAD FISHING

Sage/Partridge Graphite III
A loch-style rod (below) for increased control over a team of flies, especially when dibbling the top dropper. Middle-to-tip-action. #6, length: 3.4m. (11ft.).

Gary Loomis IMX
This is a fast-action rod (right) for fishing dry flies or nymphs when distance and delicacy of presentation are essential. #5, length: 3m. (10ft.).

Sage Graphite II
A fine steelhead rod (right) with a middle-to-tip action. It allows the angler to keep firm contact with a hooked fish but is also soft enough to be used with light leaders. #7, length: 3m. (10ft.).

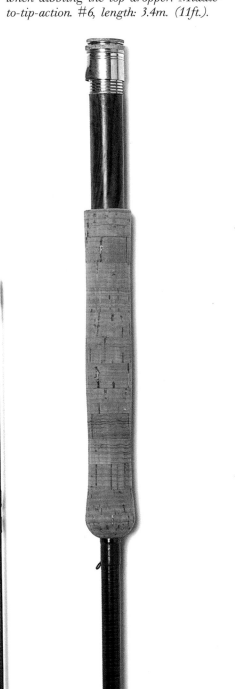

Shakespeare Worcestershire
This rod (right) is made from boron. It is a typical example of a long-range reservoir rod, permitting distance casting yet comfortable to use. #9-11, length: 3m. (10ft.).

Normark Norboron
Made from boron, this is a stiff rod (right) with little tip vibration. It is good for distance casting, especially from the bank, and for sunk-line loch tactics and steelhead fishing. #7-8, length: 3.15m. (10ft. 6in.).

Bob Church Lough Conn
Designed for loch-style or short-line drift fishing from a boat, where it is essential to use a long rod (right) with a comparative light line. This enables the bob fly to fish properly. #5-7, length: 3.6m. (12ft.).

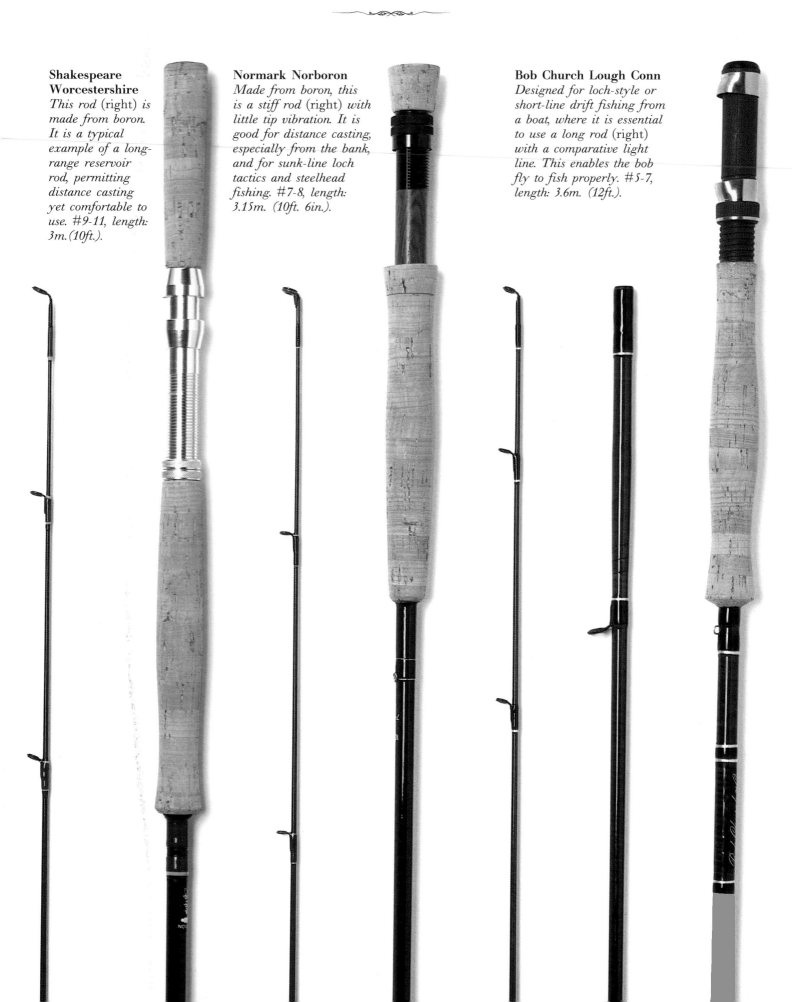

REELS
ANTIQUE

M ANY REELS IN use today are based on designs developed last century. These antique fly reels represent the everyday reels of the time. They were all precision crafted and most are still in working order.

Rochester Ideal
Circa 1900, this American reel (above) is made from nickel silver.

Brass Multiplier 3in.
Made from brass, this robust reel (above) dates from 1840.

Hardy Bros. Uniqua 3in.
Dating from 1912, this reel (above) is built from alloy and has a horseshoe latch.

Farlow 3in.
A sturdy alloy reel (above), dating from circa 1915.

Malloch Ebonite
Circa 1870-75, this brass and ebonite reel (above) has a nickel-silver rim.

Jardine 2½in.
Constructed from brass, the delicate-looking reel (above) dates from 1880.

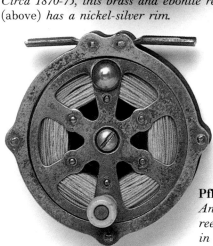

Pflueger Progress
An ornate brass reel (left) made in 1910.

Moscrop 2¾in.
Thought to be made of bronze, this reel (above) dates back to 1886.

STREAM AND LIGHT-TROUT FISHING

THESE REELS ARE used mostly with short rods and light lines. Some can accomodate #5 or #6 lines in weight-forward profiles because of their clever spool design, which also alleviates problems of line pinching or coiling.

Hardy Marquis #2/3
Ideal for very lightweight line, the Hardy Marquis reel (left) is very small. It has an exposed rim and a check system.

Hardy Golden Prince #5/6
To minimize line pinch and coiling, the Hardy Golden Prince (above) has a wide drum. It also has a drag system.

Orvis CFO 1.2.3.
One of the lightest reels made, the Orvis CFO (above) has changed little from the much-loved original model. An increased capacity makes the reel a good all-rounder.

Leeda System 2 45L
A well-designed reel (above) with increased capacity, good line lay, a disc-braking system and an exposed rim.

Maryatt MR7
Fashioned from solid-block magnesium, this reel (above) is extremely light and exceptionally strong.

ATH Traun F1
A small but capacious reel (above) incorporating sophisticated engineering.

Hardy Flyweight
A quality reel (above) from Hardy that has graced fly rods for decades.

REELS

FOR MEDIUM AND LARGE RIVERS, AND STILLWATER

THE MAJORITY OF these reels are versatile, covering most fishing styles and situations. They take the popular #6 and #7 lines with ample backing of up to 36-55m. (40-60yd.). However, some have been designed primarily for stillwater and/or hard-fighting fish, while others are better with light tippets and matching tactics.

Hardy Perfect 3¹/8
This reel (right) belongs to a series that spans nearly 100 years of production. The weight of the reel is best suited to larger rods.

**Leeda Rimfly Regular/
Cortland Crown**
Good for beginners, this medium reel (right) is popular for reservoir fishing. It is made from dye-cast aluminum and has rim control and a basic drag system.

Leeda LC80
Specifically designed for stillwater and reservoir fishing, the reel (below) has wide, interchangeable spools and a lightweight construction.

Hardy Golden Prince #7/8
Designed for steelhead and reservoir fishing, this model (above) is an excellent, light reel for use with shooting-head lines.

Orvis Battenkill 5/6
A tough reel (left) that is best suited to river fishing. Nevertheless, the counterbalance, rim control and check system make it a good reel for light-line nymphing and dry-fly stillwater fishing.

ATH Rio Orbigo F2
A good large-river, dry-fly and nymph reel (right). *Also excellent for stillwater fishing, and especially for loch-style techniques.*

Vekemans Pro. 2
An excellent hand-crafted reel (above) *with a very good line capacity, made by a small company in Belgium.*

Hardy Marquis #7
One of the most familiar sights on an English stillwater or a large American river, the Hardy Marquis (right) *is a good general-purpose reel. However, the narrow spool can cause line pinch and coiling.*

STH Airweight Gold #6
A good quality Argentinian reel (above) *with a spring mechanism on the spool.*

Hardy Princess
The Hardy Princess reel (left) *is of the cage design. Although it does not have the advantages of rim control, its lightness and drag system more than compensate.*

Orvis CFO IV
The US model (above) *covers nearly every aspect of fly-fishing – stream, large river or stillwater.*

REELS

FOR RESERVOIR, HEAVY-DUTY, SEA-TROUT AND STEELHEAD FISHING

T HESE REELS ARE designed to accommodate the heavy fly-lines and shooting heads that are used for catching large fish on large waters. The reels can be heavy and should be used with a specialist rod. Their large capacity allows for plenty of backing – essential when fighting athletic fish. The generous capacity of these reels helps when fishing fast rivers or deep stillwaters with specific tactics, such as Northampton styles.

Rimfly Magnum 200 D
Suitable for double-handed rods, this model (right) is normally used for salmon fishing. It has a good line lay and backing facility.

Pflueger Medalist 4in.
A shooting head reel (right) for lead-core and other heavyweight lines. It is also a functionable, durable steelhead reel.

Orvis Battenkill 8/9
A reliable reel (above) that uses a disc-braking system.

Sage 509
Counterbalanced to minimize spool wobble, this robust reel (above) reduces vibration down the line to the fish. This is useful when line is taken off very fast from the reel by a running fish.

Leeda/3M System Two
A rugged construction makes this reel (left) a favorite in Alaska. It has a disc-brake and rim control.

Leeda/Rimfly Magnum
This reel (right), used with a light, double-handed rod, is ideal for sea trout and certain steelhead tactics. It is also good as a shooting-head reel. It is counterbalanced and has a basic drag system.

Vekemans/RST
One of the lightest large-diameter reels (above), this reel is counter-balanced and has an exceptional drag system. Superb as a loch-style sunk-line and shooting-head reel, it is also good for steelhead.

Orvis CFOV
An excellent design (right) for reservoirs, especially sunk-line work. An upmarket shooting-head reel which is also good for sea trout and steelhead.

Hardy Marquis #8/9
An excellent reel (above) for sea-trout fishing. It has rim control, but the spool is rather narrow for distance casting.

Pflueger Medalist 7.6cm. (3in.)
This smaller model (above) is ideal for demanding sunk-line techniques.

Shakespeare Speedex
Possibly the best reservoir bank reel (left) for nymphing. The gearing system is useful for quick line retrieval and for coping with hard-fighting fish.

ACCESSORIES

Shooting Glasses
For fishing in the evening, use amber glasses (above) to extend your daylight vision.

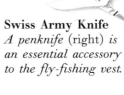

Swiss Army Knife
A penknife (right) is an essential accessory to the fly-fishing vest.

Tweezers
Use tweezers (below) to pick up delicate insects without damaging their wings.

Gink
This fly flotant (left) is known throughout the world, and is responsible for the term "Ginking."

Orvis Hy-Flote
A liquid flotant (above).

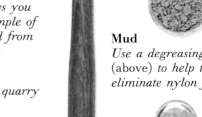

Marrow Scoop
A marrow scoop (right) allows you to take a sample of ingested food from a dead trout.

Mud
Use a degreasing agent (above) to help to eliminate nylon flash.

Priest
To despatch quarry quickly and humanely, use a priest (below).

Test-Tubes
Retain your samples of insects in plastic test-tubes (left) for later study and imitation.

Pump
A device (left) for identifying the stomach contents of a trout without harming the fish.

Aerosol Fly Flotant
For speedy application, fly flotant is available in aerosol form (below).

Nylon Cutter
To save time, fasten snippers (above) to a retractable device.

Fly Mate
For greasing or degreasing leaders quickly, this tool (above) is ideal.

Stopwatch
Carry a stop-watch (right) to work out trout feeding depths when boat fishing on reservoirs.

Permasink
*This substance
(left) can be
applied to nylon
to make it sink
– floating nylon
scares trout.*

Leaded Leader
*Use a leaded leader
(above) to turn a
floating line into
a sink-tip.*

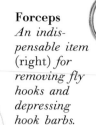

Forceps
*An indis-
pensable item
(right) for
removing fly
hooks and
depressing
hook barbs.*

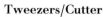

Tweezers/Cutter
*Two essential fly-
fishing tools – a
cutter and tweezers
– have been cleverly
incorporated into
this implement (left).*

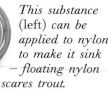

Split Shot
*Although
frowned
upon,
shot (left)
can help to place
a nymph to
trout feeding
deep.*

**Fluorescent
Bob**

Orvis Mud
*Use ointment (left)
to reduce the fish-
scaring tendency of
floating nylon.*

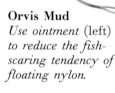

Cul-de-Canard Oil
*Extracted from the
nether regions of the
duck, this oil (above)
is a fly flotant.*

Permafloat
*Dry flies thoroughly
before applying this
flotant (below).*

Releasing Forceps
*The ingenious
roundel on these
forceps (right)
makes extraction
of the fly quicker
and easier.*

Indicator Yarn
*Fix brightly
colored yarn
(left) on the
leader to
detect a
take.*

Muciline
*A line and leader
flotant (above),
which is essential to
make fly-line tips
and nylon leaders
float high.*

Amadou
*The leather patch
(above) contains the rare
fungus amadou. The fungus is used
for drying flies. This patch is attached
to a retractable device called a zinger.*

**Line Care and
Fly Flotant**
*Clean off any
debris that clings
to the line with
this liquid (above).*

Nature Viewer
*A jar with a magnifier
(above) used to identify
aquatic creatures, which
can then be imitated.*

Tippet Dispenser
*Keeping nylon tidy can be a
problem. A dispenser (above)
enables you to carry five
tippets of different diameters
without risk of tangling.*

Telescopic Insect Net
To catch adult food forms such as caddis, upwing or mayfly, use an insect net (right). Species can then be identified and imitated: a sound policy when fishing for educated trout.

The Chest Pack
Substitute this chest pack for a waistcoat when deep wading. The harness is adjustable so fly boxes can be kept dry.

Hand Seine Net
A simple hand net (above) will unravel many a mystery. It is very easy to miss the insect species that occur in the surface film, but by using the net you can obtain this valuable information and so make the appropriate fly pattern choice.

Neoprene Gloves
These fingerless gloves (above) are a must for the early-season fly-fisher. They are warm and waterproof but allow you to retain contact with the line.

Polarized Glasses
For improved underwater vision, even on gray or rainy days, wear a pair of amber glasses (above).

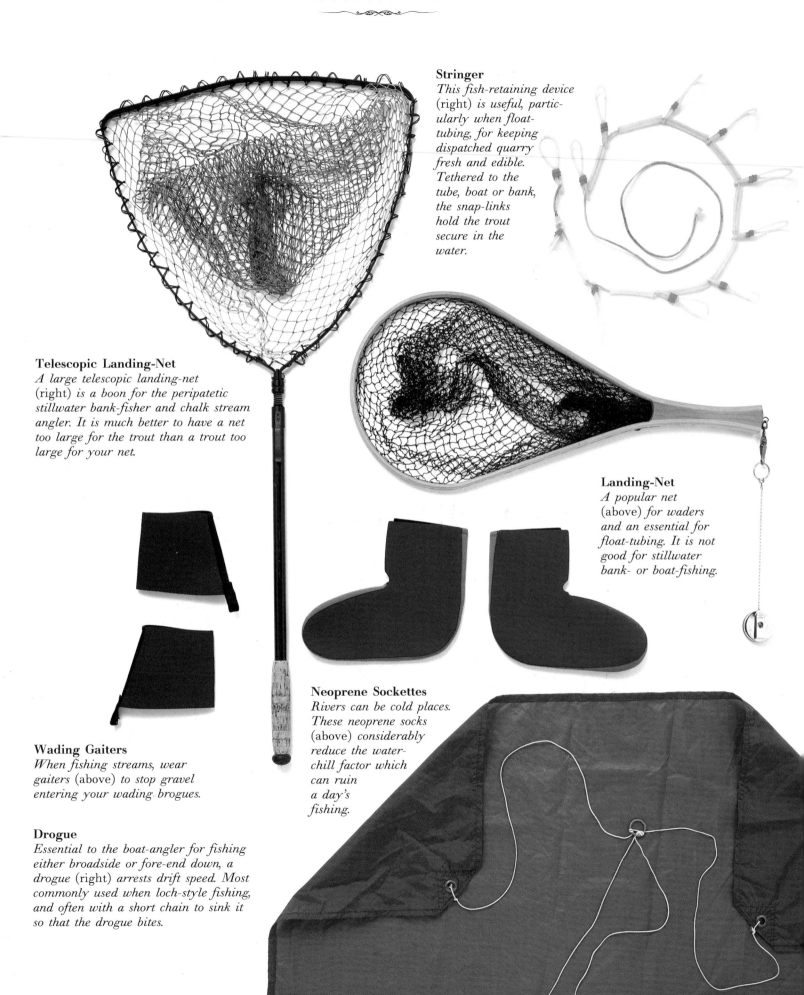

Stringer
This fish-retaining device (right) is useful, particularly when float-tubing, for keeping dispatched quarry fresh and edible. Tethered to the tube, boat or bank, the snap-links hold the trout secure in the water.

Telescopic Landing-Net
A large telescopic landing-net (right) is a boon for the peripatetic stillwater bank-fisher and chalk stream angler. It is much better to have a net too large for the trout than a trout too large for your net.

Landing-Net
A popular net (above) for waders and an essential for float-tubing. It is not good for stillwater bank- or boat-fishing.

Neoprene Sockettes
Rivers can be cold places. These neoprene socks (above) considerably reduce the water-chill factor which can ruin a day's fishing.

Wading Gaiters
When fishing streams, wear gaiters (above) to stop gravel entering your wading brogues.

Drogue
Essential to the boat-angler for fishing either broadside or fore-end down, a drogue (right) arrests drift speed. Most commonly used when loch-style fishing, and often with a short chain to sink it so that the drogue bites.

CLOTHING

F ISHING CLOTHES ARE designed to be comfortable in all weathers and conditions and to allow freedom of movement to cast and play fish. There are times when the proper clothing may even save your life.

Waistcoat
A multi-pocketed angling waistcoat (right) is indispensable. Spare spools, reels, lines, accessories, a fly box and even food can be carried about easily as you move around.

Wading Boots
For safety, select a boot with a felt or felt-composite sole.

Thermal Jacket
Warm, lightweight clothing is invaluable for cold-water wading and the early season. The pile lining of this jacket (left) is water-resistant and quick-drying.

Buoyancy Waistcoat
The buoyancy waistcoat (above) has the many pockets of an angling waistcoat. It also doubles as a life jacket.

Wellington Boots
The banks of rivers and lakes can be wet. To keep your feet dry, wear wellingtons (above). Choose a size that gives you room for an extra pair of socks.

Chest-High Waders
When you want to wade in slightly deeper pools than thigh waders will allow, chest-high waders (right) are ideal. They are available in a variety of materials, but neoprene is the best, as it is warm as well as waterproof. It is also fairly resistant to punctures and tears.

Australian Bush Hat
This type of hat (left) *is designed to protect the eyes from glare, allowing better underwater vision.*

Goretex Coat
Trout are cautious, and to deceive them you should always try to blend in with the surroundings. You will be most comfortable wearing clothes made of a modern material, for example Goretex, but choose a drab color, such as olive, tan or brown. The new fabrics, which are lightweight, wind-resistant, and "breathe" yet remain waterproof, will defeat the worst of the elements. This coat (left) *is perfect for bank or boat fishing in all but the very hottest weather.*

British Tweed Hat
A tweed hat (below) *is good for cold days.*

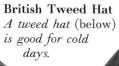

Up-Downer Hat
The up-downer hat (below) *is perfect in the sun.*

Short Wading Jacket
A short, waxed-cotton jacket is useful for wading in deep areas. The short cut of the jacket keeps everything clear of the water.

Thigh Waders
Thigh waders (right) are essential for reservoir fishing and for British chalk streams. They are more comfortable to wear for the whole day than chest-high waders, but for warm feet make sure that they can be worn over thick or insulated socks.

Midge Hat
Mosquitoes and midges can ruin a fishing trip. You are especially prone to being bitten in tundra areas such as Alaska, parts of Canada and northern Finland. Use a midge hat or head net (right) as well as a good anti-midge lotion.

THE FLY

TO CATCH A TROUT on an artificial fly is arguably the highest form of fishing. A trout, a wild creature gifted with vision and perception, possessing an uncanny survival instinct, mistakenly accepts a concoction of fur, feather, tinsel, hair or other unlikely ingredients offered as a representation of a real creature. Of course, not all artificial flies are direct imitations of food forms eaten by trout. Some resemble beings created by the overheated imaginations of science-fiction writers – overdressed, incongruous, gaudy – and yet they work. These lures or attractors appeal on a different level. A reaction of anger, or the recognition of a bait-fish shape, or the stimulus of color – all play their part. Why trout should take them is open to conjecture, but then fly-fishing is full of mysteries, and perhaps that is a good thing. Despite the appeal to trout of attractors, I believe that the essence of the sport lies in the imitation of a food form, be it insect, fish or crustacean.

A fly-tier may seek absolute realism, impressionism or merely suggestion, in the latter case offering a hint or near parody of the actual insect. This is the beauty of fly-tying, for not only can you indulge your own personal whims and fancies, but you also face the challenge of satisfying those of the fish. The ultimate goal will always be to tie a pattern yourself, creating the precise effect you desire, and then deceive a trout with it. The flies depicted on the following pages are a mere smattering among the thousands that exist. I may have left out a few favorites – local variations and obscure dressings will always, sadly, be overlooked. But you will find patterns to suit every water, most insect and small-fish forms, and the various species of trout to be found over a wide range of habitats throughout the world.

THE FLY EXPLAINED

THE ETERNAL QUESTION of which artificial fly is appropriate in a specific fly-fishing situation is rarely answered by reading fly-tying books.

However, the following selection is intended to help the newcomer select fly patterns to suit both type of water and technique.

The inclusion of antique flies and a few "classic" patterns provides a sense of history. Through this an understanding of fly design will emerge. Also included are some commercially-tied flies. Often,

substitutes for original materials have to be found, both for mass-produced flies and self-tied patterns, because of scarcity and the need for conservation. This alters the concept of the fly, so variations are constantly created.

Selecting the right fly is always a chancy affair. Confidence is crucial to successful fly-fishing and is gained only by a willingness to experiment.

Antique Fly Cabinet
Produced by Hardy Bros. Ltd., this wooden cabinet (below) *is ideal for storing flies and fly-tying equipment.*

THE DRY FLY

The dry fly is dressed to float on the surface. The hackles help achieve this, as does the tail. Dry flies represent adult flies such as mayflies, caddis, stoneflies, and midges, as well as spiders, grasshoppers, and other terrestrials. Modern styles imitate an insect set in the surface film rather than on it. Light dressings are appropriate for calm water in which flies are just hatching; well-hackled flies, often incorporating hair, for high floating in rough, fast water in which insects are hatching or about to fly off.

THE WET FLY

Also known as a "soft hackle" or, in some areas, a "flymph," the wet fly in its simplest form comprises a slim body and a few turns of soft hackle. It is designed not only to sink just below the surface, but to represent the hatching fly. Some wet flies are designed for sea trout; some are small-scale versions of salmon flies; others parody aquatic life forms. Either hackled (palmered) or winged, the wet fly is ideal for loch-style fishing or in a team of three flies on freestone streams.

THE NYMPH

The nymph is an artificial re-creation of a specific natural aquatic insect form. The term "nymph" is a generic description covering larvae, pupae, mayfly nymphs, crustaceans, such as freshwater shrimp and hoglouse, and even elaborate impressionistic forms such as girdle bugs. Nymphs can be weighted or unweighted so that various fishing depths can be reached, ranging from the lake or river bed (weighted) to just below the surface (unweighted, even buoyant).

THE STREAMER/LURE

The streamer or lure is basically an elongated wet fly which can be divided into two distinct categories. The first is the attractor which, while not imitating any particular food form, appeals to the trout through its color, movement, flash or combination of these. The second is the imitator of either bait-fish or cray-fish, or even mice and frogs. Streamers are often weighted and fished on sinking, sink-tip or floating lines, depending on the conditions and preferred style of fishing.

STEELHEAD CLASSIC

THE ORIGINS OF many steelhead patterns are to be found among the classic salmon flies of Scotland. Early developments were based generally on the principle of attraction rather than imitation, although the more drab patterns would have suggested caddis and stonefly in much the same way as the more faithful imitations do today. The style continues to be used widely along the western coast of North America, despite the vogue for egg patterns and new flies.

SPRUCE
Although designed in the 1930s for sea-run cutthroats, this pattern (*below right*) from Oregon was and still is a favorite summer steelhead pattern.

ORANGE COMET
This pattern (*above*) has an alternative name, the Howard Wortan Special. The bead eyes give the fly weight. The orange color is very effective, especially in spring, late summer, and autumn.

MICKEY FINN
When wet this fly (*above*) resembles bait-fish. It should be fished between mid-water and the bottom. Originated in 1936 by John Alden Knight, it is favored worldwide for rainbow trout.

BURLAP
Dating back to 1945, this excellent general-purpose pattern (*left*) is a favorite of many fly-fishers. Its ragged, brown-hued appearance suggests large caddis larvae or stonefly nymphs.

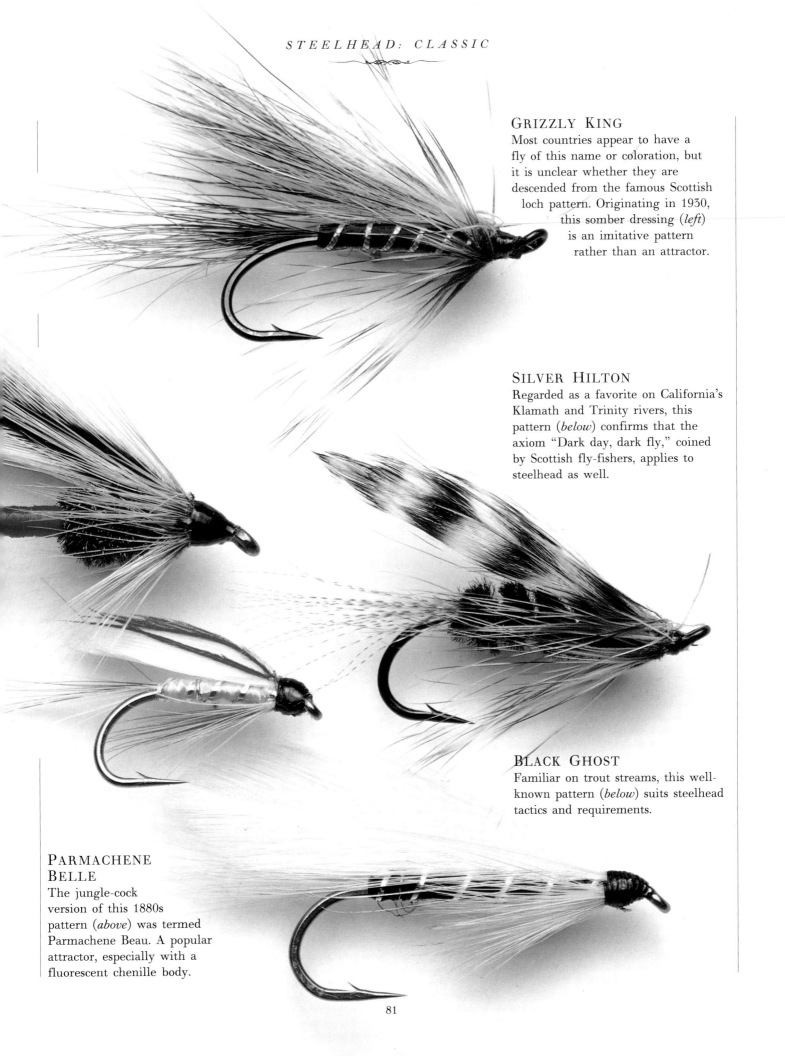

GRIZZLY KING
Most countries appear to have a
fly of this name or coloration, but
it is unclear whether they are
descended from the famous Scottish
loch pattern. Originating in 1930,
this somber dressing (*left*)
is an imitative pattern
rather than an attractor.

SILVER HILTON
Regarded as a favorite on California's
Klamath and Trinity rivers, this
pattern (*below*) confirms that the
axiom "Dark day, dark fly," coined
by Scottish fly-fishers, applies to
steelhead as well.

BLACK GHOST
Familiar on trout streams, this well-
known pattern (*below*) suits steelhead
tactics and requirements.

PARMACHENE BELLE
The jungle-cock
version of this 1880s
pattern (*above*) was termed
Parmachene Beau. A popular
attractor, especially with a
fluorescent chenille body.

ATTRACTORS & IMITATORS

THESE FLIES ARE the front line of the steelheader's attack. Many developed from traditional patterns; others have broken new ground. Colors predominate over silhouettes, and the water-moving attraction of deer-hair, hackle and other types of animal hair have an increasingly significant part to play.

FLASH FLY

Though primarily an Alaskan-silver and king-salmon fly for colored water, patterns such as this are a boon. However, ethics enter into play as this fly pattern resembles a spinner. Best fished from near to the bottom up to mid-water.

FERRY CANYON

This Randall Kaufmann fly emphasizes how steelhead patterns have altered dramatically, incorporating new materials and colors. Purple has become extremely popular for dark days and evening use.

BEAR-HAIR BUGGER

This fly is primarily for fast water. The usual tail of marabou, when fished in extreme currents, can be matt and appear lifeless. But hair reacts and pulsates, and should be chosen for white-water pockets and stretches.

BOMBER (FINLAND)

Originated in Lapland and used for Atlantic salmon on the River Tana, this pattern is also used as a trout fly during the summer, when large sedges hatch. Also useful in autumn for steelheads.

POPSICLE

This pattern is used in British Columbia for steelhead. The purple rabbit's-collar produces a sinewy motion in faster currents. A pattern for sink-tip lines and full sinkers. Fish near the bottom.

FLAMINGO ZONKER

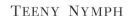

Pink has only recently come to the fore as an attractor color. Perhaps it is the hint of egg that makes it so deadly. This Masterline version is best fished on a sink-tip or a full sinker.

TEENY NYMPH

Jim Teeny is an undisputed master of steelheading. This simple fly, fashioned from pheasant in various colors, forms the mainstay of his armory and has caught most game fish, including Atlantic salmon. An indispensable pattern.

FLESH FLY

This represents decomposing salmon flesh. As unsavory as it may appear, rainbows feed on this as the salmon run the stream to spawn and die.

EGG-SUCKING LEECH
Leeches hover below spawning salmon, feeding off dislodged eggs; rainbows feed on the leeches. Fish this rabbit-strip pattern close to the bottom on either a weighted leader or a sunk fly-line.

WOOLLY BUGGER (ORIGINAL)
This pattern is one of the best producers of specimen trout in North America, especially in large sizes. Fish on a sinking line, but not in bright conditions.

MAGIC SAM
This is a Steve Parton reservoir pattern for salmon and trout. It is purely an attractor, though with a hint of bait-fish. A sinking line is best, covering mid-water to river bed.

MUSKRAT STRIP
Tanned muskrat, bead eyes and a Matuka style of dressing make this a winning combination when imitating small fish. Muskrat creates a better action in faster water. Ideal for thin and low water.

PURPLE WOOLLY BUGGER/ EGG-SUCKING LEECH
Atlantic-salmon anglers tend to agree that purple will either catch or clear the pool. If the same is true of steelhead, the color should be changed immediately.

MOUSE
Trout respond well to this mouse, especially in Alaska. Best fished on a floating line cast to the far bank and brought back across the surface with as much commotion as possible.

EGG FLIES & DRY FLIES

THESE TWO TYPES of fly are at opposite ends of the steelheader's spectrum. Egg flies are fished hard on the bottom, their ethics of use still debated; dry flies are more established, fished on the surface. Streamers are the forerunners of egg flies and flesh patterns. The use of dry and damp flies is considered to be more ethical.

RUSTY BOMBER

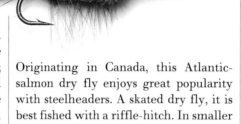

Originating in Canada, this Atlantic-salmon dry fly enjoys great popularity with steelheaders. A skated dry fly, it is best fished with a riffle-hitch. In smaller sizes, it is a very effective sea-trout fly for night fishing in warm weather.

OVERSIZE TROTH ELK HAIR CADDIS

This fly has seduced many trout, salmon, sea trout and steelhead. It is a successful fly in various sizes and suits both sedge and stonefly hatches. Best fished upstream dead drift, or slightly up and across, then allowed to swing across and downstream.

STEELHEAD CADDIS

A disturbance pattern rather than a dry fly, this is Bill McMillan's imitation of the autumn caddis/cinnamon sedge/orange caddis. Fish slightly upstream, dead drift, then allow to skate round with the current on a floating line.

GREASE-LINER

This steelhead dry fly was created by Harry Lemire for fishing in British Columbia. It is designed to move water on a floating line and is a very good imitation of the autumn caddis.

WATER-WALKER

A Lani Waller pattern that moves water, especially if riffle-hitched. Waller is one of America's most inventive steelheaders. This pattern makes full use of the floating properties of deer-hair and calf-tail. Fish across and down.

EGG FLY

This pattern has revolutionized fly-fishing, especially in Alaska. A simple ball of fluorescent yarn fished near egg-laying salmon, it has accounted for legions of fish. Fish hard on the bottom and allow to dead drift downstream.

FALL FAVOURITE

With the orange/fall caddis hatch and spawning, food matter takes on orange tones, which are attractive to rainbow trout, less so to brown trout. Fish this fly on either a floating or sunk line, across and down.

EGG-ROE CLUSTER

Why have one fly when you can have a bunch? Inspired by Randall Kaufmann, this marriage of fluorescent orange and red with a hint of Flashabou is highly visible to egg-feeding fish, even when water is murky.

POLAR SHRIMP

This unmistakable white-and-orange combination was popularized on California's Eel River in 1936. It has remained an exceptional late-season pattern, especially if weighted and utilizing fluorescent body materials.

FATHER'S BRIGHT ROE

A product of burning the midnight oil at my vise, this pattern combines the near-legendary qualities of the Babine Special with Kaufmann's enticing egg-roe cluster effect. Alaskan fish love it, and I see no reason why it should not work elsewhere.

GREEN ROE

Fluorescent green and chartreuse hold enormous attraction for steelhead and rainbow species. This pattern is useful in colored water, fished near the bottom with a weighted leader or on a sunk line with a short leader.

PINK DEVIANT

Fluorescent pink, in this case squirrel, has an odd property when fished in deep water – it changes to a deep, lustrous red. This pattern is designed for such water and works extremely well in Alaska.

SKYKOMISH SUNRISE

This pattern was devised in 1940 by Ken and George McLoud for the Skykomish River and has given George steelhead of up to 13kg. (29lb.). Its success lies in the deadly combination of red and white.

BABINE SPECIAL

Peter Alcaly advised me to try this fly in the fall. Also referred to as the "two-egg fly," it is one of the first true egg patterns. Weight the pattern and fish deep where there are loose salmon eggs.

UMPQUA SPECIAL

This 1935 pattern, attributed to Don Hunter, originated on Oregon's Umpqua River. Patterns developed for particular rivers are usually long-lasting and effective – most are still very much in evidence and exceptionally fishable.

ADMIRAL

Rear Admiral Eustace Bannan Rogers (1855-1929) created this pattern using white quill-wing, since replaced by the more mobile polar bear (now protected) or buck tail. Primarily a rainbow fly, but useful for the steelheader.

ALASKA ALEXANDER

Created for my father for his first trip to Alaska. Originally I tied this fly with a red cock-collar, but now I substitute Flashabou. It accounted for 6kg. (14lb.) and 8kg. (18lb.) steelhead on its first day, and has produced for both of us since.

RESERVOIR ANTIQUE FLIES

STILLWATER FLY-FISHING probably followed a considerable time after fly-fishing was established on rivers and streams. The patterns were more often gaudy attractors and lures than imitations of insects, and these characteristics are still present in many modern reservoir dressings.

STRADDLEBUG MAYFLY

A traditional Irish wet mayfly pattern (*below*). While the Straddlebugs and related Gosling patterns look almost nothing like the natural mayfly, their effectiveness at mayfly time on the loughs is nonetheless legendary.

BLAE & BLACK

An ancient pattern (*left*) from Scotland ("blae" meaning gray). It is considered one of the great standard representations of the duck fly, one of several species of large, black chironomids found in Scottish lochs and Irish loughs.

MURROUGH

The Irish name for the great red sedge, which occurs in large numbers on the loughs of central Ireland during summer. One of many old patterns, the Murrough (*right*) is probably the most popular. Fished on the bob and drawn through a good wave, its dense hackle creates an attractive commotion.

ALEXANDRA

This famous attractor pattern (*left*) was deemed so deadly on some waters that it became one of the very few flies ever to be banned.

COCK ROBIN

A traditional Irish pattern, the Cock Robin (*below*) is considered an attractor by most, and it still has a loyal band of followers. Some regard it as a useful fly when sedges are hatching in summer.

BUSTARD & ORANGE

The Bustard series of flies has fallen from the repertoire largely due to the lack of bustard plumage. This pattern (*below right*) is nevertheless effective for lighter, sandy-colored sedges and, at night, for sea trout.

DUNKELD

This trout fly (*below*) developed as a simplified version of the Dunkeld salmon fly (Dunkeld is a town on Scotland's River Tay). Once considered one of the great stillwater fly patterns, it is still regarded by many as an essential sea-trout fly.

PETER ROSS

Attributed to Peter Ross of Killin, Perthshire, this fly (*above*) is a variation on the Teal and Red. Enshrined as one of the most popular lake patterns ever devised, it is a very good imitation of tiny fry when fished on the point.

87

Classics

THESE FLIES REMAIN the corner-stone of modern reservoir sport, the most accessible form of fly-fishing. Here are patterns which inspire confidence and are useful for the beginner. The following are the very essence of Reservoir Classic flies, but a good fly alone will never catch a trout. Put a confidence-boosting fly into the hands of a diligent angler, and you have a winning combination.

MIDGE PUPA

This Dick Walker fly has stood the test of time and remains effective. The dressing is fairly standard, but what sets this pattern apart from the rest is the ingenious use of white feather-fiber filaments to echo the natural appendages.

OMBUDSMAN

Brian Clarke created this imitation of the alder larva, describing the natural counterpart as the Genghis Khan of the stillwater world. Ombudsman is a good all-rounder when fished close to the bottom in early season.

BLACK SPIDER

Arthur Cove's sparsely dressed nymph is a standard midge pattern that is often used on the dropper. It is a useful imitation of a variety of food forms.

BLACK-&-PEACOCK SPIDER

Created by Tom Ivens, this fly covers the majority of stillwater requirements, from midge-feeder to snail, at any depth, especially early in the season. Black-and-Peacock Spider can be fished on either a sinking or a floating line.

JERSEY HERD

This fly, created by Tom Ivens, is so-named because the original fly's body was made from a foil milk-bottle top. An enduring and realistic fly, especially as a stickleback pattern, and good for *Daphnia*-feeders and general use.

IVENS' BROWN-&-GREEN NYMPH

Perhaps the definitive stillwater nymph. This fly exudes confidence and is useful when it is unclear exactly which insects the trout are feeding on. Fish slowly, using a figure-of-eight or small pulls.

AMBER NYMPH

With his stillwater nymph patterns, Dr. Howard Bell revolutionized fly-fishing. This is just one example of his patterns and was created at Blagdon Reservoir. It successfully imitates emerging sedges.

GRENADIER

This large red or orange midge, tied by Dr. Howard Bell for use at Blagdon Reservoir, is mandatory when the natural is hatching. It is best fished either singly or in a team, loch-style. It can also be dressed dry.

CHOMPER (SERIES)

Dick Walker was arguably the greatest innovator on the stillwater fly-fishing scene. Like Bell and Cove patterns, there is an air of simplicity about his creations, perfectly illustrated in this thin, white *Corixa*-like pattern.

COVE'S PHEASANT TAIL

Simplicity and sharp observation have created this impressionistic midge. Fish this fly anywhere, at any depth, at any time of day or season, and it is guaranteed to bring results. Always fish it slowly.

COLLYER'S BROWN NYMPH

A Dave Collyer pattern. This general-purpose nymph suggests many creatures, particularly lake and pond olives and brown midges.

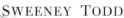

BUZZER

Dr. Howard Bell created this midge pattern during the early part of the century. This simple, effective fly is still used today.

BABY DOLL

In 1971 Brian Kench devised this simple white fly. It immediately found favor with both anglers and trout, but especially with fish feeding on fry. The fly loses its effectiveness once the fluorescence fades or becomes soiled.

SWEENEY TODD

The "demon barber" inspired Dick Walker to create this crimson-throated hair wing. Good for both brown and rainbow trout, and useful in a variety of sizes and at all depths. It is particularly effective during late evening.

APPETIZER

Among the greats of stillwater fly-fishing is Bob Church. His Appetizer, created in 1973, is one of the most successful fry imitations around. Bob landed eight Grafham trout (a day's limit) totaling 14kg. (31lb.) on this fly.

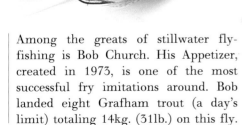

BLACK-&-ORANGE MARABOU

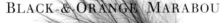

During the late 1960s, the formative years of the UK's stillwater boom, Taff Price devised many streamer patterns. This one, which utilizes marabou, is still an effective dressing. A good early-season fly, best fished deep and slow.

MUDDLER MINNOW

Dan Gappen created this truly classic fly, but Tom Saville must be thanked for introducing it to British stillwater fly-fishing circles. In large sizes it is a great small-fish pattern; it is better still in small sizes for imitating hatching sedge.

DRY FLIES

MORE THAN ANY other branch of stillwater fly-fishing, this area has undergone enormous change in the last five years. Rising trout are quarry for the dry fly but not necessarily candidates for a light-wire nymph or pupa. This change has created a wealth of new ideas and patterns, particularly to imitate sedges and midges. The secret in stillwater dry-fly fishing is to resist pulling the fly or fishing it static.

DADDY-LONGLEGS

Dick Walker devised this stillwater pattern, paying unaccustomed attention to detail on the legs. It remains one of the most effective reservoir dry flies of all time. Simply cast it out on a long leader and leave it.

HAWTHORN

Many designs are based on this terrestrial, found in stillwater between the middle and end of spring. Most depict the natural's gangling back legs. The insect is best fished in rather than on the surface.

GREY DUSTER

This fly belongs in every stillwater fly-fisher's box. Excellent in sizes 18-20, especially when *Caenis* are on the water, but also effective fished static, when unknown surface activity suggests that dry-fly tactics need to be employed.

GRAFHAM HOPPER

The use of dry flies during the past decade has been revolutionary. Fished static and cast accurately, even at short range, this single fly has accounted for legions of trout. The body may be orange, olive or claret.

LAKE/POND OLIVE DUN

Because the differences between these species of upwing are so slight, I settled on a single pattern for both, utilizing the *cul-de-canard* feather for its buoyancy. The fly works when trout are feeding heavily on the insect in the surface film.

GREENWELL'S GLORY

It is believed that the late Canon William Greenwell devised the wet version of this fly while fishing the River Tweed. This dry version remains one of the best stillwater olive patterns and is mandatory in reservoir anglers' boxes.

BRISTOL HOPPER

John Hornsey devised this West Country variation of the Grafham Hopper for fishing at Chew Reservoir. It is very much a Bristol fly with more than a hint of buzzer. It is very successful when fished static or cast to rising fish.

BOB'S BITS

Bob Worts designed this emerging midge pattern for his home water, Grafham. It is a general representative tying, most useful in black, covering other species of insect besides *Chironomidae*. Fish static when trout are rising to hatching midge.

BLACK BOB

Another effective, if unlikely, creation from the Bristol school. This loose but adequate interpretation of black beetles, midges, and flat-wing flies appeals to trout in a ripple.

PARA MIDGE

I created this fly for that infuriating period when trout are shouldering in flat calm, usually to feed on emerging buzzers. This attempt at the stage between pupa and adulthood works well when fished static to observed trout.

HARE'S-FACE MIDGE

The properties of the Hare's-Face are well known when fish are feeding on midge. On its first outing at Blagdon, my dry fly accounted for six fish. Since then, it has seldom been off the leader when trout are rising in a gentle wave.

REALISTIC DRY MIDGE

I tied this version of midge to produce close-copy patterns merely by changing color schemes. In this way, various species can be mimicked when flat calms and trout behavior so demand. Fish singly to observed rising trout.

ELK-HAIR CADDIS

The fluorescent yellow butt (which casts light green) echoes the female caddis's egg cluster. It works extremely well when natural adult caddis are about, especially during late evening when the females return to lay eggs.

GODDARD & HENRY SEDGE

John Goddard and Cliff Henry made this sedge imitation to overcome the poor floating properties of patterns created in the 1960s. A favorite with river and stillwater fishers the world over, it is very good static or as a wake fly.

SAVILLE'S SUPER SEDGE

Tom Saville is one of stillwater's pioneers. His adult sedge works extremely well on the Midlands reservoirs, when naturals hatch during the summer. This pattern is always worth a wetting during the evening.

GROUSE-WING

Though not overenthusiastic, trout can be persuaded to accept an imitation of the grouse-wing, as long as it is small. Sadly, two successive droughts have all but wiped out this insect. This pattern still works, however.

SPENT CADDIS

Dawn often reveals a residue of female sedges that have died after the previous evening's egg-laying exertions. This imitation spent caddis is best fished static in darkness or early dawn even if no naturals are seen.

INNOVATIONS

S TILLWATER TROUT FISHING is a comparatively new branch of the sport offering exciting new designs and departures from traditional fly-tying. Many of the pioneering fly patterns have been refined. Some benefit from modern materials – the Fiery Grenadier, for example; others, such as Dave Shipman's floating buzzer, offer a new tactical style. A few, such as the Fidget, herald an exciting departure from old styles.

ST CLEMENTS

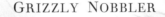

Devised by Steve Newsome specifically to attract "stockies" from reservoirs. This garish fly has taken fish in bright weather conditions, especially during heat waves. Fish very slowly on Hi-D lines at depths of over 3m. (15ft.).

FLAT ROACH

Probably the most lethal dead or dying fish imitation available. Troublesome to tie, it is nevertheless worth the effort. Fish static on a floating line in and around fry activity or weed beds. The occasional twitch often gets a response.

CONCRETE BOWL

An all-purpose fly suiting most retrieves and line types that can be dressed in varying colors. The deadliest are white and green; pure red; orange-and-yellow. The flies are attractors rather than specific imitations.

GRIZZLY NOBBLER

Steve Parton designed this fly pattern during the summer of 1984, when perch disease was rife. When dead or dying, perch become off-white, perfectly matched by the grizzle hackles on this fly. The lead head simulates death throes.

CARNHILL NOBBLER

A variation on the Trevor Housby original, with a shorter hook and collar hackle. The long tail creates an undulating motion. A fly for most lines, the Carnhill Nobbler is best retrieved using short, intermittent pulls.

PINK PANTHER

Gordon Fraser concocted this face-saver for those days when nothing seems to work. How it operates is unclear. It is possible that below 1.5m. (5ft.) or so, pink becomes a deep red and trout take the pattern for a giant bloodworm.

CAT'S WHISKER

The allure of this fly lies in its color combination. Devised by David Train, the original had white cat's whiskers, which can be difficult to obtain, for the tail support. Fish at all depths on all lines, using various speeds of retrieve.

DATCHET RAZZLER

Once an imitation of a bullhead, this fly pattern is now standard fare for static or ultra-slow retrieves on Hi-D lines or lead-cores, in very deep water or near the lake bed. Trout take these flies very confidently in a variety of colors.

RABBIT ZONKER

A Steve Parton pattern for fish feeding on fry. It is especially good during late summer into autumn, using a sinking line and various retrieves, or a floating line and figure-of-eight retrieves around weed beds.

SHIPMAN'S BUZZER

Dave Shipman's fly suggests a chironomid emerging or hatching in, or on, the surface. This fly should be "Ginked" to float and fished either static or slowly figure-of-eight style, singly or in a team.

GREEN-BUTT GRIDDLE BUG

Steve Parton adapted this American pattern for reservoir use, adding a fluorescent butt and longer rubber legs. It is best fished from spring to mid-summer, on an intermediate or Wet Cel II line in long, steady pulls or quick jerks.

MINK SPUDDLER

My own fry pattern, based heavily on American and British patterns. It may seem unnecessary to carry many similar flies, yet small fish form so large a part of the reservoir diet that it can be a mistake not to do so.

OAKHAM ORANGE (PEARL)

In the hands of Dave Shipman this pattern has undergone change, acquiring an arc-chrome tail and pearl Lurex body. He suggests it should be used in bright conditions with a floating line as a middle or top dropper.

BEWL GREEN

Designed by Chris Ogbourne to cope with a heavy green midge hatch, this pattern has proved deadly when green chironomids are on the wing. Fish either deep on a Hi-D line or on the surface with a floater.

FIERY GRENADIER

This established Dr. Bell pattern has been updated with the addition of a fluorescent orange tail. Best fished in traditional, wet-fly mode in a team of three flies, it is very much a summer pattern for use on a floating line.

FLASHBACK NYMPH

This American general nymph pattern has enjoyed considerable success as a point fly in traditional team formation, and singly when bank fishing. The iridescent back imitates hatching insects. Fish either very slowly, or static.

FIDGET

This unlikely creation from John Hatherall has proved to be one of the best floating fry patterns I have used. On one occasion, at Grafham, I landed 12 trout. This pattern is also a good attractor/disturbance pattern.

LURES & ATTRACTORS

NO ONE KNOWS quite why trout chase lures and attractors. It may perhaps be because they provoke an aggressive instinct in the trout, imitate a favored food substance or simply make the trout curious. Indiscriminate use has tended to give lure fishing a bad name, but for the beginner, this type of fly offers the best chance of success on a reservoir.

THE WAGGY

To exclude Peter Gathercole's pattern, popularized by Fred Wagstaff at Rutland, would be unfair. It has caught a great many large trout on big reservoirs. However, I leave you to decide whether or not this is a "sporting" fly.

BLACK CHENILLE

Bob Church created this to imitate the dark cases of caddis flies. It is a favored early-season pattern in small sizes, on any line, depending on area and depth.

APPETIZER

Fry-feeding trout can become preoccupied with a certain size of food. You must have a pattern that imitates it. This tandem offers a considerably longer fly and can be essential during summer and autumn at Rutland and Grafham.

RABBIT VIVA

The Viva is probably the most successful lure of the last decade. Fish it throughout the year, fairly slowly, at all depths. Reaction from trout is almost guaranteed with this pattern.

GOLDIE

This pattern was created by Bob Church specifically for fishing big brown trout, utilizing both a lead-core line and Northampton-style tactics. It remains a superb pattern, especially for sea trout and brown trout.

RASPUTIN

Dick Walker was angling's colossus of the post-war period. He was always innovative, and this pattern of his was one of the first to incorporate Ethafoam. The Rasputin imitates a bullhead.

WHISKEY FLY

Orange, so prevalent in North American steelhead patterns, was brought to the fore in the UK by Albert Willock, at Hanningfield Reservoir, Essex. An immediate success, especially in high summer.

MUDDLERINE

Steve Parton has done more to rationalize reservoir lure fishing than any other fly-fisher. This muddler-type fly overcomes the problem of hooking and chasing rainbow trout on the surface.

JACK FROST

Bob Church created this pattern for fry-feeding trout, specifically those feeding on small bream. It has caught enormous amounts of fish and is an extremely potent fly at most depths. A slow retrieve appears to work best.

MINNOW STREAMER (MALE)

Taff Price was one of the first to draw attention to flies that imitate bait-fish, are purely attractive or provoke attack. Many he based on American concepts. This is just one example of the early reservoir style.

FLOATING FRY

The idea of floating fry created a style of fishing that is the ultimate in excitement and, arguably, provides the best chance of a specimen trout from a reservoir. Primarily an autumn pattern, best cast near weed beds and simply left.

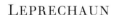

LEPRECHAUN

This fly found particular favor at Grafham, where trout would soup in great numbers of *Daphnia*. If orange, the traditional color for *Daphnia*, is unsuccessful, then this fluorescent green fly will generally work.

SINFOIL'S FRY

Another early reservoir style. When bailiff at Weirwood, Ken Sinfoil found great success imitating the pin-head fry trout were so fond of. He did this by utilizing clear plastic sheeting, fashioning an almost transparent body.

MISSIONARY

The late Dick Shieve adapted this from an earlier New Zealand pattern. It was superseded by marabou patterns but is still effective, especially on a slow-sink line. Use long draws interspersed with short pulls.

COMPETITION WET FLIES

OVER THE LAST decade, competitions on reservoirs have boomed, creating specific rules and tactics. Some of the flies are well known; others are kept secret. While owing something to tradition, these flies represent more modern trends, but show how competitive fly-fishing can offer the pleasure angler new twists, patterns and ways of fishing.

RED-ARSED WICKHAM

Summer is the time for sedges on British reservoirs, lochs and lakes. The fluorescent red tail makes it highly visible, either at range, in low light, or in peat-stained water. An all-round pattern, fished as a top dropper on a floating line.

JC VIVA

The Wet Cel Hi-D line allows teams of flies to be fished at depth. Black, the ever-popular early-season color, is almost a mandatory point-fly color, and succeeds in making this pattern deadly.

TOFFEE-PAPER WICKHAM

Designed by Grafham fly-fisher John Ielden for the top- or middle-dropper position on a floating line. It is especially useful in summer and/or during sedge activity. An interesting variation, which can prove to be the undoing of trout.

ANNABELLE

This top- or middle-dropper pattern is named after my daughter. Bob Morey, the respected Bedfordshire fly-fisher, uses it on a floating or sunk line almost all season through. I see it as a sedge imitation for a floating line from summer.

PEACH BOOBY

When slowly nymphing through over shallows proves troublesome because of constant weed hang-ups, a buoyant fly such as this on the point overcomes many of the problems. It also succeeds in attracting trout.

PEARLY WICKHAM

Steve Parton and Steve Newsome created what has since become an almost definitive modern palmer. It is best suited to the top or middle dropper, fished on a floating line, and is an exceptional sea-trout loch pattern.

WHITE PALMER

Chris Ogbourne developed this into one of his top sedge patterns. I have added a tail of pearlescent Spectraflash. It is now my best small-fish pattern, fished either on the point or dropper.

KILLER

While adhering to competition size limits, John White's design imitates the damsel nymph tied on a heavy wire hook. It is an ideal point fly for digging deep using a floating line in flat calms.

VINDALOO

Created during the heat wave of 1989 by the Bristol School for use with a Hi-D line in near-flat calms and at depth. Deadly as an attractor on the top dropper, it is one for use on hot days in bright sun.

TOOGOOD'S WHITE

Another Bristol pattern from the noted angler of the same name. A good early- and late-season point fly, this stark creation came into its own during the 1989 drought. The fluorescent red provides obvious target points.

LIGHT BULB

John Hornsey from Bristol has quickly established himself as one of the more adaptable, reservoir fly-fishers. This pattern is a departure from his usual imitative approach, though it is nonetheless effective for all that.

ORANGE WIGGLER

A point fly for fishing with nymphs above. Again, best suited to a Hi-D line, but also effective on an intermediate line when trout are feeding on *Daphnia* near the surface in dull weather.

MINI APPETIZER

Another point-position fly by Bob Church, this is arguably the best sunk-fry imitation about. Excellent the whole season through at most depths, but in a class of its own from summer through to autumn.

PEARLY HARE'S EAR

David Shipman's Hare's Ear variation is very successful during fry time. It is most useful in autumn, around weed beds, when it should be fished on the point position, using a floating line and long leader.

ORANGE PRIEST

Sometimes small flies are to be preferred, even at depth. John Moore designed this fly, suited to any leader position, but perhaps best on the top dropper when employing strip-and-hang or nymph-and-hang techniques (loch-style).

FLUORESCENT RED PALMER

Very much a Grafham top dropper, this pattern is extremely useful in rolling waves and overcast conditions. It is fished fairly quickly in order to make a discernible wake.

PEACH DOLL

I believe it was England's National Team captain Geoff Clarkson who inspired this pattern. It came to the fore when England won the 1987 World Championship. Fish strip-and-hang style on a Hi-D line in cold water.

LARGE NYMPHS

SMALL STILLWATERS HAVE created their own methods, fly patterns and tackle requirements. Although stocked regularly with sizeable trout, small stillwaters are not necessarily easy to fish. Special tactics and flies are often required. This section covers a range of colors, shapes, sizes and foodstuffs that have all caught fish. Never be frightened to change patterns, as the offbeat often works where the more predictable has failed.

MAYFLY NYMPH

This pattern (*below*) has been effective so often when the naturals are not present, one wonders just what trout take it for. Dick Walker created this long-shank nymph, which appears to be as good on rivers as on stillwater. It is truly ubiquitous.

RABBIT-STRIP DAMSEL (ZONKER)

I have tinkered with David Fynsong's original to produce a fly (*below right*) with the characteristics of the natural. It caught rainbows weighing 4kg. (8lb.) on its first outing. It is worth trying in a bright, flat calm.

FLUORESCENT-GREEN MONTANA

Everyone succeeds with this stillwater pattern (*below*) except me! One of the major patterns of the last five years, it is almost essential to every fly box.

GAME PIE

A mad fit at the vise one day created this pattern (*left*). Rabbit, partridge, hackle, and pheasant were all incorporated, plus fluorescent yarn.

PULLING DAMSEL
I required a close-to-nature copy of a damsel nymph (*right*) that incorporated hot-spots. These I depicted as fluorescent yellow eyes to offer trout a target. The marabou tail works in a similar way.

LAMBSWOOL DAMSEL
This Richard Walker dressing (*two below*), was one of the first to cover this insect's nymphal form. A parody of the natural, it hints at body shape.

BLUE DAMSEL
Bill Sibbons, the Hampshire big-trout master, realized that trout chasing adult blue damsels cannot tell the difference between above or below the surface. This simple fly (*left*) is fished at speed just beneath the surface.

ALDER LARVA
Many patterns depict the alder larva. This one (*above*), is most useful during the spring. Fish it slowly on the bottom.

YELLOW EARS
Fish this pattern (*above*) slowly on a floating line and long leader when damsels are about.

NYMPHS & SMALL ATTRACTORS

THIS GROUP OF FLIES forms the foundation of the small stillwater fly box. A logical sequence of presentational variations can work far better than continuous fly changes. A diminutive fly can be the undoing of a mighty fish because the trout does not feel intimidated by it to the same extent as it would by a long-shanked nymph or large, gaudy lure.

BROWN NOBBLER

This style of fly – especially the mini variety – offers both alluring movement through the water and weight, enabling it to sink quickly to cruising depths. Brown is good for some species of damsel nymph and dragonfly larvae.

ORANGE TADPOLE

A pattern best reserved for bright, sunny days. Like most small-water attractors, this is best fished on a slow-sink or intermediate line, using either a constant figure-of-eight retrieve or long, steady but slowish pulls on the line.

HERN WORM

Large fish in small, clear lakes are often scared by large flies, yet small flies do not sink quickly enough to the desired level. For the perfect solution, pinch a small lead-substitute shot on a small Pheasant Tail.

YELLOW NOBBLER

Color is the important factor here. On sunny days, and for no apparent reason, trout will target yellow. Yellow is also extremely good for use in cloudy water and algae blooms, being one of the more visible colors, as is, oddly, black.

PINK LADY

Steve Newsome's early-season reservoir fly is also effective on small lakes. Bead-chain eyes achieve a sink-and-draw action, which is enhanced by the marabou tail tied short to prevent annoying plucks at the fly by following trout.

WIGGLE-TAIL HARE'S-EAR

Devised on the spur of the moment from remnants of marabou strewn across my fly-tying bench. Three rainbow trout over 4kg. (8lb.) confirmed my earlier faith. I vary the tail color to incorporate white, black, yellow and olive.

ORANGE CUT-DOWN

Orange is a superb color for early in the day or for getting trout to react and chase. It should, however, be changed quickly if the trout show signs of upset or alarm.

WOBBLE WORM

Christened "the gentleman's dog-nobbler," Peter Lapsley's pattern was designed to imitate bloodworms in a variety of sizes and colors. By varying head, body and tail coloration, many insect permutations can be covered.

VIVA TADPOLE

This great performer works in a variety of depths, ranging from deep in early season, through middle and top layers for the rest of the fly-fishing year. Indispensable, but best fished slowly and steadily.

PATTERSON RED SPOT

A shrimp pattern with fluorescent red yarn spots. Broadly appealing, though only when freshwater crustaceans occur. A targeting fly that is particularly deadly if presented to fish already observed feeding or slowly cruising.

PHANTOM PUPA

This is a scaled-down version of a Dave Collyer pattern and represents the *Chaoborus* spp. of *Diptera*. It is best fished on a slow-sink line and a long leader of 5-8m. (18-20ft.), with a very slow figure-of-eight retrieve.

DAMP CRANE FLY

Dever Springs in Hampshire is one of the more recent big-fish waters. Fishing a dry daddy-longlegs near to the bottom on a fast-sinking line works extremely well here. Use a slow figure-of-eight or small draws on the line.

YELLOW CORIXA

The late Dick Walker created this alternative to the normal brown-back/white-body variety. A good change fly best suited to target fishing – that is, spotting a trout and delivering a fly to it in its feeding path.

LEAD SPECK

This Bill Sibbons fly pattern offers the trout a tiny speck (size 16-18 hook) that looks edible and is unobtrusive. I added the marabou tail to create the illusion of free-falling movement.

COCKWILL'S HARE'S-EAR SHRIMP

This versatile fly has caught trout for me worldwide. Bob Church even lured a Russian brown trout weighing 4kg. (9lb.). It is wonderfully "insecty" and edible. A must in every fly-fisher's box, it suits all fly-fishing methods.

LEAD BUG

A heavily weighted pattern that does not scare or give offense to wary trout is difficult to create, but Peter Cockwill has succeeded with this example. For targeting fish rather than random pulling.

GREEN-WAISTED WHITE

Where standard fry flies and white patterns fail to work, this one often succeeds. It has caught sufficient trout to be included in a fly box. Fish on a slow-sink line with long, slow draws and medium-to-fast retrieves.

FORMATIVE PATTERNS & ODDITIES

P UT-AND-TAKE fly-fishing and clear-water fly-fishing both have a short history. These water types have spawned their own patterns, tied to outwit educated trout. Here are some curious and original examples, together with their historical forebears.

VOSS BARK NYMPH

Conrad Voss Bark is just one of Two Lakes' eminent anglers. His leaded Olive Palmer is a wonderful all-rounder suggesting damsels, shrimps and olive nymphs. Fish on a floating line and long leader, either blind or to observed fish.

SHORT DFM GREEN PARTRIDGE

Large trout cruising in shallow water can be frightened by weighted flies and lost if small hooks are used. They are, however, susceptible to tiny flies. Dick Walker's solution was to tie a small fly on a large hook – and it worked!

BRASSY PHEASANT TAIL

Dick Walker, in his book *Modern Flydressings* (1980), gives the recipe for a Brown Damsel. This Pheasant Tail uses the same technique, but substitutes a brass ball-bearing for the split-shot lacquered head.

ORANGE SHRIMP

A great favorite with the Damerham regulars during the early 1970s. This comparatively gaudy pattern can out-fish a more natural olive – even on streams. Always a pattern to carry when fishing clear waters.

BW OR BARRIE WELHAM NYMPH

Originally named Brown Wool, this fly is known as the BW or Barrie Welham Nymph, primarily because of the champion caster's consistent success with this bug. It is faintly reminiscent of a midge pupa and other aquatic forms.

OLIVE DOG-NOBBLER

This updated version of Trevor Housby's Ice Jig comes from Kevin Hart, a leading reservoir bank angler. Devised primarily to catch trout sticklebacking on Queen Mother Reservoir near London, it has proved a deadly damsel imitation.

ORIGINAL MAYFLY NYMPH

The use of ostrich herl gave Dick Walker his initial killing pattern, which was superseded by the angora yarn version. I prefer the original which, although fragile, gives the illusion of feathery life in a more natural manner.

RED DIDDY OR RUBBER-BAND FLY

Devised by Arthur Cove to mimic the frantic writhings of a bloodworm or chironomid larvae. Used on small lakes (weighting the body for deeper fishing), it is very successful, especially on fish that have seen it all.

HINGED DAMSEL

At best, movement is self-produced, as with this articulated damsel. On its first trial, I landed three fish over 2kg. (5lb.). Best fished on a neutral or slow-sink line in short pulls interspersed with long, slow draws on the line.

ORANGE TWINKLE NYMPH

A range of nymphs has evolved. Their appeal lies in their color or flash. Orange is a useful color in hot, bright weather, especially at depth. This fly pattern has proved particularly deadly when fish are feeding on *Daphnia*.

TWINKLE DAMSEL

J.W. Dunne, the great dry-fly theorist, was moved to paint hooks white to echo the nymph's sparkle and inner reflection. This dressing shows how effective modern materials can be in the same capacity.

FUZZY CRAWLER

Barry Unwin's oversized and ragged Hare's-Ear Nymph has led to the downfall of many canny brown trout. Fished very slowly along the lake floor with a floating line, it suggests damsels, dragonfly nymphs, and other food forms.

DRAGONFLY NYMPH

The dragonfly nymph is on the trout's menu all year round. This commercial pattern should be fished very slowly along the lake bottom. Use a floating line and long leader, at times momentarily speeding-up the retrieve rate.

PEACHY

Often, rainbows will chase this fly for long periods, then surge forward and strike. Sometimes they turn off at the last minute. Different days produce varying reactions. Fish this fly fast, but use sparingly. It is not a standard pattern.

MONTANA WASP

An effective change pattern – that is, once familiar patterns have failed, on goes the outrageous. This fly pattern is best fished on an intermediate line and long leader, brought back in figure-of-eight movements.

MONTANA CAT'S WHISKER

Perhaps not the purest of insect patterns, this fly has met with considerable success recently. I find it best fished on an intermediate line using a fast figure-of-eight retrieve or slow, lengthy pulls.

POPPET

This buoyant, "insecty" fly works best in a midge hatch. Fish on a fast-sinking line, left to rise and fall through ultra-slow figure-of-eight retrieves. Good on hot days or early in the season.

CLASSICS

OF ALL THE GROUPS of artificial flies of historical importance, there can be none better documented, more strictly adhered to or which have bequeathed such a legacy to fly-fishers than these classic chalk stream and limestone patterns. Despite being almost 100 years old, many are still enjoying success. Others are reminiscent of an era of tranquillity and of rivers that are now either threatened or lost to fishing for ever.

AMERICAN BLACK GNAT

Larger than the English version and also sporting a tail, this pattern represents one of the earlier American dry flies, the original body appearing to be formed from chenille.

GRANNOM

As a boy I remember seeing blizzardlike hatches of grannom (*Brachycentrus subnubilis*), Britain's earliest sedge, hatching in spring. This commercial pattern is a combination of the Russell, Ronalds and Courtney Williams versions.

IRON BLUE DUN

Representative of the dun stage of *Baetis niger* or *B. muticus*, which tend to hatch in blustery conditions and, when emerging, have a habit of monopolizing the trout's attention. The magenta tag is not present on the natural.

SHERRY SPINNER

This commercial pattern, differing from the original's seal's-fur body and hare's-ear, was tied by G.E.M. Skues to represent the imago stage of the blue-winged olive (*Ephemerella ignita*). Conservation now suggests a floss body should be used.

TUP'S INDISPENSABLE

This commercial pattern is named after the wool coming from a tup's (ram's) hind quarters. It is a superb pale watery pattern originated by R.S. Austin, although G.E.M. Skues named it with typical aplomb.

LUNN'S CAPERER

This pattern was first tied by the Test's great river keeper, William Lunn, to represent the Welshman's button or caperer sedge, *Halesus digitatus*. The yellow band would seem to suggest a cluster of eggs.

LUNN'S YELLOW BOY

This modern, store-bought fly is a passable attempt at the pale evening spinner (*Procloeon bifidus*), apricot spinner (pond olive, *Cloeon dipterum*) and large spurwing (*Centroptilum pennulatum*).

HOUGHTON RUBY

Named after possibly the most exclusive club and stretch of the Test, and originated by its most famous keeper, William Lunn. This commercial pattern is an excellent imitation of the egg-laying female iron blue (imago stage).

RED SPINNER

A general imago tying for a number of upwing olive species, this commercial version was originated by G.E.M. Skues. Seldom exceptionally effective, the Lunn's Particular is much preferred, as are other, more modern patterns.

LIGHT CAHILL

An American pattern originated by Mr. Cahill, a Dublin *émigré*. Of the two versions – Light and Dark – the lighter is a wonderful imitation of the olive *Baetis* spp. such as *B. ascentroptilum* and, in larger sizes, *B. heptagenia.*

PALE MORNING DUN THORAX

This remarkably effective pattern is by the American fly-fishing master Vince Marinaro. Marinaro dressed flies with wings and hackles in the middle of the shank, thus creating a silhouette.

RED SEDGE

This commercial pattern is based lightly on Skues' Little Red Sedge and remains a standard chalk stream fly. Although the modern sedge/caddis interpretation is now far more lifelike and accurate, this older pattern still works.

PALE WATERY

This fly is a modern derivation of G.S. Maryatt's original. With H.S. Hall, Maryatt developed the eyed hook as we know it today. This fly represents the dun of *Baetis fuscatus.*

GREENWELL'S GLORY

Even now, over 130 years since its inception, there are few better olive patterns than this, especially for the early and late hatches of *Baetis rhodani*, the large dark olive. Indispensable.

BLUE-WINGED OLIVE UK

This commercial pattern may be attributed to G.E.M. Skues and Commander C.F. Walker. Both, it seems, felt that the blue dun appearance was more important than the natural's olive/brown body coloration.

LUNN'S PARTICULAR

One of the most famous chalk stream flies of all time. Though I have found most success with it during a fall of blue-winged olive spinner, it is usually regarded as a general olive pattern imitating both dun and spinner.

GINGER QUILL

This represents the standard American recipe. There is also an English winged version and a spinner version. All are extremely similar and fill a general dry-fly role, suggestive of many species yet not specifically imitative of any one.

Mayfly Adults

T HE BRITISH MAYFLY (*Ephemera danica* and *E. vulgata*) has captivated fly-fishers for over 100 years. Every season is guaranteed to produce another pattern or idea. There can be few insects that have been so well documented and accurately imitated. These are just a few examples of the many and various styles and patterns that represent this sublime insect, whose emergence takes place between late spring and early summer.

EMERGER

This is a hatching nymph between its juvenile and dun stage. Cream furry foam forms the body, deer-hair the wings. The thorax contains pearlescent Spectraflash strands that imitate the nymphal outer skin.

LOUGH ARROW

Named after the Sligo lake, and justly famous during the local mayfly carnival. This fly's sweptback, flowing hackle and fused colors always remind me of the ecloding, or hatching, fly.

STILLBORN

This pattern, conceived by the Orvis Company of Vermont, blends old and new. Swisher and Richards recognized the importance of casual ties amid a heavy hatch of flies. These tend to be the first cropped by the trout.

STRADDLE BUG

Despite the appearance of a traditional wet pattern, this is fished dry on chalk streams. The body can also be formed from natural garden raffia. The late Dick Walker set great store by the color orange during a mayfly hatch.

GOSLING

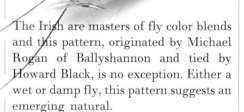

The Irish are masters of fly color blends and this pattern, originated by Michael Rogan of Ballyshannon and tied by Howard Black, is no exception. Either a wet or damp fly, this pattern suggests an emerging natural.

FLOATING NYMPH

When I developed this pattern I opted for a body of dubbed deer-hair for its floating properties and Antron for the embryonic wings. The wood-duck tail gives this pattern a softer outline.

MAITLAND'S HATCHING MAYFLY

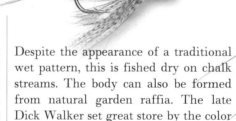

This fly was fashioned primarily for the River Kennet in Berkshire and uses entirely traditional materials. The pheasant tail echoes the nymphal stage; the seal's-fur, the emerging adult. Deer-hair wings add prominence and buoyancy.

DROWNED MAY

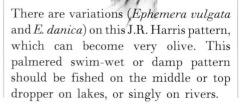

There are variations (*Ephemera vulgata* and *E. danica*) on this J.R. Harris pattern, which can become very olive. This palmered swim-wet or damp pattern should be fished on the middle or top dropper on lakes, or singly on rivers.

FRENCH PARTRIDGE

This is a "buzzier" version of the Courtney Williams classic, which had a crimson rib rather than palmered hackle. During the 1940s, when traditional mayflies were at their height, hackled varieties were equally recommended.

NEVAMIS

This is one of John Goddard's earliest patterns, devised to overcome the bad hooking quality of some patterns. The clipped and palmered head tackle, coupled with the hackle wing, make this a durable and buoyant pattern.

SHADOW MAYFLY

This imitation of a mayfly dun is one of the best patterns in use today. Created by Peter Deane, the remarkable Eastbourne fly-tier, it has proved useful, in my experience, in spinner falls.

LIVELY MAYFLY

By chance, I picked up a book by Chauncy Lively in the Fly-Fishers' Club, and, by adapting one of his patterns, evolved this fly. It enjoys considerable success and remains my most successful dry-dun pattern.

GREY WULFF

Mention the mayfly on the streams in Hampshire and its anglers will, in the same breath, mention this pattern. Lee Wulff's pattern has been the first choice for two decades at least.

FLY-LINE MAYFLY

A fusion of the traditional with the off-beat. However, someone (Dave Whitlock, I believe) had the bright idea of turning old fly-line into fly bodies. This is the spinner version, semi-spent.

SILHOUETTE OR THORAX DRY MAYFLY DUN

The Orvis Company extended the series of thorax flies they have made so popular with this somewhat dark *Ephemera danica* dressing. It works superbly well because of the low-slung profile.

GREEN DRAKE WULFF

For the important American *Hexagenia limbata* (yellow may), *Ephemera simulans* (brown drake) and *Ephemerella grandis* (green drake), this Lee Wulff pattern fits the bill, with some color variation where appropriate.

LUNN'S SPENT GNAT

William Lunn achieved immortality through his work as river keeper on the Test. This version of the imago stage illustrates his uncanny ability to imitate nature on a hook. He has created an enduring imago pattern.

Nymphs

For every floating fly ingested by the trout, five or more subsurface food forms will be eaten. Fishing the artificial as an actual food form demands great skill, for method is far more important than choice of pattern. Once a certain level of competence is achieved in nymph fishing, in your hands will lie the most potent method ever devised for catching trout in alkaline water. It takes time, but it is time well spent.

SAWYER'S PHEASANT-TAIL

This simple but highly effective concoction uses the fibers from the tail of a cock pheasant and a length of dark copper wire. If you carried only this one pattern, you could catch trout the world over, almost irrespective of water type.

TROTH PHEASANT-TAIL

Any fly from Al Troth is worth including in a fly box. The use of peacock herl for the thorax gives the fly a slightly midge-like air and a bit of sparkle. I have found this pattern to be better than the Sawyer original in fast water.

KILLER BUG

A rather nondescript, maggot-shaped fly made of darning yarn, but nonetheless it has caught salmon, trout and grayling in great numbers. Perhaps trout mistake it for a shrimp or caddis grub – or even a maggot!

PINK SHRIMP

I added a tail of partridge and two pearlescent Flashabou horns to this shrimp imitation. On the Derwent during a fly-fishing exhibition, I extracted four rainbows and three grayling on it in only half an hour.

GERR-OFF

Created by John Goddard for fishing during the 1976 UK drought. It sinks by the hook weight alone. Effective for slow areas, low-water conditions and around and below mid-water, where trout are feeding on nymphs and shrimps.

SHRIMPER

Another Goddard pattern and the first, to my knowledge, to use PVC to imitate the natural's shell back. Shrimp imitations are confidence flies and, where allowed, can be deadly for trout lying in deep areas and pockets.

HOGLOUSE

Last year I realized that I was missing out on the potential offered by *Asellus* spp. This pattern has equipped me better. It shows potential as a lake pattern, especially at depths of 12m. (40ft.) or more; also for streams.

BLUE-WINGED OLIVE NYMPH

Ephemerella ignita in the UK and *Baetis* spp. in the US are well known to chalk and limestone stream fly-fishers. I suspect this pattern best imitates the pale morning dun. River trout are usually susceptible to olive-based patterns.

SQUIRREL NYMPH

Grey squirrel pelt uncannily resembles a hare's-mask and is a nymph-tier's godsend. This general-purpose nymph is just one example. It has fished extremely well for me, especially first thing in the morning, just after the early hatch.

GREEN SQUIRREL

Immersed in a fluorescent green dye, the pelt becomes olive-hued. This pattern has been extremely effective in *Baetis* activity, as well as in a more general nymphing capacity, fished upstream and dead drift.

BOW-TIE BUZZER

Another Sawyer's Pheasant-Tail version. The yarn allows the fly to revolve around the nylon. The angler threads the nymph up the leader, ties on some white yarn and adds the leader tippet to it to create a free-moving midge pupa.

GREY GOOSE

I have used Lady Amherst pheasant instead of herl-fiber tail. Goose or pheasant is one of the best small *Baetis*, *Brachycercus* and *Caenis* spp. materials there is. Best fished upstream, dead drift, in the classic Nether-Avon style.

PVC

An alternative general nymph when the pheasant tail is spurned. John Goddard's cleverness fuses new (PVC) with old (feather fiber) to deadly effect. I prefer sparse flies, but added weight makes the pattern a shade fatter.

GOLD-RIBBED HARE'S-EAR

The Gold-Ribbed Hare's-Ear and Pheasant Tail between them cover all seasons. You could confidently fish this indispensable pattern in any water, in most styles, and expect to catch fish.

GE NYMPH

This pattern of mine is now my first choice as a nymph pattern. It has a little more buzz than Sawyer's Pheasant Tail and a leaner form than the Gold-Ribbed Hare's Ear. Best fished upstream, dead drift or induced. Weighting is optional.

HATCHING BUZZER

Mick Huffer from Nottingham has made the *Chironomidae* a life study. These insects are an important part of stream hatches. Patterns such as this one will deceive trout when other imitations fail.

POLY-RIB BUZZER

Chalk stream make-up is changing because of pollution. With change comes the ascendancy of *Diptera*, rather than *Ephemeroptera*. Best for selective trout feeding on midges. Fish this pattern just under the surface, dead drift, upstream.

EMERGERS

NATURE, BAROMETRIC PRESSURE, the intensity and angle of light – all probably have a role, decreeing that nymphs migrate surfaceward and hatch. The surface tension, or meniscus, creates an enormous barrier for them, causing some to die, others to be trapped, with most at least held motionless for varying amounts of time. Trout capitalize on this comparatively easy prey – a fact that the fly-fisher should never overlook.

GREY SUSPENDER PUPA

A factotum is always worth carrying, and this is it as far as emergers are concerned. Grey imitates caddis, mayfly and even terrestrials. Fish on a 4-5m. (12-15ft.) leader upstream to rising fish or toward known feeding activity.

MARCH BROWN FLOATING NYMPH

Although *Rhithrogena morrisoni/hageni* (US) and *Rhithrogena germanica* (UK) are similar, the American fly enjoys a protracted season. Fish without drag in the surface, in slack-water areas such as pools, or behind rocks.

MOSER EMERGING CADDIS/ SEDGE

This comparatively simple fly works on two levels: first as a newly emerged caddis, and second as a hatched amber-brown upwing dun. Fish either up or downstream, dead drift. Especially good in the evening.

CREAM SUSPENDER

If the Grey Suspender Pupa does not work, this one probably will. It covers most upwings, especially the smaller *Baetis* family. This particular style represents the nymph with its wing-case about to explode.

STILLBORN OLIVE

I became aware of the importance of stillborns when I read Doug Swisher and Carl Richards' books. During heavy hatches, some flies die. Trout often feed selectively on such flies, and so specific patterns such as this are called for.

RED SEDGE EMERGER

Best fished in or near to the surface rather than mid-water. A sink-and-draw on a steady figure-of-eight retrieve works well after the fly has been allowed to swing down and across stream.

FLOATING NYMPH (JARDINE)

I have included my own floating nymph variation purely because it works! This style is quite familiar, but the addition of a parachute hackle has appeared to increase its allure. Fish up or downstream, dead drift, without a hint of drag.

KAUFMANN FLOATING NYMPH

Somewhat easier to tie than others, the dubbing ball on top of the thorax has been replaced with Antron fibers, curved as a loose wing-pad cover. Very realistic, this is a personal favorite of mine, especially for smaller species of mayfly.

EMERGER II (JARDINE)

At certain times, especially during heavy hatches and evening periods, trout get remarkably fussy about what they eat, so accurate patterns are important. This one has wings and soft leg hackles, and is designed for use in heavy hatches.

EMERGING MARCH BROWN

This pattern also works in hatches of caddis, *Ephemera danica* and *E. vulgata* as well as *Rhithrogena*. Antron wings and a dubbed deer-hair body give it great buoyancy and create an illusion of struggling life.

MUSKRAT EMERGER

A pattern I conceived for stillwater but a good general emerger on rivers too. The long tail represents the discarded nymph shuck; the muskrat body suggests a wide range of insects. Fish in the surface film dead drift, without drag.

LAST LIGHT SPECIAL

How well the angler can see a fly is often essential to its success. Fluorescent Antron wings – orange (good on gray days), white (fast water) or yellow (evenings) – maintain high visibility. Fish as other emerger patterns.

COLLYER DEER-HAIR MIDGE PUPA

Before Gink and floating nymphs, keeping a fly in the surface with the leader sunk posed a problem. The late Dave Collyer solved it by using deer-hair/muddler techniques for the head of this chironomid imitation.

RAIDER

The curved body imitates many species (mayfly, midge or caddis) during the hatch. The parachute hackle keeps the fly's position in the surface film. Fish static, drag-free, on rivers and lakes using a 4-5.5m. (12-18ft.) leader.

GODDARD'S SUSPENDER PUPA

John Goddard's self-buoyant fly demonstrates its creator's ingenuity. Midge pupae play a very important role in chalk stream fishing. This pattern is indispensable when trout are feeding on the natural.

CARNHILL'S ADULT BUZZER

On the Test, trout rarely move more than a few inches to take a fly, so when they move a metre or so, as they did to take this one, it must be special. Use this fly from summer to autumn.

LITTLE GREEN MIDGE

Trout can become preoccupied with tiny creatures in the surface, usually tiny *Chironomidae*. This small apple-green pattern can also be tied in black, brown or dark olive. Do not overdress. Fish it with a fine tippet.

FLOATING ADULTS

ONCE HATCHED, THE adult fly is still at peril from the trout's attention. Mayflies wait for their wings to dry before flying off the surface. Even caddis need some drying time. On damp days this takes longer, and therefore dry flies should be low-floating; on clear dry days, hatching is swift, meaning that high-riding (full-hackle) patterns are appropriate.

GULPER ADAMS

Very often trout, especially fussy ones, expect flies (both natural and artificial) to be pinioned to the surface film. This pattern does just that while at the same time the wing offers a very good visual aid. Low-riding.

SPARKLER

I came up with this pattern when small *Baetis* were hatching in vast numbers on my local stream. It was designed to offer a bit of sparkle amid the sea of naturals preoccupying the trout. Low-riding.

LOOP-WING ADAMS

It was Gary Borger's video *Dry Fly Fishing* which inspired me to try this pattern. Though fragile, this fly can often encourage fish that have spurned other patterns to rise – even the standard Adams. High-floating.

MILL EVENING DUN

Developed by fellow guide, Nick Mitchell, to overcome problematic blue-winged olive hatches on England's Test and Itchen during the evening. It worked extremely well and has since remained a favorite. High-floating.

FUNNEL DUN

Each of Neil Patterson's flies is worthy of inclusion in any fly box. This pattern is tied to be fished upside-down, but obviates the delicate artistry of John Goddard and Brian Clarke's upside-down duns. Low-riding. Flush.

ADAMS

I would be utterly lost without this essential American fly. Since I was first introduced to it, it has traveled the world with me and been used on every conceivable type of water that requires a floating fly. High-floating.

BEACON BEIGE

The Americans have the Adams, the British this essential fly. More sparse than its American cousin, it remains one of the best adult-olive imitations in existence. It was popularized by master fly-tier Peter Deane. High-floating.

SPARKLE DUN

This pattern was first shown to me by John Goddard on the banks of the River Traun, in Austria. After his fifth grayling weighing over 1kg. (3lb.), I became curious! This compara dun theme fishes well. Low-riding and flush.

HARROP DUN

If not legendary, then certainly Bonnie and René Harrop's fly-tying expertise is revered. This fusion of a compara dun, a Troth Elk Hair and thorax is especially useful in riffling water and choppy glides. Low-riding. Flush.

UPSIDE-DOWN DUN

Having experienced the fragility of the excellent Goddard/Clarke pattern, I set out to devise a similar, durable concept. In sizes 14-20 and in various colors, it works extremely well on ultra-shy and fussy rising trout. Low-riding. Flush.

NO-HACKLE DUN

Carl Richards and Doug Swisher altered significantly the approach to stream fly-fishing. When fish are feeding in the surface film or on hatching or newly hatched duns, this is *the* fly for them. Low-riding. Flush.

DUCK'S DUN

It was Fratnick who first utilized the preen-gland feather from a duck to fashion a dry fly. My version combines a thorax style. Restricted to one dry fly, in various sizes and colors, I would choose this one. Low-riding. Flush.

KITE'S IMPERIAL

Mention Sawyer and, in the same breath, you must mention Kite when discussing upstream nymphing tactics. His dry flies are timeless and very effective, the Imperial being one of the best *Baetis* dun patterns I know. High-riding.

PARA DUN

Having acquired a vast quantity of turkey flank feathers for tying the more usual thorax patterns, I experimented further and this small *Baetis* is one of the results. Good for selective trout in flat or calm water. Low-riding. Flush.

MICRO CADDIS

This pattern started life as both a stillwater and a *Mystacides longicornis* pattern. Trout seem to take it with complete confidence, even when feeding on upwing duns. A very good general pattern. Low-to-medium riding.

FLUTTERING CADDIS

Chironomids are now a stream-fisher's alternative hatch. This Leonard Wright design is a very good general pattern for those instances, as well as for caddis. Medium- to high-floating.

TENT-WING CADDIS

I once cast this to cover a rise underneath a bridge spanning the Itchen and 25 minutes later I landed a 2.5kg. (5lb.) rainbow, bearing the hallmarks of a steelhead. I still wonder whether I caught the first Itchen steelhead on a dry fly.

SPINNER & SPENT

AFTER LAYING THEIR eggs, mayflies and caddis become enmeshed in the surface film, creating a great food opportunity for trout. These patterns mimic the spinner and spent forms and are fished to recreate the insect's motionless state as it lies in the surface film. This is the last stage of interest to the trout until the underwater nymphal stage.

RICHARD WALKER'S SEDGE

This pattern is similar to Wright's Fluttering Caddis, except for the arc chrome butt. The butt resembles the caddis' egg cluster and can prove irresistible to trout, especially if fished late in the evening.

POLYWING SPINNER

This pattern can be made in any color or size to fit upwinged spinner (or imago) types. Swisher and Richards' effective hen-wing style has been superseded by polypropylene yarn. Best fished in the surface film.

BROWN MILLER

Calf-tail wings make this a good dead or dying caddis pattern. Shown me by American Will Thomas, it can be successful fished when female caddis or moths have fallen into the stream, especially at dawn, or very late at night.

TERRY'S TERROR

An exceptional general-purpose fly brought to prominence by master fly-tier Peter Deane. It was devised by Messrs. Lock and Terry, who recorded it as a hatching olive, but I have succeeded with it as an egg-laying caddis imitation.

FALLEN SPINNER

Based on an idea by Dave Whitlock, this durable spinner pattern uses hackles clipped top and bottom which suggest the natural's outstretched hyaline wings by creating dimples on the surface film.

DEPOSITING CADDIS

I created this for stillwater, but use it on rivers when caddis are laying eggs. Best fished around trees, where the caddis seem most at peril. The muddler-style head provides a good wake across the surface, which is desirable if not purist.

SUNSET SPINNER

Like most chalk stream anglers, G.E.M. Skues wrestled with the problems of imitating the blue-winged olive spinner. When trapped on the surface, flies hold an aura of red/orange light. I designed this successful pattern on that premise.

PATTERSON SUNK SPINNER

A variation on Neil Patterson's copper-wired pattern. This represents the drowned female imago of the *Baetis* family. Especially useful on southern English chalk streams.

JARDINE'S SUNK SPINNER

Once, when fishing the evening rise, I noticed hosts of small, light-cream spurwing spinners (*Centroptilum luteolum*) appear. Their folded wings resembled flashing mother-of-pearl. This is the resulting pattern.

RUST SPINNER

This Bonnie and René Harrop pattern uses hackle fibers at the thorax area. It represents the pale morning dun (*Ephemera infrequens/inermis*) and the blue-winged olive (*Baetis* spp). Good when fish feed on spinner.

CAENIS FALLEN SPINNER

I have opted for a clipped wing of hackle over-and-under. Rather a parody of the real insect, the wings are not white like those of the natural. Fished to individual trout on light tippets, this pattern has been very successful.

SPARKLE SPINNER

Spectraflash imitates the iridescence of the upwing imago. The reddish-brown body resembles many egg-laying *Ephemeroptera*, including the blue-winged olive and some *Baetis*. A general pattern where falls are expected.

WHITE WING (BLACK)

Black tricos (*Tricorythodes* spp.) hatch out in vast numbers and trout quickly become preoccupied with these tiny food items. Flies must be small and tippets fine. The pattern here is a thorax dun style.

POLY CAENIS

This commercial pattern has a dark thorax and dense polywings, echoing the natural. The transition from sub-imago to imago in some *Caenis* species takes place directly after hatching, and in *Tricorythodes* spp., after only two hours.

BAETIS SPINNER

A striking feature of the female egg-laying adults of this group is the definite, bright yellow segmentation along the abdomen. When preoccupied with a spinner fall, trout can be very selective, so attention to detail is essential.

ANGLER'S CURSE

The genus *Caenis* can easily be found on sluggish parts of a chalk stream, where it hatches in great numbers throughout the summer. The fly is lighter-colored than the closely related *Tricorythodes* sp.

ADAMS MIDGE

In sizes 20-26, this standard version is one of the best all-round small-fly imitations. River flies can appear larger than they are, so a small pattern will catch a trout that has previously refused an array of larger dressings.

TERRESTRIALS

LAND-BORNE INSECTS and fauna are a much overlooked aspect of fly-fishing. Certainly the annual "hopper carnival" on many alkaline rivers in America is exceptional. Spiders, ants, beetles and grasshoppers are vitally important to fly-fishers. It is advisable to carry the less familiar patterns at all times, especially if fishing in daylight during the warmer part of the season where there are trees overhanging the river.

HAWTHORN FLY

From the middle to the end of spring, *Bibio marci* (hawthorn fly) hover in colonies around hawthorn bushes. Some get blown into the water where trout feast on them. Fish this Taff Price pattern in the surface film.

BLACK SPIDER

During the hot, listless days of summer, I doubt that it is necessary to carry many patterns other than this general-purpose imitation. In various sizes it imitates midges, smuts, beetles, even spiders. Good when fished beneath trees.

HALFORD BLACK GNAT

Frederick Halford was a dry-fly purist but was also a perceptive man of great fly-tying skill. This pattern represents *Bibio johannis*, which occurs frequently on chalk streams.

LETORT CRICKET

Letort, the famous Pennsylvania stream, has offered fly-fishing a rich legacy of characters, such as Charlie Fox and Vince Marinaro, and patterns. Letort was the first place where my eyes were opened to terrestrials on alkaline rivers.

BLACK ANT

Flying ants provide one of fly-fishing's unpredictable high spots. Not to carry at least a couple of these important flies may well render you fishless, since trout become extremely fussy and preoccupied when feeding on them.

BLACK BEETLE

Beetles and other creatures fall from trees or are blown into the water by winds. Trout usually take advantage of such windfalls. This pattern is a good general imitation and should be fished in the surface film.

SOLDIER BEETLE

I have yet to hear of trout feeding on soldier beetles, but doubtless they do. G.E.M. Skues, never one for overfilling a fly box, thought them sufficiently important to imitate.

LADYBIRD

On occasion, especially during hot summers, great masses of this beetle are in evidence. It seems likely that trout will eventually feed on them, although I am told large quantities of ladybirds can make them sick.

BLACK MIDGE

A rather simplified version of Halford's Black Gnat. This pattern is actually size 22, though smaller ones are used in high summer, especially on rivers, pandering to some picky trout behavior.

BROWN MIDGE

Quite what trout take the Brown Midge for is open to conjecture. Possibly tiny chironomids, just hatched, or perhaps tiny terrestrial beetles. They are, however, essential to the fly box. Use tippets no heavier than 1kg. (2lb.) breaking strain.

BLACK EMERGER

Though it is exceptional on stillwater, I have also enjoyed considerable success with this Barry Unwin pattern in small sizes (18-22) on rivers. I believe trout take it for an emergent midge.

INCHWORM

During the peak summer months, trout are said to leap clean out of the water to seize caterpillars (*Lepidoptera* spp.) as they dangle from trees. It is wise to carry a pattern or two!

CROWE BEETLE

Devised by John Crowe, this pattern is noted for deceiving larger-than-average brown trout. The semi-muddler head affords a degree of water movement that can be very attractive to trout, especially if skated then left inert.

FLYING ANT

This winged/resting version of an ant further emphasizes the importance of *Hymenoptera* in fly-fishing on stillwater as well as rivers. I suggest carrying various kinds in a mixture of guises and colors at all times.

BROWN ANT

To John Goddard, the brown/red or wood ant is reminiscent of "those old pictures of Victorian women – large chests and hips and tiny waists." He concluded that patterns should imitate them for success.

McMURRAY ANT

Ethafoam and Plastazote have superseded cork, but the concept is still sound. Created by Ed Sutryn of McMurray, Pennsylvania, this ultimate ant pattern can be fished anywhere and at any time when ants are in evidence.

ETHAFOAM BEETLE

This Ian Warrilow pattern is a good all-rounder, as much at home on stillwater as it is on running water. The foam back keeps the pattern afloat in the surface film, imitating the natural. The dubbed body offers an illusion of life.

CLASSICS

PATTERNS DEVELOPED ON the tempestuous and more acidic rain-fed and spate rivers have a long lineage. Many tactics have been developed to fish them. Yet many areas, especially the North of England, Scotland and many parts of Europe, still adhere to a traditional doctrine, echoed by the following selection. Rain-fed rivers are more common worldwide than chalk streams, so the fly styles are more varied.

ADAMS IRRESISTIBLE

A variation on the timeless Irresistible proper. In fast, broken waters there are few better dry flies, either for buoyancy or imitation of many insects. Good in and around pocket water in caddis hatches or as a search pattern.

RENEGADE

This fly is unusual in that a hackle is placed at the bend of the hook and conventionally to the fore. Jack Dennis, the famous Wyoming fly-tier, rates it as "one of the top rainbow-trout flies in the West," which is recommendation enough.

WICKHAM'S FANCY

Arguably one of the top ten dry flies ever conceived. An excellent caddis/sedge imitation and general dun pattern, and not purely on freestone rivers – stillwater and chalkstream fish also rise to Dr. T.W. Wickham's Fancy with alacrity.

GREY WULFF

The British have the Wickham; the US has this classic fast-water fly from Lee Wulff. This fly could feature in fly-fishers' boxes from Maine to the Drakensbergs, it is that indispensable. In sizes 6-14, most insects can be covered.

BLACK GNAT

Bibio johannis is endemic to most waters. A trout that has refused closely imitated examples of naturals will seldom refuse this Black Gnat in sizes 18-20. A good all-round fly for quiet areas and pools rather than fast water.

COCH-Y-BONDHU

This classic Welsh beetle pattern is representative of *Phyllopertha horticola*, an insect very much in evidence throughout the summer on particularly rough streams and acidic lakes such as Vyrnwy in Wales.

BI-VISIBLE

This fly covers a range rather than a specific fly pattern. It is designed to remain visible to the angler when fishing fast-broken water. The body of palmered hackle aids floating and can be varied to suit the angler's needs.

ALDER

Sialis lutaria or *S. fuliginosa* is, in my experience, seldom taken in the adult form, yet the larvae appear very popular with trout. On fast, rough and freestone streams it is extremely successful in its dry form. This is the classic dressing.

COACHMAN

I caught my first trout with this fly when I was six years old. It remains a timeless classic, still good for trout and sea trout in tumbling streams. Exceptionally effective at dusk and as a night fly.

MARCH BROWN

Here we find the traditional version of *Rhithrogena germanica* and *Ecdyonurus venosus*, the true and false March brown. It masquerades extremely well as a hatching dun on northern and far-western streams in Britain.

PARTRIDGE & ORANGE

A classic wet fly of fast rocky river origin. When fished early season, across and down, in traditional three-fly teams (it is an excellent middle dropper), the method is the crystallization of rough-stream trout and grayling fishing.

GREENWELL'S GLORY

Some authorities suggest that this style was the invention of Canon Greenwell, the dry version coming after. There is no better imitation of an olive fished in classic wet-fly style down and across, or upstream in teams of three.

SILVER MARCH BROWN

To quote G.E.M. Skues: "The March brown is an excellent fly and, as generally tied, quite a poor imitation of the natural fly and quite a passable one of anything else!" This pattern fits that category admirably. It is a fabulous sea-trout fly.

HARE'S LUG

This fly simply cannot be bettered. When used as a hatching/ecloding nymph at the surface, the Hare's-Ear variety is arguably all one could wish for. Despite being fashioned as a freestone spider, this fly is equally at home on stillwater.

SNIPE & PURPLE

This T.E. Pritt pattern conveys the deadly simplicity of the North Country spider. Sparse, drab and very insecty. Fish three flies on the leader, a soft-actioned rod, across and down, combined with upstream mends or simply upstream.

BLACK SPIDER

The original James Baillie pattern had the hackle palmered a third of the body up to the eye. It was said to have seldom been off his leader and was "the most killing artificial" he knew.

RED TAG

Perhaps the oldest fly in the literal sense, its history stretching back at least 150 years, possibly longer. Very much a grayling pattern, red is widely agreed to hold great attraction for the "lady of the stream."

SMALL NYMPHS

ALTHOUGH THESE FLIES represent only a few of the imitative nymphal forms available to trout on rivers worldwide, they do not differ drastically from those found on alkaline waters. There is perhaps a slight bias toward the caddis, rather than the mayfly, yet both naturals will be present. River flies, especially the smaller ones, do tend to overlap, but localized emergences can sometimes dictate a special pattern.

TRAUN RED-SPOT SHRIMP (SCUD)

A fusion: a bit of Neil Patterson's Red Spot deadliness, combined with Traun River Products' Spectraflash II as the shellback, which imitates the shine of the naturals admirably. A very good fly for fast or colored water.

STRAW SHRIMP

A duller shrimp for quieter areas such as slack water, pools and back eddies. This fly is a close imitation of the natural's grayish/olive tones. Fish on a floating line and leader over about 2m. (6ft.) depth, dead drift.

SMALL GREEN CADDIS

Caddis are prevalent on most rivers. Carry various sizes, colors and aspects in order to meet hatch requirements. This one imitates the hatching or ascending green-colored juvenile sedges such as grannom and *Rhyacophila*.

TRAUN PUPA

Named after the organza-type wing material marketed by Traun River Products. Best fished dead drift either up or downstream in mid-water. Some weighting might be necessary.

DEEP OLIVE PUPA

Gary La Fontaine's fly patterns indicate his extensive knowledge of caddis. Antron, a tri-lobal material to which air bubbles cling underwater, is used to imitate the natural fly. A superb pattern.

AMBER LONGHORN PUPA (EMERGENT)

A useful river pattern primarily for stillwater. It is a fusion of Jorgensen's Fur Pupa and La Fontaine's Sparkle Pupa series. I added silk horns as a recognition point. Fish 30cm. (1ft.) below, up to and including the surface film.

GLITTER PUPA

Pearlescent Mylar suggests trapped air and haemoglobin pockets under the pupal skin. Although good for the smaller caddis, this also makes a very good midge pattern. Fish near to the surface, dead drift.

MUSKRAT (PELLIS)

A few general-purpose fly patterns are absolutely essential to every fly box. This is one. Originated in Pennsylvania by Tom Pellis, it suggests a host of creatures, from caddis and shrimp to mayfly nymphs.

ALL-PURPOSE DARK (ORVIS)

Designed to offer the fly-fisher a series of general representative nymphal-shaped flies. In various sizes (8-16), tied in the light and medium versions, with some examples weighted, almost every upwing from surface to river bed can be covered.

HENDRICKSON

The American hatch *Ephemerella subvaria* rivals the large, dark olive (*Baetis rhodani*) of the UK, as the herald of spring. If you fish such areas of the US, be sure to carry this nymph and its adult counterparts.

MARABOU NYMPH

This American general-purpose nymph pattern tied in various insect colors affords a marvelous degree of movement and texture. Trout, especially rainbows, seem mesmerized by marabou. An all-rounder for all waters and most tactics.

MAHOGANY NYMPH

Although palish purple in color, this pattern suggests many of the *Leptophlebia* spp. This commercial nymph is categorized as a labored swimmer and should be used in quieter areas of a river (such as pools) and some stillwaters.

LIGHT CAHILL

A general pattern accommodating cream-colored upwinged insects. In America this may be *Callibaetis* or *Heptagina*; in Britain, pale wateries *Baetis fuscatus*, and *B. scambus*. In various sizes (14-20) this is an accurate facsimile.

FILOPLUME MAYFLY NYMPH

Randall Kaufmann introduced me to filoplume, the secondary feather at the base of the breast and flank feathers on most game birds. A more mobile action one could not find. Deadly between mid-depth and near-surface.

COPPER NYMPH

This fly fulfills the need for a slim, spare fly suggestive of many forms of aquatic life, from midge to mayfly. It sinks quickly through the surface film, even in small sizes. I am happy to report that it met with approval from the trout.

ADAMS FLASHBACK

The effectiveness of the Dry Adams is well known; less-well known is the nymph version. A good all-rounder, with an attractive thorax and back of Flashabou. Best fished close to the river bed, but comfortable in all methods.

MARCH BROWN

I have darkened Al Troth's original body color and used hare's-fur tinged with red to represent our own *Rhithrogena germanica* and *Ecdyanurus venosus* spp. Fish in areas of large boulders and medium flow, near to the bottom.

Heavy Nymphs

FREESTONE RIVERS CREATE the ideal habitat for larger insect forms such as hellgrammite, *Pteronarcrys* nymphs and some very large caddis species. These food forms dictate the trout's diet and therefore the angler's approach. The nymphs featured here suggest #6 - #8 line and rods of about 3m. (9ft.), often requiring floating, sink-tip and sunk line. The majority of the following nymphs translate well into other fly-fishing areas.

Tellico Nymph

A favored American search pattern that works on many water types (even British reservoirs) when fished sink-and-draw on a floating line. Possibly trout mistake it for a caddis pupa. Fish dead drift, or allow to swing across current.

Bread Crust

Not a fly I use very often, but extremely popular in a general role with American fly-fishers. Good on most rivers, throughout most of the season, at most depths. Reminiscent of a caddis pupa, which may account for its effectiveness.

Montana Nymph

A general-purpose fly that has found favor all over the world, on all water types. This pattern can be tied in various sizes and covers most of the darker stonefly nymphs, attracting exceedingly well due to its color scheme and shape.

Prince

All praise to Doug Prince for one of the most useful nymphs an angler can carry. I have enjoyed great success with this pattern on fast rivers, particularly in Europe. Fish dead drift with a weighted leader or fly.

Zug Bug

Popularized by the great American fly-fisher Arnold Gingrich on the Esopus Creek, this fly seems to be the alternative popular choice to the Prince, but it has a softer profile.

Large Black Stone

A direct imitation of the large stonefly nymphs, which abound in areas stretching from Colorado to Wyoming, Idaho, and Montana. Trout find no difficulty in accommodating their bulky form and do so with relish.

Girdle Bug

This impressionistic pattern of a large stonefly nymph is good in fast, boisterous areas, which vibrate the rubber legs. Fish heavily leaded, around boulders and close to the bottom. A favorite on Rocky Mountain rivers.

Ted's Stonefly

If trout are feeding on brown stonefly nymphs, it is wise to offer a brown pattern. This works admirably, especially fished near to the bottom, with a weighted or sunk line. Originated by American nymph specialist Ted Trublood.

BOTTOM-SCRATCHER

An unlovely name for an unlovely fly! I created this pattern after visiting Austria. The Austrians' use of deer-hair and gold beads to weight flies is ingenious. This dressing imitates several creatures: cased caddis, stonefly, and dragonfly larvae.

CREAM CRAWLER

Designed by Col. Unwin to represent a wide range of light-colored, bottom-dwelling aquatic forms – golden stonefly nymphs and mayfly nymphs. This pattern should be heavily weighted to fish well with a floating line on fast water.

DAVE'S STONEFLY NYMPH

A prime example of the superb fly-tying of America's Dave Whitlock and about as good an imitation of a golden stonefly nymph as it is possible to find.

CASUAL DRESS

E.H. Polly Rosborough first tied this fly on the Upper Big Deschutes, Oregon, in 1960. In so doing, he created one of the best all-rounders, utilizing his fuzzy style of dressing. This pattern exudes life – a *must* for the fast-river fly-fisher.

KAUFMANN STONE

Randall Kaufmann has created numerous patterns that are skillful, simple and realistic. Fish heavily weighted on most streams to overcome fast currents when *Pteronarcrys californica* and *Acroneuria californica* are active.

BOX CANYON STONE

This tying originates from Ery's Fork River in Idaho, perhaps the best fast-water stretch of trout fishing in America. The pattern imitates the larger stonefly species and is heavy enough to overcome considerable currents.

GOLDEN STONE NYMPH

Another Rosborough pattern. This large pattern relates to the nymphal forms of *Calineuria californica* and *Doroneuria baumanni*. Fish when naturals are in evidence and active.

ORVIS STONE

An upside-down-style dressing, when the hook is fished point upward. Swiss straw represents the hard abdominal back and wing-cases. This pattern imitates *Pteronarcrys californica*, *Acroneuria californica* and hellgrammites.

EARLY BROWN STONE

This pattern imitates *Brachyptera*, which are found on opening day in Pennsylvania, in mid-spring in other eastern areas, and up to the end of spring in the West. The pattern will suffice, with size variations, for most species.

STREAMERS

FREESTONE RIVERS OFFER a form of fly-fishing that would be dismissed as unsporting on the more placid chalk streams in many parts of the world: that is, the use of streamers or bait-fish imitations and attractors. Mostly these are employed on large-nymph tackle, with the same tactics and in similar areas. These tactics can be combined with streamers, especially Black Woolly Buggers, at nightfall for patrolling brown trout.

COLORADO GOLD MUDDLERBOU

I simply did not know what else to call this pattern, which I was given on the banks of the Frying Pan River, Colorado. It has a proven track record as a late-season fly for big brown trout, although it is a sculpin imitation. It works well on the upper Colorado River and elsewhere in that state.

WHITE MARABOU MUDDLER (DAN BAILEY)

This fish-like fly is the perfect river streamer. The deer-hair head creates underwater disturbance and the marabou wings make enticing movements. Essential for fast-water fly-fishers.

BELGIAN SCULPIN

Crafted by Paul Vekemans, this pattern adapts American ideas to suit specific requirements. Vekemans fishes this fly in the rivers of Germany (generally Bavaria), and north and south-west Belgium, during early and late season.

MUDDLED BLACK MINK ZONKER

Primarily for fishing after dark on rivers and stillwater, the ragged appearance of this pattern works well in dark pools, by tree roots and by boulders. Fish on sink-tip or full-sinking line, down and across.

TROTH BULLHEAD

Initially I recoiled at the large size of this pattern, but I have since appreciated the need for such flies. Use this bait-fish imitation in brawling currents for large trout. One for the sunk or sink-tip line, it is also a good night pattern.

PULSATA

WOOLLY WORM (BROWN)

BLACK ZONKER
This Dan Byford pattern is an adaptation of the New Zealand rabbit (Matuka) series. The main difference is its body of Mylar tubing. A known catcher of big trout in fast, turbulent water.

This fly was introduced to me as a successful rainbow-trout fly, but it also takes browns. The rabbit strip enclosing the whole hook and muddler-style head give it a unique pulse action. Excellent when a big fly pattern is required.

Reminiscent of both nymph and bait-fish attractors, this has even been classified as a wet fly. Very popular in America, both as a lake and river pattern, and best fished near to the bottom.

WOOLLY BUGGER

THREADFIN SHAD

FURNACE MATUKA VARIANT

One of the best modern creations. Designed by Russell Blessing, its role embraces that of bait-fish imitation, damsel-nymph, dragonfly-nymph, and other nymphs in small sizes. It is also a plain attractor of trout.

This gray Mylar-bodied pattern by André Puyans is as "fishy" as one can get and very effective when trout are harnessing tiny fish on river shallows and elsewhere. An exceptionally good lake pattern.

I was given this fly when guiding on southern England chalk streams. The pattern is effective in various countries, especially for brown trout during the evening and after nightfall. It has also proved excellent for sea trout.

OLIVE MATUKA

ROYAL COACHMAN
BUCKTAIL STREAMER

SILVER DARTER

Swisher and Richards popularized this New Zealand style in the US. Its straight-plane mode of movement gives the fly a unique action. In Britain, it briefly found favor as a reservoir style.

This is probably the definitive American streamer, which, apart from the Matuka and other New Zealand patterns, did as much as others of its ilk to make this style of pattern universal. Still effective, especially for rainbow trout.

An old-school American streamer by Lew Oatman of New York State. It is effective as a bait-fish imitation – a field that the American angler has fashioned into a fishing art-form that is still evolving and being improved upon.

DRY FLIES

Pocket water, riffles and fast runs drown lightly dressed patterns. Hair and good-quality hackling is essential for the buoyant effect needed. Fast-water dry flies tend not to imitate specific insects. An impressionistic caddis such as Troth Elk Hair or the stonefly parody Sofa Pillow is ideal in this capacity. The Yellow Humpy or Goofus Bug is a most attractive fly in fast or broken water, yet it is not a specific imitation.

SOFA PILLOW

An imitation of *Acroneuria pacifica*, which hatches in the western US between spring and autumn. Fish as for a normal dry fly, but twitches across the current can lead to explosive takes.

WHITE WULFF

White is an easy target when fading light and broken water create poor visibility. This is a useful imitation of the coffin fly or green drake spinner (*Ephemera guttulata*), especially good on eastern US waters.

STONEFLY ROGER

Roger Wooky, the Derbyshire professional fly-dresser and publisher of *Modern Trout Fly Dressings*, created this pattern, which was at the time one of the first (if not *the* first) to incorporate the hackle-point wings that he favored.

GRIZZLY WULFF

This Wulff dry fly, suffused with the color of a Humpy and an Adams, is successful in a variety of applications, especially as an imitation of *Epeorus* duns and *Hexagenia limbata*, the yellow may duns, (sizes 6-8).

ROYAL WULFF

This rainbow fly is a favorite with many fast-river anglers. Oddly, it worked on England's River Itchen in smaller sizes (16-18), even catching sophisticated brownies. A harder testing ground for a fly I cannot imagine.

GOLDEN STONE

This fly represents the larger species of the *Perlidae* family stonefly found in the US. Although also found in Europe, it is considerably smaller than *Acroneuria californica*. This pattern is a commercial version of the insect.

YELLOW HUMPY OR GOOFUS BUG

Universally popular with fly-fishers in the US. In England I have enjoyed great success with it, especially as a hatching mayfly (*Ephemera danica*) pattern. Always carry in all sizes (8-18) to cover most freestone situations.

RAT-FACED McDOUGAL

An intriguing name! I believe this started life as a salmon dry fly but was soon transported to freestone trout streams in smaller sizes because of the buoyant deer-hair body. It has, however, been superseded by the Adams Irresistible.

IRRESISTIBLE WULFF

This white-winged version of the original is an effective fast/broken-water pattern at range. Curiously, it seems to encourage larger fish to the surface, possibly because of the dense outline. One to be carried in sizes 10-16.

FLUTTERING CADDIS

Leonard M. Wright's *Fishing The Dry Fly As A Living Insect* is required reading for anyone who thinks fly-fishing is simple! Not surprisingly, he has radical thoughts about fly design and this is just one – an effective one too.

MARCH BROWN (DRY)

So many patterns imitate *Rhithrogena germanica/Ecdyonurus venosus* that it is hard to choose just one. This version is featured in Courtney Williams' *A Dictionary of Trout Flies* as representative, placing it in the 1940s.

GODDARD CADDIS

Known as the G. & H. Sedge in Britain, this adult caddis pattern's natural outline and buoyancy make it popular in western US. Size 16 or smaller makes good wake flies for dibbling the surface or retrieving noisily after nightfall.

HENRYVILLE SPECIAL

A good adult caddis imitation on any water, emphasizing the importance of this branch of insects to fast-water fishers. This Hiram Brobst pattern started life on Broadoaks Creek, Pennsylvania, which makes it more of a limestone pattern.

OLIVE DUN

On boulder-strewn rivers there can occur large hatches of *Ephemeroptera*. This is a winged version of Skues' Medium Olive *Baetis vernus, B. tenax* or *B. buceratus*. Equally effective in stony or chalk rivers.

TROTH ELK-HAIR CADDIS

Never be without one of these in any trout-fishing water, be it lake or river. I have known trout take this fly when there is not a sign of caddis. Fish up or downstream, dead drift or skated. Carry large (8-12) and small (down to 20).

COACHMAN

A British old-stager, that still works well, especially toward evening and nightfall when moths are about. Its invention is attributed to one H.R. Francis in around 1870.

BADGER HACKLE

This is one of those effective British patterns that have proved untraceable to a definite source, although perhaps attributable to T.J. Hanna. A good, buoyant fly in the traditional palmered sense that makes a good search pattern.

LARGE DRY FLIES & NYMPHS

LARGE NYMPHS TEND to spawn large adults. Grasshoppers, moths, and craneflies also fit the "large mouthful" category in the trout's diet. A fly box should always accommodate this fact and patterns should be fished in the same freestone rivers as large nymphs. Impressionistic patterns can cover a great many fly-fishing contingencies.

GODDARD CADDIS

This salmon version not only has proved the scourge of steelheads when high in the water during summer, but makes a good disturbance/stonefly pattern for the larger species, such as salmon flies and giant golden stoneflies.

HENRY'S FORK HOPPER

Mike Lawson observed that when on the water, the natural is flush to the surface and the body very significant. His pattern makes full use of the buoyancy of deer-hair and the floating properties of an extended body. Good for selective trout.

DADDY-LONGLEGS

A definitive Dick Walker pattern for stillwater use. He did river anglers a great service, too. From early to mid-autumn, trout and grayling happily feed on the cranefly.

MOSER'S ADULT STONE

Roman Moser's use of natural and man-made materials is first-rate. His organza-designed wing is fused with a dubbed body of deer-hair. A pattern for dead-drift situations more than skittering fish. Fish up or downstream.

JOE'S HOPPER

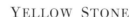

The forerunner of modern terrestrial design, also referred to as the Michigan Hopper. Devised by Art Winnie in the 1950s, this pattern is still widely used. An occasionally useful caddis pattern on English reservoirs.

EXTENDED-BODY DADDY-LONGLEGS

Craneflies occur throughout the summer as *Nephrotoma crocata*, the yellow-bodied summer variety, proves. This large, heavily dressed fly remains buoyant due to the use of a small hook.

YELLOW STONE

I have combined some of Moser's caddis and stonefly ideas together with accepted hair-wing styles. A good pattern fished either dead drift or skittered in a hatch of *Isoperla grammatica* (*I. patricia* or *I. marmona* in the US).

DAVE'S HOPPER

Dave Whitlock is among America's most innovative fly-tiers. Here he has achieved good floating properties through inspired use of deer-hair. Essential worldwide in any freestone-river fly-fisher's box.

HOOLET

This pattern was devised by Geoffrey Bucknall to represent a moth at dusk. It is effective for trout and sea trout. I suspect that it is often taken as a large caddis as well. This fly incorporates an underbody of cork to aid flotation.

STIMULATOR

This yellow, green and orange Randall Kaufmann fly covers stoneflies and terrestrials such as hoppers and caddis flies. A good general fly, it also covers many floating-fly requirements. Carry in various sizes, from 6-16.

SIMULATOR

This is an extremely successful pattern from Randall Kaufmann. It meets the general needs of nymphing trout based on concepts conceived by Charlie Brooks and Polly Rosborough.

FLUTTERING GOLDEN STONE

An effective fly when *Acroneuria pacifica*, *A. californica* and *Classenia sabulosa* are in evidence. For such large patterns, however, heavier line sizes (#6 and #7), plus larger-diameter leader tippets will be necessary to effect good turnover.

LITTLE BLACK STONEFLY

I created this pattern on return from fishing in Finland, where the natural was very much in evidence. Subsequently, this little grayish fly has worked well in early-season hatches of *Taeniopteryx* spp. and *Leactra geniculata*.

BITCH CREEK

Jack Dennis' most versatile nymph, this works in salmon-fly activity and generalized nymph operations. The hackle-and-rubber appendage makes considerable underwater disturbance that always succeeds in attracting trout.

MacSALMON

Originally designed by Al Troth utilizing orange macramé yarn for the body. This fly is the adult imitation of *Pteronarcrys californica*, *P. princeps* and *P. dorsata* – the salmon flies.

CATERPILLAR

A North of England pattern, based on a fly I received from McHardy's of Carlisle, Cumbria. Fish this pattern wherever branches overhang a trout stream. I term this whole concept "drop-off" fishing, for obvious reasons.

BLACK STONE

Curiously enough, realistic flies seem to hold little attraction for the trout. This ragged and bedraggled plain "buggy" pattern wins every time over slavish adherence to the natural.

AUSTRALIA & NEW ZEALAND

NEW ZEALAND AND Australia have created many patterns using the Matuka and fur-strip styles that hail originally from New Zealand. This small but diverse array concentrates on the fly patterns that have been mastered in fur and feather.

BLACK MATUKA

Matuka is a style of fly-tying. This version (*below*) has a tied-down wing, which enables the fly to be fished on an even plane, preventing the annoying twisting that can sometimes occur in streamers with a loose wing.

RABBIT

New Zealand anglers were the first to see the merit in the Matuka style of tying, using readily available rabbit's-fur as a wing. The sinewy movement of this pattern (*above*) imitates small fish, leeches, and even damselflies.

HARE & COPPER

Most countries have a nymph pattern that uses these materials. The variation here (*above*) is the marked wing, which suggests a hatching caddis or upwing mayfly. Fish in the surface area on a floating line.

CORDULLID

This pattern (*right*) represents the larva of the mud eye, a dragonfly specific to Lake Eucumbene, other large Australian waters and Lake Peddler, Tasmania. It can evoke both a rise and selective feeding. This suggests that a close copy is essential.

MRS SIMPSON

Arguably the definitive New Zealand pattern, this fly (*left*), named after the late Duchess of Windsor, has found favor worldwide as a bait-fish imitation and dragonfly nymph. It can be fished on still or running water with equal effect.

GOVERNOR NYMPH

This is not a specific insect imitation (*right*). Rather, its shape suggests food, its color being particularly visible. The peacock-herl thorax is reminiscent of a midge pupa.

HORNED CADDIS

Representative (*above*) of a cased caddis, horns suggesting the natural's legs protruding from the case and thorax region. Usual species include *Oateapsyche, Hydrobtosis colonica, H. umbrepennis,* and *H. pynocentrodes.*

PARSON'S GLORY

This Matuka-style pattern (*above*) uses cock hackles back-to-back. Designed by Phil Parsons for the legendary trout of Lake Taupo, it is tied to resemble small trout, which are preyed upon by their own kin.

GERMANY & AUSTRIA

NEW MATERIALS AND the cross-pollination of ideas between various countries have revolutionized fly-dressing. Germany has been influenced by some American styles and has created some ingenious patterns. The Traun area of Austria has, through Roman Moser and his companions, created some truly innovative fly-fishing concepts.

WOELFLE EMERGENT CADDIS

Thomas Woelfle is one of Germany's leading fly-tiers. He excels in the blending of artificial with natural materials. This emergent sedge has wings of clipped, pre-formed and marked organza made by Traun River Products.

DEER-HAIR EMERGER

The deer-hair body, which is dubbed then clipped to shape, suggests the dishevelment caused by hatching. Fish dead drift with a floating line, or allow to swing down and across stream.

GOLD-HEAD PUPA

This style of dressing is commonly used in Germany and Austria, though it is now found all over Europe. It represents the caddis, the metal ball forming the gold head. This gives the pattern enough weight to fish in fast, deep water.

MOSER SEDGE PUPA

A simple, easy-to-tie pupa pattern that is, nevertheless, deadly. Fish in all kinds of flows, just beneath the surface, when the naturals are on the wing.

FEMALE CADDIS

This pattern imitates the female sedge laying eggs under the surface, while her head stays in the film. It is also an excellent hatching pattern, especially on stillwater. Fish without drag, on a floating line and leader.

GOLD-HEAD PUPA II

The Gold-Head can be gold-plated or duller brass to imitate any shade of caddis. If a more realistic, clear-water fly is required, brass is the better choice. Fish this pattern dead drift on a floating line and long leader.

BALLOON CADDIS

Originating from the Traun, this pattern represents caddis emerging and hanging in the surface film. Roman Moser designed an Ethafoam head to support the pattern. Fish it dead drift on a floating line and buoyant leader.

DARK CADDIS

When trout become preoccupied with a certain species, they will accept no other food forms. At such times, fly patterns must appear realistic. This pattern is designed to be fished in the surface film and offers a plausible caddis silhouette.

LIGHT CADDIS

This lighter version of the Dark Caddis has mottled wings of colored raffia, resined and clipped to shape. Use when grayling and trout are feeding on adults or in the surface. Floating-line and dead-drift tactics appear to work best.

TRAUN-WING CADDIS

Rudi Hegar's organza wings are dyed, printed with markings, clipped to shape and added to the dressing. This makes for a durable, realistic wing, which should be mixed with deer-hair or hackle fibers to provide an illusion of life.

GAMMERUS

Roman Moser gave me this freshwater-shrimp tying when fishing in Cumbria. Best used in conjunction with a sunk leader or with lead added to the fly, this pattern has proved invaluable on water where the gammerus crustacean abounds.

CHIRONOMID PUPA

A Moser tying for quieter areas of the stream and stillwaters. The clipped wings of raffia, deer-hair thorax and sparse abdomen create an illusion of life. Fish in the surface film with floating line and long leader (floating butt/sunk tippet).

SPARKLE (BAETIS/EPHEMERELLA) NYMPH

This fly is one of mine. It was tied while fishing the River Traun when both trout and grayling were being ultra-selective, having endured a whole season of anglers. The size 16 nymph with a bottom-bouncing leaded leader worked well.

NUMIADES NYMPH

Paul Vekemans' sparse, general olive nymph is used in the Black Forest area for grayling. It works well on English reservoirs for trout, too. Fish with floating line, longish leader and dead drift, or swing across and down with the current.

GRAYLING NO.1

A Vekemans Black Forest dry fly which, although used primarily for grayling, has caught trout. A general pattern not representing either a midge or amber spinner, but that has allure through a Spectraflash wing. Fish dead drift.

"F" FLY

Another non-specific artificial fly. Europe has established a rapport with the feather *cul-de-canard*, first employed by anglers on the Jura over 100 years ago. It is now used in a great many dry flies, of which this is just one variation.

ANTRON DRY EMERGER/DELTA WING

This fly's wing starts life as carpet pile! Antron is tri-lobal, repels water and traps air bubbles, making it resemble a hatching sedge at the surface film. Fish on the surface, cast upstream, allow to drift downstream and swing.

FRANCE, SPAIN, ITALY, & YUGOSLAVIA

THESE PATTERNS TRANSLATE well, beguiling trout worldwide. A Luxembourg angler of my acquaintance wrought havoc among the English chalk stream population by using two French mayfly patterns: the Pont Audemer and Panama. The following is a random selection of styles which are effective throughout the trout-fishing world.

PALLARETTA

A traditional Spanish wet fly, with an air of sedge pupa or uncased larva. The wing is formed from Coqs de Leons hackles, which are famous worldwide. This Pyrenees pattern is normally tied with the glossy, stiff hackles.

MAVE

Purple is, generally speaking, an uncommon color in trout flies. Only now is it gaining popularity in North America for steelhead patterns, although the English Snipe and Purple is much-used when hatching olives are about.

COCCHETTO NYMPH

This Italian pattern was originally tied from the silken fibers of an indigenous moth cocoon and intended for grayling. I see no reason why it should not be just as deadly for trout. The pattern imitates an uncased caddis larva.

OSSOLINA EMERGER

Originating in the Ossola Valley, Italy, the hook bend is formed after the pattern is made. Apparently there are only a few people left who construct in this traditional way. Again, the shape is reminiscent of caddis.

VALSESIANA

This is part of a series of spider-type flies originating in Piedmont, where they have caught trout and grayling since the mid-1700s. The hooks are eyeless. The array of colors in the series suggests a range of hatching aquatic river forms.

PRÉCIEUSE

A French pattern, which forms part of a series, from the hands of Guy Plas. Its subtle gray is beloved by river fly-fishers because it imitates various mayfly species so successfully.

THE DORMOUSE NYMPH

This pattern hails from Yugoslavia and was originally tied with dormouse-tail fur. Use blue rabbit or gray squirrel for a more conservationally desirable substitute. Designed by Marjan Fratnick to cover most ephemerid species.

BARTELLINI SPIDER

This red-and-white pattern from Turin, Italy, is reminiscent of the North of England spiders. I can vouch for the effectiveness of the series from which this pattern comes when reservoir trout are feeding on midge pupae.

LA RUE

This French pattern, I am informed, represents a stillborn fly, half in and half out of the nymphal shuck. The coloration suggests an emerging caddis. One wing is tied along the fly's side to emphasize hatching dishevelment.

OLIVA

Despite its bulky appearance, this Spanish pattern is used as a wet fly to represent various olive species. Its hackle is wound fully around the shank instead of the more familiar half-turn wing. Primarily a river fly.

UCERO

The caddis theme revisited. This pattern, which represents a hatching type of fly, is from Spain's Luis Antunez. It is probably best fished in the surface film.

"F" FLY

Marjan Fratnick, a Yugoslav now living in Spain, popularized the Swiss idea of using the duck's buoyant and waterproof preen-gland feathers. This is one pattern of a series and is almost indispensable for trout grayling.

HOZ SECA

Named after the River Hoz in Spain, this fly incorporates the popular styles that employ man-made fibers. Antron is used to create the wing on this particularly convincing adult olive pattern.

TAJO

This distinctive orange-bodied fly suggests that the Spanish and Portuguese who fish the River Tajo have hatches not dissimilar to the UK's blue-winged olive. A very passable imitation of the spinner stage.

VERANO AMARILLO

Another Spanish dry fly from Luis Antunez, representing an olive species. I have not encountered the European *Ephemerella* spp. in the UK, but in small sizes this pattern would work well in that capacity.

MOUSTIQUE 1

This light-colored pattern, which comes from the Jura region of Switzerland and France, covers the smaller olives and utilizes the duck's preen-gland feather as a buoyant hackle.

UNIVERSAL CADDIS

Originating in Switzerland, this pattern underlines the importance of caddis species in Europe. It has two lacquered, quill-segment wings tied on top of each other, creating the unique configuration of the natural's tent-wing shape.

SCANDINAVIA

T HE MODERN FLY-DRESSER knows no bounds. New materials and ideas exert their influence on fly patterns. Not broadly representative of Scandinavia as a whole, the dressings depicted have, in the main, emerged from Finland and show how advanced the techniques and imitative concepts are becoming in terms of the caddis. Most of the patterns shown here are very transportable indeed between water types and countries.

ORANGE PUPA

This Juha Pusa pattern is a loose interpretation of a caddis pupa. It uses Antron to indicate the natural's ability to gather air bubbles about itself, especially in fast water.

GREEN-ANTRON PUPA

Trout like this *Rhyacophilodae* imitation. Caddis in far northern Europe are much larger than in southerly regions, making big patterns essential. This fly is heavily weighted for fast streams and boiling pocket water. Fish across and down.

RHYACOPHILA PUPA (CURVED/TUMBLING)

Trout in rough streams can be fussy when harvesting a particular food item. Lacking the right size or tone of this pattern could well mean a fishless day, especially when the natural is abundant.

RHYACOPHILA LARVA (REALISTIC)

Rhyacophila do not build cases like most other caddis larvae, preferring a free-swimming existence. This makes them vulnerable to trout. A very successful pattern by Veli Autti, I find it is best fished dead drift, upstream.

NALLE PUH

This superb general-purpose dry-fly pattern utilizes bear-hair for its wing. It has caught many trout, especially those feeding on mayfly. Also a good golden stone adult imitation.

NALLE PUH/STONE (DARK)

During the spring, just after ice-off, many rivers receive an impressive hatch of small, dark stoneflies. Fished either upstream static, dead drift or down and twitched, this pattern is excellent for the rises that can occur.

NELSON CADDIS

I believe this pattern was first tied in the US, although the design is now a firm favorite on fast, caddis-rich water in Scandinavia, especially Finland. This is due primarily to the buoyancy of its layered deer-hair.

VA-SEDGE

Top Finnish fly-dresser Veli Autti collaborated with a graphic designer to create this printed, veined wing material, which imitates the adult caddis. This style is prevalent throughout Europe.

RACKELHANE

This Juha Pusa caddis pattern is a good resting pattern, but is still biased toward fast flows. Also good fished drowned or damp when *Rhyacophila* spp. or other green-based caddis hatches abound.

DRAGONFLY NYMPH

Scandinavian lakes give rise to enormous amounts of *Odonata* spp. To me, this pattern is more imitative of the *Zygoptera* (damselflies). I would fish this pattern with confidence when *Zygoptera* were on the wing.

GROUSE-WING SCULPIN

Autti Pirinen created what I believe is the best sculpin or miller's-thumb pattern. Fish on a sink-tip line, down and across, early season and at night, when big brown trout can be expected.

MYSIS RELICTA

Running through Tampere is a small section of river that spans two lakes; the white-water flows make it a first-class fishery. I believe this prehistoric shrimp thrives there, and in Lake Baikal, and trout feed quite selectively on it.

STONEFLY NYMPH

The early black and brown stonefly appear to be abundant on freestone rivers worldwide during the spring. Trout greet their emergence with gusto. This nymph pattern is a realistic Finnish interpretation of the insect.

FLAT-HEAD SCULPIN

Sculpin are feeding targets for trout. Very much a freestone fly, lakes and reservoir fish may respond to its use. The varnished head is flattened to give the fly a unique swimming movement. Fish on a sink-tip line, down and across.

PARALEPTOPHLEBIA NYMPH

This nymph is known in Britain as a turkey brown or ditch dun, and in America as a blue dun, or red or blue quill. It is an extremely good facsimile in a naturalistic manner.

MUSKRAT MUDDLED ZONKER

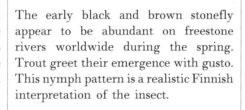

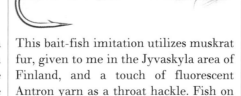

This bait-fish imitation utilizes muskrat fur, given to me in the Jyvaskyla area of Finland, and a touch of fluorescent Antron yarn as a throat hackle. Fish on a sink-tip line, down and across.

PERCH FLY

Excellent on English reservoirs, especially during the autumn, when roach and perch congregate near weed beds. Tied in Scandinavia by Perthi Kaira.

WALES

WALES HAS A tradition of producing effective trout and sea-trout flies. Its lakes and streams have given birth to many international patterns such as the Coch-y-Bondhu. The tendency is to overlook many as being nondescript, thereby missing their value as skillful interpretations of natural food forms. Even the sea-trout patterns, often gaudy in other areas, are not so in Wales, but for all their sobriety they are deadly.

DOG'S BODY

Harry Powell, the late Usk fly-tier, was asked to tie a batch of flies. The body color presented a problem, but the solution came via a mongrel sheepdog with a foxy coat. This is an excellent olive and caddis pattern.

DAIWL BACH

This pattern is the wet dressing as distinct from the nymph version. It was created by Welsh anglers for fishing reservoirs, especially Chew and Blagdon, where it proves most successful toward the evening.

CONWAY RED

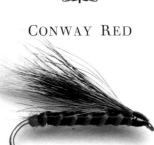

The River Conway in North Wales is a first-class sea-trout river. It has spawned a variety of patterns of which this is just one. The original contained the now protected badger hair, but gray squirrel is just as effective.

HEREFORDSHIRE ALDER

I deliberated over whether to include this pattern, since to do so might upset Welsh readers due to this fly's usage on the Marches. I hope not. Devised by Ralph Penny, it is a good general olive pattern, rather than strictly an alder.

HARRY TOM

While this is classified as a sea-trout fly, I have enjoyed most success with it on stillwater as a hatching somber sedge or general crustacean. A middle-dropper fly on stillwater or a point fly on rivers.

MOC'S CERT

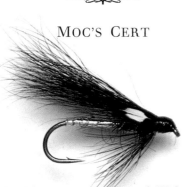

Moc Morgan, sea trout and Wales are almost synonymous. Moc is the perfect ambassador for Wales and, as a fly-fisher, the scourge of its sea trout. A quintessential sea-trout pattern.

WILLIAMS' FAVOURITE

This pattern was devised by Courtney Williams. Although it is classified as a sea trout pattern, I have personally had more success with it on reservoirs during a black-midge hatch.

HAUL-A-GWYNT

"Sun and Wind" is the English translation of this pattern from the reservoirs of North Wales. Very much a point, or better still, middle-dropper fly. I fish this pattern with the utmost confidence.

DAI BEN

According to Taff Price and Moc Morgan, this pattern originated from David Benjamin Glynn Davies for the River Towy and was nicknamed Dai Ben. One of the best known sea-trout flies in Wales, though not so common elsewhere.

TEIFI TERROR

Moc Morgan recommends this fly pattern for sea trout. Fish either singly or in tandem, subsurface, especially during daylight hours and on a falling flood or in fairly low water.

COCH-Y-BONDHU

This dressing has traveled all over the world, and more to the point, is used to deadly effect both as intended – a beetle pattern – and also as a general dry fly. There is also a wet version.

WELSH PARTRIDGE

Designed by Courtney Williams, this is really a damp pattern, neither entirely floating or sunk. It is an excellent pattern and one I have used to great effect as an emerger on chalk streams and reservoirs.

RED TAG

This pattern's origins lie in Worcestershire, but its inclusion introduces a grayling pattern. The Dee is renowned as a grayling river and worth very close inspection, as these attractive fish can attain a good weight.

LEWIS' GRANNOM

Brachycentrius subnubilis, or grannom, is a fluctuating hatch and appears to be susceptible to pollution. Nevertheless, it still occurs during spring. The pattern was designed by the Rev. Edward Powell, one of the greatest Welsh fly-fishers.

KELL'S BLUE

This fly was devised for the River Usk. The originator, the late Eddie Kelly, was a caster of extraordinary skill and an instructor par excellence. This *Baetis* pattern fulfills the Imperial's wet role.

YORKE'S FAVOURITE

This does not look much like a dry fly to me, yet I am told that it is a popular pattern when the heather fly, *Bibio pomonae*, is about. In Scotland, this close relative to the hawthorn fly (though this has red legs) is called the Bloody Doctor.

GREY DUSTER

This is the hackled Adams, and is essential in every fly box. Its origins are unknown, but it was born out of the Alwen, a stream which feeds the Welsh Dee. Whoever devised it did fly fishing a great service.

SEA TROUT

TACTICS PECULIAR TO sea trout play a vital role. Equipped with a few offbeat dry flies such as the Grey Duster, nymphs such as the Pheasant Tail, the more traditional choices such as hairwings, terrors and tandems, and a touch of insomnia (sea-trout fishing is traditionally a night-time escapade), you will be prepared for your first sea trout, which will transcend most other angling experiences you can imagine.

BLACKIE (WADDINGTON)

This pattern represents the black-lure concept on a considerably larger scale. It is useful for fishing pools in darkness on a sunk line. Most effective from summer to autumn between daylight or twilight and in low water.

SURFACE LURE (PLASTAZOTE)

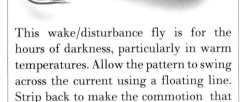

This wake/disturbance fly is for the hours of darkness, particularly in warm temperatures. Allow the pattern to swing across the current using a floating line. Strip back to make the commotion that is so attractive to trout.

RUANE'S FANCY

Professional fly-tier Terry Ruane here represents the nocturnal fare of sea trout. The yellow dots are created by mixing yellow paint with fabric glue. A useful change pattern on a sunk line during darkness in slower areas.

TERROR

Always popular with sea-trout fly-fishers, this pattern relies on the combination of blue, silver and a hint of red, which fish freshly introduced into the river system find appealing.

GOLDIE

Bill Pennington, noted Lancastrian sea-trout fisher, swears by a large fly even during daylight. Fish this yellow-and-black pattern on either a floating or sunk line in appropriate places, using across-and-down tactics.

PETER ROSS

This curious wet fly is one of the most popular lake patterns. It is employed as a point fly in a team of three. This is the river version, created specifically for moderate to high water levels.

HEADLEY'S SPECK

So named because the idea originated with Stan Headley, talented Orcadian fly-fisher. This tiny treble with a turn of hackle is very useful in ultra-low water or bright conditions. It is best fished on floating line in thin water.

MEDICINE (MALLARD)

This deadly blue-and-silver pattern was developed by Hugh Falkus. It is a river fly and an ideal all-rounder, suiting most conditions, water-brightness and light levels. For fishing on either a sunk or floating line.

WICKHAM'S FANCY

Another timeless example of a general-purpose fly that is successful with sea trout, and as good today as it was in 1884. Best fished loch-style, in the same way as the Silver Invicta.

BA PRETTY

I designed this little spider for Scotland's west-coast, small-spate rivers, particularly for Finnock. It has caught innumerable trout when fished from twilight to dawn in riffle water (which occurs at the heads and tails of pools).

FLASHABOU ALEXANDRA

I used this fly in Norway in low water and almost impossible conditions. It caught four sea trout up to 4kg. (8lb.) in one evening on a floating line. Not a standard pattern, but good when you have tried everything else.

BLOODY BUTCHER

Though a derivative of the old standard pattern, this fly, which has more red (the hackle), has itself become a classic with sea-trout fishers. Use it to fish either loch or river. For drifting, it can be used as the tail fly in a team or singly.

LOCH ORDIE (DAPPING)

Dapping is probably one of the oldest forms of presenting a fly. Use a 4-6m. (12-18ft.) rod, with a light floss line that can billow with the wind, and allow the bushy fly to trundle, kiss and furrow across the surface like a hatching fly.

SILVER INVICTA

The classic wet fly for either stream or lake. It is best used on loughs and lochs, where it should occupy either the middle-dropper or tail position when short- or long-lining from a drifting boat using a floating line.

RED STUART

This fly, with its origins in yesteryear, has recently enjoyed a revival thanks to Brian Peterson and Steve Parton. It is an excellent loch pattern for drifting, specifically as a point fly. It has taken fish to 7kg. (14lb.).

RED PALMER (DAPPING)

Like the Ordie, this pattern is representative of a group of flies designed specifically for dapping. They have a lot of hackle, and so create disturbance, and are very buoyant.

SCOTLAND

SCOTTISH FLY PATTERNS are among the most difficult to catalogue. So many Scottish artificials have become the very cornerstone of fly-fishing. The following are inner-sanctum patterns, most of which easily make the transition from one country to another, especially in stillwaters. Not generally seen as imitations - you have only to look at the Black Pennell or McLeod's Olive to see that insect interpretation is often overlooked.

DOOBRY

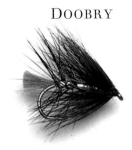

Stan Headley, the great Orcadian fly-fisher and dresser, devised this pattern for fishing colored water on bright days and on clear water on dull days, often in conjunction with a dark point fly. Hints of color make it sparkle.

LOCH ORDIE

Originated from a dapping fly and developed into the now well-known top-dropper pattern by J. Yorsten, who conceived the idea, and W.S. Sinclair, who tied it. Successful as a top dropper for emerging sedges (caddis).

KATE McLAREN

Named after the wife of the great sea-trout fisher Charles McLaren, this pattern is widely used as top dropper, especially in a big wave. It is just as good for reservoir rainbows as for traditional brown and sea trout on big lochs.

CLAN CHIEF

This is a modern, traditionalist fly by Captain John Kennedy from South Uist, where it is used to deadly effect on trout (sea and brown) and, I am told, salmon. I imagine that reservoir rainbows might also like it.

KE-HE

A 1930s Orcadian pattern devised by two fly-fishers, Kemp and Heddle. It is recommended as a point fly, especially for bright summer days when there is a wave, working on either peaty or clear water. Best in size 10.

ZULU

The definitive loch-style fly for darker days, the adage "Dark day, dark fly; bright day, bright fly" remaining as true as ever. A top or middle dropper, or even the point fly. A catcher of trout and sea trout throughout the British Isles.

GOAT'S TOE

This fly is apparently attributed to both Scotland and Ireland. It sports a fluorescent red yarn tail instead of the usual plain red yarn. More a middle- or top-dropper fly, it is also a successful salmon pattern on lochs.

BLACK KE-HE

Along with Orange and Benbecula, this point fly is a very useful variation. It is especially good early and late in the season and as a dusk pattern, probably because it bears more than a passing resemblance to hatching black midge.

BLUE-TAG RED PALMER

This is yet another variation on the ancient Red Palmer theme. The blue tag is Stan Headley's addition, and the pattern has proved very successful for sea trout as well as loch trout.

BURLEIGH

A potent pattern especially as a point fly when lake and pond olives begin to hatch. Its reputation on lochs for being good from early summer onward would support this. One of the enduring dressings from Loch Leven.

BLACK PENNELL

This turn-of-the-century pattern by Cholmondley-Pennell is one of Scotland's greatest exports and is found in most fly boxes. Especially good during the early season as a point or middle dropper when black midge are hatching.

MACHAIR CLARET

Although this pattern, devised by Captain John Kennedy, hails from Uist in the Outer Hebrides, there is more than a hint of Irishness about it. A water-moving fly, it is heavy hackled and lively-looking, in the Bumble tradition.

HECKHAM PECKHAM

Invented by William Murdoch of Aberdeen, this is one of those patterns that fall in and out of favor. It was, for example, once used widely in America. A good fly in bright conditions for loch sea trout, as middle-dropper or point fly.

MALLOCH'S FAVOURITE

This pattern is named after the Mallochs of Perth, the venerable Scottish tackle dealers. Although dowdy, the pattern has a lovely insect-like quality and is very useful as a point fly when midge are hatching.

WHITE-HACKLED INVICTA

This W.S. Sinclair pattern suits colored and peat-stained waters in either the middle- or top-dropper position. At times wonderfully effective, at others hopeless, this is a useful pattern on reservoirs as well as lochs.

McLEOD'S OLIVE

This point or middle-dropper fly could almost be an Irish or English olive pattern. Most countries have a similarly designed wet or emerging olive (*Ephemeroptera*). The gold butt is effective in peaty water or on dark days.

YELLOW OWL

This fly appears to hail from Loch Leven, which produces world-famous brown trout. Use on midsummer evenings as a point fly or middle dropper. These positions and the color suggest an emerging sedge or caddis.

IRELAND

THE HISTORY OF fly-fishing in Ireland is a rich tapestry of tradition based on sound local entomology. The loughs with their abundant fly life have given rise to many mayfly, sedge and chironomid patterns and, despite looking absurdly impressionistic, they deceive where more accurate patterns fail. Most have, like Scottish patterns, transferred admirably to stillwaters the world over, especially to English reservoirs.

GOSLING (SAM ANDERSON)

This quintessential mayfly pattern combines the Mayo with the Lough Erne Gosling and is actually supposed to represent the hatching mayfly, which can be almost epidemic on some Irish lakes. A middle- or top-dropper pattern.

GREEN PETER

This ubiquitous pattern represents a sedge or caddis (*Phryganea varia*) that could be a wet or dry fly. It is usually fished wet, in the top-dropper position. Good on almost any stillwater in the evening when large sedges are about.

OLIVE BUMBLE

The Irish judge T. Kingsmill Moore created many lake patterns. The Bumble series are among the most traveled. Essential in any drift angler's box and superb as a top dropper in a big wave, from Lough Conn to Loch Harray.

MAYFLY NYMPH

The Irish-style mayfly nymph, resembling the emerging insect or, more accurately, the drowned adult. Loose mayfly imitations work well on Irish waters, bearing out the advice, "Obtain local knowledge and local flies."

BIBIO

There can be few more famous flies for lake-fishing than the Bibio. Oddly for a palmered fly, it works in any position on the leader. Excellent in hatches of dark to black midge or any occurrence that calls for a black fly with a hint of color.

CLARET BUMBLE

Very good toward evening or darkness and especially in peaty water. Kingsmill Moore regarded this pattern as his best sea-trout fly. I can only confirm this finding. A top-dropper fly and best in roughish conditions.

MURROUGH

This pattern is by Sam Anderson, one of Ireland's better-known fly-tiers and anglers. This is the sedge and a fine one at that. Though looking more like a dry fly, it is in fact a top-dropper fly.

MELVIN BUMBLING BIBIO

I devised this pattern at Lough Melvin, when it was obscured by horizontal rain and clothed in a gray pallor. Three days later, as the weather cleared, over thirty trout had fallen to the design. It works especially well in rough weather.

CONNEMARA & BLACK

A classic that has found favor abroad. Variations from English reservoirs sport a fluorescent green tail, which has proved excellent in a midge hatch. A superb point fly, especially during the early and late months of the season.

FIERY BROWN

This fly has developed a reputation for being an excellent sea-trout pattern. I know it as a wet-sedge design. In that role, especially from summer to autumn, it is excellent, either as a point or middle-dropper pattern.

SOOTY OLIVE

There are countless versions of this fly. They all imitate the *Baetis* sp. which hatches on the great loughs, generally between spring and summer, and again in autumn. This point fly is one version of the hatching insect.

MELVIN OLIVE

This general olive pattern represents the *Ephemeroptera* spp. Malone gives two dressings of which this is the lighter, the second having a sooty olive body. A good point fly for lake and pond olives.

KINGSMILL

A T. Kingsmill Moore pattern updated with a fluorescent green butt that is attractive to rainbows. The body of ostrich herl is a near-perfect material, reacting with light better than most and becoming translucent underwater.

MELVIN OR ROGAN'S EXTRACTOR

Another pattern from Lough Melvin around which have grown specific patterns such as this one by the legendary Michael Rogan of Ballyshannon. I have given it a lighter look by using wood-duck wings.

BALINDERRY OLIVE

The master Irish fisher T. J. Hanna was way ahead of his time in his perception of insects as fly patterns. He always used traditional materials to great effect. The yellows, oranges, reds and browns in this pattern show olive when in water.

IRISH MALLARD & CLARET

This is an effective sea-trout pattern for the evening and in peat-stained water. A useful point fly, especially on dark days. I have added jungle-cock cheeks and a fluorescent tag in place of the ordinary wound floss used in the original version.

HARE'S-EAR

On a rough day on Lough Erne, I caught ten brown trout, all over 1kg. (1.5lb.) with this pattern. Each fish was overflowing with hoglouse (*Asellus* spp.) and I know of no better imitation of that insect than this.

NORTH AMERICA

WHITE MARABOU MUDDLER

ROYAL COACHMAN

THE UNITED STATES is the dominant force in the introduction of innovative styles and materials. The following includes older patterns, reminding us that there are few ideas that are truly revolutionary, since many were designed centuries ago. It would, however, be to ignore the demands of conservation to overlook the modern and attractive approach: these patterns use materials that do not harm our fragile ecosystem.

This fly incorporates two deadly materials: lithesome marabou for the wings, and deer-hair. An excellent imitation of many bait-fish species. Fish this pattern near the bottom, weighted or with a sunk line.

Arguably one of the definitive flies of North America. This wet version is a derivative of John Haily's 1878 dry version and was named by L.C. Orvis. It is still popular today, often effective when nothing else works.

GREY GHOST

THUNDER CREEK

ROYAL COACHMAN TRUDE

This fly represents the classic featherwing streamer style, but is also effective for the salmon-family species in general. A Carrie Stevens pattern, of which there is also a longer-shanked trolling version.

Created by Keith Fulsher, this fly is totally innovative in terms of its profile and design. Both wings and head are formed from buck tail, which, when in a stream, almost breathes with life.

A modern variation of the original pattern and one of a series devised by Dick Surette, known as riffle flies. These are designed for fishing in fast, broken water on freestone rivers. The white wing offers good visibility.

DAVE'S CHAMOIS LEECH

DARK HENDRICKSON

ZONKER SCULPIN

Craig Matthews was the first, to my knowledge, to use lambswool as a substitute for a deer-hair head. A zonker strip gives mobility, producing a bait-fish imitation that is good at night.

Trout, especially those in deep lakes and reservoirs, eat leeches. This successful imitation uses chamois leather, which undulates in the water, as tail and back. It should be fished deep in steady 1m. (2ft.) pulls and draws on the line.

The wet fly differs from the dry in wing shape: the wing fibers are raked back, whereas in the dry version they are divided upright. Devised as a commission by Ron Steenrod in 1915, this pattern has remained a classic ever since.

LIGHT CAHILL

This pattern, created by Don Cahill, is an imitation of a particular species, *Ephemerella subvaria*. There are wet, dry and nymph versions of this pattern in existence.

FILOPLUME MAYFLY EMERGER

One of a new wave of American fly-tyings, using the secondary or aftershaft feathers from game birds. Fish this Jack Gartside pattern, which mimics hatching dishevelment, in or near the surface.

CUT-WING DUN

Realism and a wide range of dry-fly effects have been the hallmarks of modern American fly-fishing. This parachute pattern is in the style of the master fly-tier Paul Jorgensen, and is very effective for selective trout.

CAREY SPECIAL

Col. Tom Carey's pattern suggests hellgrammites, stonefly nymphs and other drab, bottom-living creatures. Popular with both trout anglers and steelheaders, it is best fished near the bottom.

BROOKS' STONEFLY

This *Pteronarcrys* imitation was created by the undisputed freestone master, Charlie Brooks. Fish it near boulders and river beds in fast water. His theory of offering the trout the same view of a fly from any angle is brilliant.

POLYWING SPINNER

Another innovation is the use of hackleless flies. This pattern represents the last stage of an upwing's development, when the natural lies inert in the surface film. The polypropylene wings pinion the fly to the surface film.

MUSKRAT-WIGGLE NYMPH

I first came across this type of articulated dressing in Swisher and Richards' *Selective Trout*. The principle has been used by Dave Whitlock in his damsel patterns. Useful when trout are feeding on active nymph forms.

QUILL GORDON

This very serviceable general mayfly imitation was created by Theodore Gordon. Dating back to the 1890s, it shows how quickly split quill wings were ousted in favor of more durable bunched and divided fibers in the US.

FOAM ANT

As well as leaving few stones unturned in the quest for new fly-tying materials, the US also leads the field in developing land-based alternative food forms, of which this ant pattern, made from microcellular foam, is one example.

CASTING

O PLACE A FLY delicately and accurately at a distance where trout are feeding is the essence of fishing with the artificial fly. A good cast is, quite simply, the single most important factor in successful fly-fishing.

To a passerby, the sight of the fly-fisher moving his fly rod back and forth in precise, controlled rhythms would appear to suggest that the physical demands of casting are not great. Mastery of the mechanics of casting techniques is, for some people, easy to acquire. For others, indeed for the majority, a good casting technique is a particularly difficult skill to acquire.

The beginner tends to see difficulties rather than the attainable side of casting. Once dissected into manageable portions, however, a thorough working knowledge can soon be achieved.

Casting is best approached and practiced with a professional instructor, school, or a proficient friend. It is impossible to reach the necessary level of expertise from the written word alone. There is no immediate need for water — a lawn, field, and parkland have created many a fly-fisher. In the early stages, casting is best learned through repetition and practice. Visualize the cast as a house under construction. A solid foundation is laid and the basic overhead cast is mastered. Then comes the first layer of bricks, and shooting line is learned. At second-floor level are the false cast, and the single and double haul and the roll cast. The finishing touches are side casts, loop control, shooting roll casts, parachute casts, reach mends and other tactical casting maneuvers. These should not be tackled until a firm foundation is laid. Learn the mechanics of the basic overhead cast, and the rest should fall into place. Presented properly, a pattern with little allure will perform better than a slavish imitation presented badly.

ROLL CAST

THE ROLL CAST IS a way of casting the fly without using a back cast. The line is lifted off the water to the side of the angler and cast forward in a circular, rolling movement. It is very useful in confined spaces where overhanging trees or bankside vegetation makes the overhead cast impossible. It is also the only cast that does not rely on starting with a straight line between rod tip and fly and is useful when you have a jumble of line lying at your feet.

The roll cast contains many of the same components as the overhead cast, such as the lift, forward cast, and follow through. The arm should move from the elbow with the wrist firm. However, it does not use a back cast to load the rod. This is achieved by the line being held on the water and the line belly positioned behind the angler as the forward cast begins. The cast requires a forceful hammer action on the forward cast. The roll cast is difficult to execute on grass and best learned on water.

Nymph-fishing Tactics
Roll casting (below) *is vital to many nymph-fishing tactics, especially in medium- to fast-moving water. Cast into pocket water with a leaded leader to reach deep-lying trout.*

1 THE LIFT

Begin by flicking the rod out to one side (**A**, see below) so that the line and fly are clear of your body. Move the arm from the elbow to lift the rod back and up to the vertical, describing a semicircle. At (**B**), with the rod at the 1 o'clock position, the rod has reached its maximum height. The line travels across the water while a section of the line must remain on the water's surface.

2 CREATING IMPETUS

More impetus can be given to the roll cast by tilting the rod hand back and up slightly, so that the rod is at the 1:30-2 o'clock position (**C**). The loop in the line behind the rod, and the angler's side should be obvious.

3 FORWARD CAST

Start the forward cast when the line is looped behind you at point (**D**), using a strong hammer action of the forearm to roll the cast down and forward. A brisk, powerful action is required to get the line to unfurl forward.

A   B   C   D   E   F   G

4 LOADING THE ROD

At point (**E**) the line is about to roll forward. In the roll cast the rod is loaded by the end of the line being held in the water surface at this point in the cast. The rod hand is reaching maximum force and is moving down and forward to gain more momentum.

5 THE ROLL FORWARD

Full force has been injected into the rod and line at point (**F**). This condenses the loop, allowing it to unfurl and shoot forward. By stopping the action a little sooner (at 9:30-10:00) or later (at 8:00-8:30), you can make higher and wider or narrow and lower loops to cope with the various waterside situations. The follow-through at (**G**) ensures a smooth turnover.

ROLL-CAST PROBLEMS

The line leaves the water early.
When the line shoots out of the water beside your feet or under the rod tip, you have done one of two things incorrectly. You have either applied too much force when moving the line across the surface, or you have not left sufficient line to adhere to the surface film.

The line or fly hits you.
If you are forced to duck or flinch out of the way of the line, leader, or fly, you have lifted the rod in front of you. To avoid this, flick the rod and line out to the side before starting the lift.

Failure to roll forward.
The line may not unfurl in front of you and shoot forward properly. If this occurs, you have not used enough force when making the hammer movement with your forearm.

The line falls onto the water.
You have stopped the hammer action either too soon or too late if the line goes up in the air in front and then falls back, or fails to roll forward, hitting the water with a splash.

Loch-style Fishing
Roll casting is also useful during loch-style fishing (above). Having started the dibble (raising the rod tip to make the fly skate along the surface), you may run out of the necessary lift and arm movement to make a conventional overhead cast. A roll cast allows either for the flies to be re-presented immediately or for the rod tip to be positioned near the water.

WATERS & TACTICS

HETHER IT IS A SMALL, brackish, Scottish Highland burn or a rampaging, boulder-strewn western American river, a freestone river relies for its water on either rainfall, snowmelt, or its tributaries.

Freestone rivers are, in general, less alkaline-rich than the chalk streams or limestone rivers, which means that freestone trout seldom grow very large. Freestone rivers often have fast currents, and rocky passages which create runs, riffles, rapids, and pockets that demand particular fishing styles and tactics.

Chalk streams invariably originate amid chalk or limestone hills when rainfall percolates through porous rock into underground pools, then surfaces through alkaline-rich springs. They meander placidly through wide valley basins, allowing weed beds and insect populations to thrive.

The creation of lakes and stillwaters that cater specifically to the needs of fly-fishers is a recent phenomenon. There are two basic types of manmade stillwater: the gravel pit, often large and opaque, and the smaller alkaline pit.

The creation of such waters means that the sport has thrived when pollution and development might have impeded it.

Lochs and loughs demand a specific angling style. Fishing from a boat with a team of three or four wet flies is a favored tactic. Reservoirs provide water supplies but are also places for recreational sport. Many provide excellent trout fishing and bear witness to the fact that man can create stillwater that offers trout sport and trout habitats of the highest caliber.

FREESTONE AREAS

AN ABILITY TO read water accurately
makes catching trout a far easier
task. The first concept to grasp,
especially where freestone rivers are
concerned, is that what you see on the
surface can be utterly misleading.
Frequently, the fast surface water can
give way to negligible flow nearer
the river bed.

Current variations are not the only
criteria that can fashion tactics. Time
of season and time of day affect
where the fish will be lying. In the
early season, the deeper areas, such as
pools, deeper runs, and undercut banks,
provide warmer water and shelter. In
the middle to late season, the river is
more responsive to the angler.

The location of fish also depends
on the time of day. During darkness
and at dawn, shallows, riffles, runs,
and thin water to the side of pools are

Perfect Location
A typical glide or flat (above) *where
excellent dry-fly and subsurface-nymph
fishing can be found.*

Freestone Lies
*The riffle immediately downstream of
the angler will hold trout, as will the
flat beyond* (below).

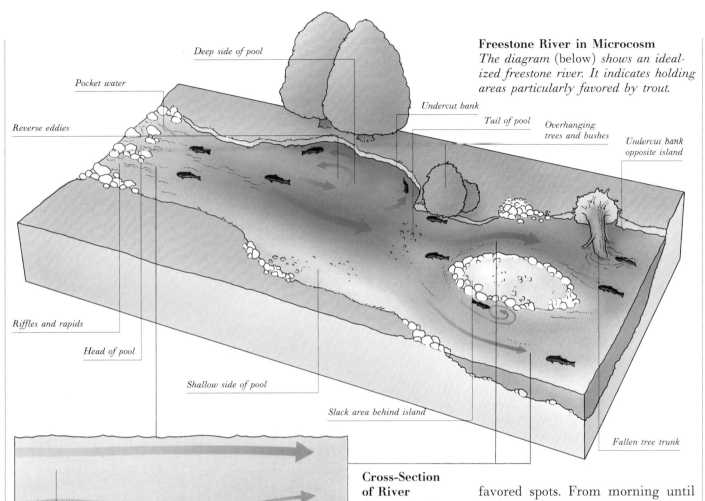

Freestone River in Microcosm
The diagram (below) *shows an idealized freestone river. It indicates holding areas particularly favored by trout.*

Deep side of pool

Pocket water

Reverse eddies

Undercut bank

Tail of pool

Overhanging trees and bushes

Undercut bank opposite island

Riffles and rapids

Head of pool

Shallow side of pool

Slack area behind island

Fallen tree trunk

Cross-Section of River
Nymph tactics predominate on runs. Potholes and depressions (left) alter trout behavior and call for careful searching of the river bed.

Fast current at the surface

Slow current at depth

Seine Net
A large seine net made from two broom handles and a nylon net is pushed upstream against the river current (left). This dislodges pebbles, sand, and small stones to uncover indigenous aquatic creatures that can then be imitated.

favored spots. From morning until midday and afternoon, especially during warm periods, deep runs, shaded areas, obstacles bounded by deep water, undercut banks, and well-oxygenated water are prime locations for trout. Early evening into darkness is usually the same as for dawn, but reverse eddies in pools, undercut banks, and around fallen trees or logs may also be important.

LATE-SEASON HOT SPOTS
In late season, stream inlets, shallows, riffles, and runs are favored. As the instinct to mate and spawn develops, fish need to feed up for winter.

Riffles and, in particular, runs are areas that tend to fish well during the whole season, irrespective of time of day or hatch. Wade a new stretch of river carefully before fishing it. Remember that the fast current, potholes, and shifting river bed of a freestone river can be unpredictable and dangerous to wade in.

Fast-Water Nymphing

WHERE THE WATER is fast-moving and boulders create pockets of slack water, the fly-fisher's opportunities are fleeting. When fast-water nymphing, it is best to cast out and let the line swing around in the current, to search the river bottom. Regardless of the speed of the current, let the fly sink to the trout's feeding depth. A fully sinking or sink-tip line and weighted fly or leader sinks the fly more quickly. Either fish the pocket water, or try "shotgunning" (see p.176). Deep runs, with potholes, boulders, and depressions, are also superb trout habitats.

Fishing a Run or Riffle
Great care must be taken when wading (above right), especially in fast water. A buoyancy aid and wading staff are essential in unknown waters. Where possible, use a guide.

Weighting Arrangements
*Various arrangements (below) are available: **A** (twist-on or spiral of lead wire) and **B** (split shot) both allow the fly to move naturally along the river bed; **C** (leaded fly with floating or sinking line) sinks fast; **D** (sink-tip or fully sinking line) is for fishing the middle depth only and **E** (leaded or weighted braided leader) can be used to sink very small, light flies in fast water, simulating natural movement.*

Releasing the Catch
This rainbow trout was caught in a deep hole upstream. Release the fish carefully into shallow water, holding its head into the current (above).

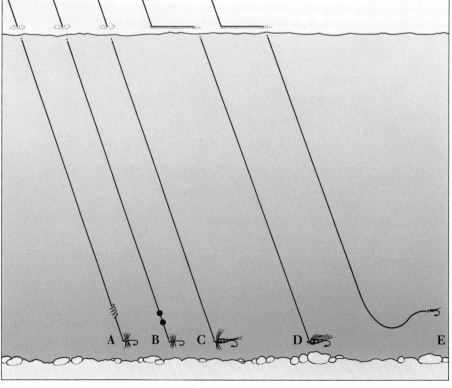

Searching Riverbed Pockets

After casting, lower the rod to allow the fly to search pockets on the bottom while keeping a curve in the line (above). If the line straightens, a trout has probably accepted your artificial, and you should strike immediately.

The Dead-Drift Swing

You should cast the line either slightly up or directly opposite, or slightly downstream. Allow it to swing around at the same speed as the river current. As the fly-line curves around, it will speed up. This raises the fly in the water (right).

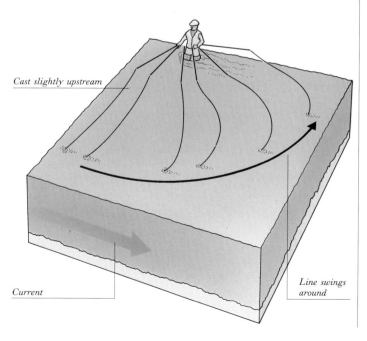

Cast slightly upstream

Current

Line swings around

QUIET-WATER NYMPHING

IN QUIET AREAS of the river many different insect types are found: caddis species, ephemerids (mayflies), shrimp (scud), and, if tree-lined, terrestrials. Your choice of fly should imitate these natural food forms. In general, it is advisable to use only small patterns.

FISHING NEAR THE SURFACE

The across-and-down method is effective for taking fish feeding near the surface. Cast carefully across the stream so that the fly, or team of flies, swings across the current in a concave curve and ends up downstream. Let the line keep pace with the current, allowing only very slight acceleration on the line swing. You may need to release a little line to overcome surface drag.

DEEPER FISH

An alternative method, for fish feeding deeper, is to cast a weighted pattern upstream and let it fish dead drift (see p.175). This tactic is suited to bank-fishing or wading in either fast or slow water. Likely areas are usually upstream of the angler. These include pockets and wide runs or riffles. It is best to divide each riffle into zones, tackling each zone systematically. This technique is known as "shotgunning." You will seldom, if ever, feel a fish take the fly. Watch the line carefully for a visual "stop" or draw forward, either of which indicates a take. Always retrieve slack line outside the rod tip, so that you can make a quick strike.

A Faster Run
A shallow bar gives way to a 2m. (6ft.) run (right) that holds both rainbow and grayling. The best approach is to cast upstream with a leaded leader and small nymph, allowing it to dead drift.

Slack Water
Cast slightly across the stream (left) into the edge of the fast water and use the across-and-down method. When you retrieve the fly, create some disturbance to imitate a pupa furrowing under the surface.

Shooting Roll Cast
This cast (above) *is also known as the switch cast. It overcomes the problems of heavyweight leaders and bankside foliage by creating an extra-wide shooting loop. A sight bob indicator will help you to detect takes as far as 18m. (20yd.) downstream. As soon as you feel a take, strike upstream with a long, sideways sweep.*

The Tuck Cast
The tuck cast (above right) *is often used on freestone rivers in Europe because it allows the nymph to penetrate the surface film before the fly-line lands on the water. It can therefore achieve a quicker descent, as there is less resistance from the water on the line. To execute this cast correctly you must tap upward and high, holding the line back on the forward shoot.*

Kicking-Nymph Method
The diagram (right) *shows the steps involved in the kicking-nymph method:*
A *The nymph drifts downstream in the current;*
B *Line is trapped against the rod butt to make the nymph jump in the water;*
C *The line is released and the fly sinks down toward the river bed again.*

THE UP-AND-DOWN SWEEP

The up-and-down sweep combines both the across-and-down and the dead-drift method into one tactic. It is best practiced wading in water with a fairly fast current and at a depth of 0.6-1.8m. (2-6ft.).

The cast, which can be quite short – between 4.6-12m. (15-40ft.) – is made upstream with a leaded or unleaded pattern and a sinking or non-sinking leader. Throw a small downstream mend in the floating line. Slack will indicate any takes. Raise the rod tip, still maintaining the mend, to keep constant control on the line. Takes at this point can be savage, so be prepared to raise the rod tip and give line.

DEEP-LYING FISH

The kicking-nymph method can be used for deep-lying trout on fast runs. Use a leaded nymph and a tuck cast. This allows the nymph to penetrate the surface and achieve a quicker descent before the line lands.

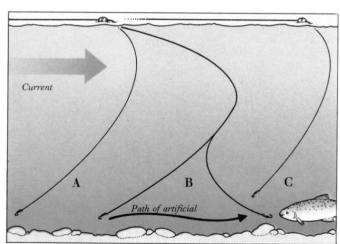

Up-and-Down Sweep
The line straightens out downstream (left). The tension of the line will make the fly rise like a natural through water. The diagram shows:
A *The artificial nymph pattern sinks to trout's depth;*
B *The nymph floats downstream;*
C *Tension on the line causes the nymph to rise.*

CHALK STREAM TACTICS

THE PLACID, ALMOST comatose, temperament of a spring creek or chalk stream is, of all habitats, probably the best for trout. Gentle flows, rich, verdant weed beds, and alkaline-rich water mean that foodstuffs are plentiful and easily obtained by trout.

READING THE WATER

It is easy to misread the meandering water of the chalk stream. Trout can frequent any number of subtle lies, and these are often overlooked by anglers. Many such trout-rich areas are located hard into the inside line (side of the riverbank), especially where reeds, tall grass, or iris overhang. There are also more obvious locations, such as by weed beds, channels, and areas of debris and collected weed on weed racks and bridge pillars. Natural or man-made hatch pools offer the same fishing opportunities as freestone pools. The overall depth of chalk streams and limestone rivers does not vary quite as drastically as in the rain-fed/freestone variety. This means that trout can be encountered almost anywhere along a stretch. Careful reconnaissance, preferably un-encumbered by tackle, should always precede your efforts with rod, line, and artificial.

Shallows tend to be less important on chalk streams than on freestone rivers, except during the evening or early morning, when surprisingly large trout will venture into the area to feed. In autumn trout will migrate to such places before spawning.

Fish that are either rising or actively feeding can be "marked down." To do this, walk the beat carefully, (crawl if necessary) peering at the water and noting or "marking down" any moving or rising fish with a twig on the bankside, away from the water's edge. You can then return at leisure, positioning yourself well back from the river to engage the trout without having disturbed it.

WATER CLARITY

Remember that any fish you spot in the extremely clear chalk stream water can also see you, and from a considerable distance. Therefore, it is sometimes better to cast from a kneeling position, particularly when there is no bankside cover. Always be prepared for the unexpected when fishing chalk or spring creek rivers. A moment's absentmindedness and you could be obliged to witness the shadow of a large trout drifting slowly away, disturbed by your presence and made wary and uncatchable for the immediate future.

Wooden Bridge
Bridge supports (above) collect weed, providing a larder and cover for the trout. Ovipositing baetids may climb down the supports to lay their eggs. They sometimes get swept away, making this an ideal place for the sunk spinner.

Mid-Stream Cast
Cast from a mid-stream position (far left) into the river bank, which is a prime lie for trout, since the vegetation offers protection. An overhead cast may be used to good advantage here, as there is no ob-struction behind.

Weed Channels
Channels (left) between the weeds are a favorite holding spot. Trout sheltering in these places have a tendency to be more nervous because of their exposed position. Careful casting, wading, and presentation are therefore essential.

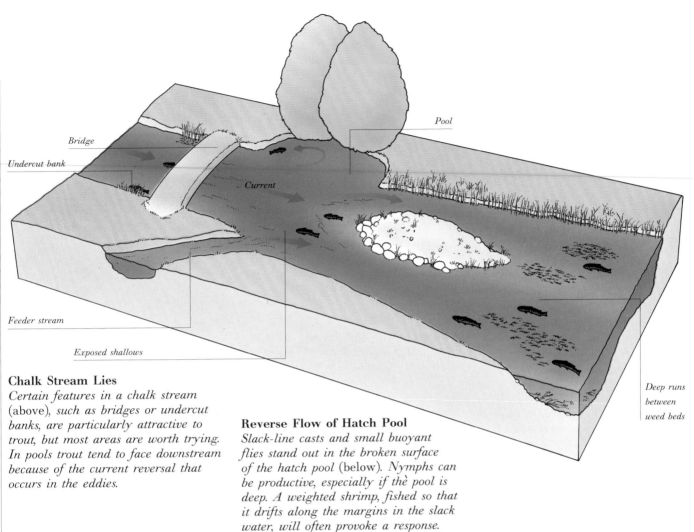

Bridge

Undercut bank

Current

Pool

Feeder stream

Exposed shallows

Deep runs
between
weed beds

Chalk Stream Lies

*Certain features in a chalk stream
(above), such as bridges or undercut
banks, are particularly attractive to
trout, but most areas are worth trying.
In pools trout tend to face downstream
because of the current reversal that
occurs in the eddies.*

Reverse Flow of Hatch Pool

*Slack-line casts and small buoyant
flies stand out in the broken surface
of the hatch pool (below). Nymphs can
be productive, especially if the pool is
deep. A weighted shrimp, fished so that
it drifts along the margins in the slack
water, will often provoke a response.*

THE ANGLER

MOST FLY-FISHERS of spring-fed rivers agree that how an angler presents himself is almost as important as the way he fishes the fly. To stand bolt upright wearing white or brightly colored clothing and stride boldly along the bank is inviting disaster. Fishing chalk streams and spring creeks is like jungle warfare, in which a crack from a broken twig strikes a discordant note and can alert the enemy to your presence. You are an intruder into the fish's environment, and to be a successful fly-fisher, you must try to harmonize with the surroundings. Clothing should therefore echo rather than fight with the colors around you. Against a background of grass and blue sky, err toward lighter colors; with trees or bushes in the background, clothing should likewise be darker.

AVOIDING SHADOWS

Shadows are a constant enemy. Accidentally cast your shadow across the stream and you will see fish flee for cover. So, whenever possible, fish from the side that will cast your shadow harmlessly away from the water. If this is not practicable, then kneel down to reduce your outline or conceal yourself in bankside cover to break up the image. When wading, be heedful of vibrations that may be sent out by clumsy footfalls – these can be picked up by the trout's lateral line (see pp.20-21) and will alert it to approaching danger.

When struck by sunlight, heavily varnished rods can scare trout, as can fly-line speeding through the air. Whenever possible, use dark-colored fly-line when you are fishing against a background of trees or heavy shade.

Keeping a Low Profile
It may be necessary to creep along the bank on all fours (below) *and cast from a kneeling position.*

Fishing at Dusk
As the light fades (above), *insects, especially caddis and upwings, become active, and trout lose some* *of their innate caution. By wading you will present an even lower profile to the fish, merging easily with the background.*

Bankside Cover
Reeds and grasses (left) *break up the silhouette, and, if you wear the correct clothes, offer good camouflage.*

Correct Approach
Move quietly, cast delicately, and read the water accurately, and you will come away with the prize (above).

SAWYER METHOD

THIS NYMPHING TECHNIQUE was developed by Frank Sawyer, who was an influential keeper on the River Avon, England. It revolves around the tactic of casting sufficiently ahead of a rising fish to enable the fly to descend to its level. Then, at the last moment, the rod tip is twitched upward, causing the artificial fly to speed away from the trout.

LOCAL KNOWLEDGE

A good foundation knowledge of fish-holding areas in the chalkstream is necessary for this style of fly-fishing. You must also be aware of your position in relation to the trout. By placing yourself immediately downstream and directly behind a fish, you could "line" and spook it. A wider angle may therefore be necessary to enable you to cast ahead of a fish without sending the line or leader over the trout. It is important that the first and only thing the trout see is your artificial nymph – not you, your line, or your leader.

CURRENT VARIATIONS

You must ascertain where the trout is lying in the current, at what depth, and in what speed of flow. Match your imitation fly accordingly. The nearer the surface a trout is holding, the closer you must cast to it. However, when trout are stationed at a depth of 60cm. (2ft.) to 1.3m. (4ft.), this can present problems. Try timing a leaf, twig, or bit of debris floating down the river, noting how long it takes to reach the trout from a certain point. This will give you an idea of the distance and time you need to allow for your nymph to meet the trout.

Fishing Between Weed Beds
Fishing the channels between weed beds demands accurate casting (right). You must not frighten trout holding in the prime lie.

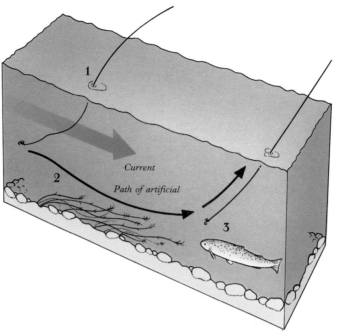

Current

Path of artificial

Sawyer Method
The method (left) is visual, not tactile. If the fish moves right or left or makes a sudden dart, strike. If you see a flicker of white by its nose (this is actually the inside of its mouth), strike. On windy or overcast days you may simply see a dark shadow or a silver flash: strike with conviction.

1 Upstream Cast
This gives the fly time to sink to the fish's level.

2 Dead-Drifting
Allow the fly to dead drift toward the trout.

3 Lifting the Fly
Raise the rod tip just as the fly approaches the trout to make the artificial lift in the water.

Choice of Tackle

Using the correct tackle (right) *and fly is particularly important for this method of fly-fishing. Leaders should be at least 30-60cm. (1-2ft.) over-depth and treated to sink. The fly should be weighted. Light lines #4-#5 are also advisable, as are fast-action rods. Artificials can be ejected extremely quickly, so speed in tackle and reaction is essential.*

Maintaining Contact

The Sawyer method relies on upstream casts, so slack line (as in upstream dry-fly fishing) must be created to enable you to strike at the right moment. Pull line back through the rings with the line hand (below), *at the same time as you raise the rod tip. Maintain contact and control of terminal tackle all the time.*

Classic Stretch

Weed growth (left) *in this stretch of chalk stream guarantees hosts of nymphs. The water is clear, ideal for spotting trout "on the fin."*

Pattern Choice

A Sawyer Pheasant Tail (below), *a Grey Goose, and a Killer Bug are all you need for this style of fishing.*

EMERGERS

FISHING AN EMERGER — a nymph pattern that resembles the hatching fly at the surface — depends on good observation and accurate casting. In many ways it parallels dry-fly fishing in that you are looking for specific rise forms. However, these will not be surface upheavals but underwater swells and contusions. You must be able to deduce, therefore, whether a trout is feeding in or on the surface, just subsurface or in the surface film.

Adopt the same technique as was used in upstream dry-fly fishing, aiming just above the trout's feeding zone so that your fly descends to the exact feeding depth (this will not be very deep). The last 15-30cm. (6-12in.) of leader tippet should be treated so that it sinks. This avoids the problem of shiny nylon and ensures that the fly cuts through the surface tension.

SELECTIVE FEEDING

Trout feeding close to the surface can be very selective, scorning rough, impressionistic flies in favor of more realistic designs. Hatching mayflies with embryonic wings can be very effective. It is also important not to overlook the possibility that midge pupae could monopolize the trout's attention, especially during warmer months and in areas of water that cover a silt bottom. Presentation is important and must be delicate. Trout will be very near the surface or operating in a shallow depth-range. Any splashy casts will either put the trout on alert or scare it off the feed.

FISHING LIGHT

Leader tippets should be as fine as you dare fish. Over 1.4kg. (3lb.) b.s. is rarely used unless in conjunction with a large nymph (over size 12). This usually is the domain of the small fly (sometimes as small as size 20-24), when hatch or situation demands. Fine nylon must be balanced by a softer-action (light) tackle system.

The indications that a trout has accepted your artificial are subtle. It may be a movement of the floating part of the leader (this and the line tip should be treated with flotant) either down or sideways or unnaturally against the current upstream; or a boil or whorl underwater. You may see the trout's mouth open and close in proximity to your fly, or the trout may drift to one side, or even tilt upward to intercept the free-drifting pattern. At the slightest hint of a trout taking your fly, lift the rod tip and set the hook gently but firmly.

Fishing Emergers
A thick surface film (below), which holds the ecloding insects, is essential when you are fishing emergers.

The Stillborn
In heavy hatches of mayfly a proportion will die during hatching. A pattern such as the Stillborn (below), should be carried in sizes 14-22, in various shades of olive, to mimic this state.

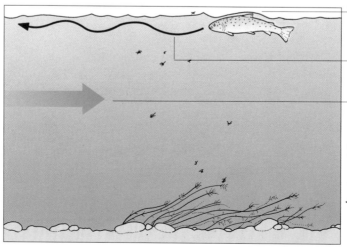

Bulge

Trout's direction of travel

Current

Nymphing Trout
The nymphing trout creates a bulge in the water's sur-face (left) as it swims along, taking flies off the surface. Occasionally its nose and tail may break the surface.

Perfect Conditions
A sedate current and calm surface (left) *provide the perfect conditions for upwing and chironomid hatching activity. You should try to use the rod as a shock-absorber against any sudden movements that occur when a trout takes your fly. This type of chalk stream river (the River Test, Hampshire, England, in this instance) often demands long, accurate, and delicate casts.*

Quarry Deceived
Unhook the trout carefully (below). *Always use a hook with a pinched barb: once the hook is taken out, the fish can then live to fight another day.*

Targeting Trout
You must be very accurate with the cast, landing the fly about 10cm. (4in.) *upstream from the trout's nose and then allowing it to drift to the target* (above).

RISE FORMS & PRESENTATIONS

BEING ABLE TO read the water and deduce lies and holding areas where trout may lurk is an enormous advantage. An understanding of the trout's diet and the way food is ingested is particularly important, as is the ability to spot and respond quickly to a presentation and rise. The rise, when the fish inspects or takes the fly, is preceded by the presentation, when the trout breaks through the surface, or makes a definite movement just underwater, so disturbing the surface.

The spring-creek fly-fisher must be able to read rise forms, as they indicate the presence of feeding trout. By recognizing the shape and significance of a particular rise form, you can deduce the type of insect that the trout is feeding on, and even the stage of development that the insect has reached. This will enable you to choose your artificial fly with great accuracy. Broadly speaking, rise forms and presentations occur throughout the entire fly-fishing season.

The Straightforward Rise
Circular rings fan outward when a trout takes a fly from the surface (left), though the size, length, and shape will vary in different water types and conditions. A trout sees a dry fly only from beneath, which is why it is a waste of time tying a pattern with elaborate wing detail on the upper side. However, the wet fly or nymph may be seen from any angle, including from above.

Nebbing
The trout pushes its nose (for which "neb" is an archaic term) silently through the surface (above) as heavy hatches of duns or spinners hover over its head. This rise form usually occurs during the morning and evening and in dull or cloudy weather. A trout is unlikely to rise in this, or any other way, during bright, sunny conditions.

Sip or Kissing Rise
The trout audibly kisses the surface, leaving tiny rings and a bubble (left). This rise form occurs either when insects are stuck in the surface film or when tiny terrestrials and Diptera such as gnats and midges are active. It is commonly seen on stillwater on hot, muggy days, when insects become trapped in the glue-like meniscus.

B Upward Drift
The trout allows the current flow to lift it to the surface.

C Simple Rise
The trout engulfs the fly as it drifts past.

D Compound Rise
A suspicious trout delays taking the fly until this point.

E Complex Rise
If the trout is still doubtful about the authenticity of the floating form it has encountered, it will continue to inspect the surface-bound object. It may then ignore the artificial or take it with its head facing downstream.

A Field of Vision
The trout is lying in a particular position in the river (a station) and is ready to feed. A fly comes into the cone of vision (right).

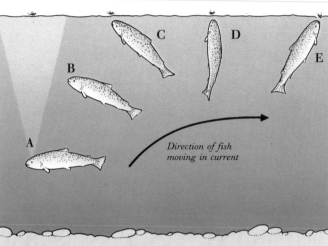

Direction of fish moving in current

Splash or White-Water Rise
This rise (below) *is the least common of all rise forms. The violent action required to complete it demands considerable effort on the part of the trout. It occurs in the late evening when either the mayfly or adult caddis species abound, but is also common on freestone rivers during general feeding times.*

DRY-FLY FISHING

FOR GOOD FLY presentation you need to cast accurately and delicately. It is also important to spot a fish and cast to it without being spotted yourself. The first thing the trout should see is the fly, so it is better to cast short than to overshoot. When the trout rises to the fly, resist the temptation to strike immediately. Instead, tighten the line and lift the rod definitely but slowly. Fly choice is always problematic. Often a general-purpose fly such as Adams or Beacon Beige will suffice, but if you base your pattern and color on the size of the natural in evidence, you should not go far wrong.

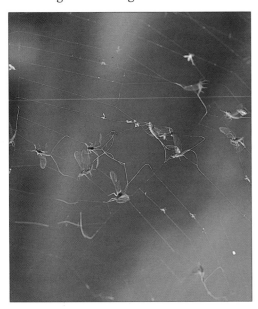

Observing the Natural
Nature and observation combine to provide clues as to pattern choice for the dry-fly fisher. Flies caught in this spider's web (above) are Baetis spinners from the previous evening, indicating the appropriate species, size, and coloration of the artificial.

Preventing Drag
A dragging fly (right) alerts trout to danger. A slack line (upstream or reach mend) lengthens the fly's floating period, delaying onset of drag.

Nearside Bank Fishing
Often trout rise very close to the bank, where they are easily overlooked. Inspect the bank closely and you may see half a rise or dimple. When fishing the nearside bank (above), cast directly upstream, slightly above target. The best approach is to aim high to achieve a soft descent.

Overgrown Areas

Hooking trout in densely weeded surroundings creates problems. Hold the rod above your head to force the trout to fight on the surface. This gives better control of the fish, enabling you to avoid potential hazards more easily.

The Duck's Dun (below)

Twilight Fishing

A brown trout comes to the net (above). At this time of night trout can swiftly turn their attention from dun to spinner. A prudent angler will watch for this.

Chalk Stream Habitat

Lush water meadows, verdant banks of weeds, and an even flow of water provide a habitat for terrestrials, flies, nymphs, and crustacea, so guaranteeing a constant food supply for trout.

The Prize

Handle trout carefully (right), if you want to put them back in the water again.

STILLWATER TACTICS

THE TEMPTATION IS to imagine that all stillwaters are the same, but this is not so. Like rivers, lakes can be divided into various categories, each requiring different tactics. The smaller, "put-and-take" stillwaters tend to divide naturally into two distinct types: the clear, usually spring-fed, chalk/limestone, alkaline variety; and the opaque, which may be less alkaline or merely prone to periodic algal blooms. Opaque stillwater requires the same tactics and strategies as those that are employed on reservoirs. However, clear stillwater requires an approach similar to that of the chalk stream angler rather than the opaque stillwater fly-fisher.

TERRITORIAL BEHAVIOR

When introduced to these crystalline lakes, trout soon carve out a territory for themselves. Once acclimatized, they can be seen patrolling a particular area, keeping to a precise route. They do this partly to familiarize themselves with their surroundings, and partly to keep out intruders.

These well-defined routes are also feeding excursions. A prime tactic is to ambush the trout. To do this, you must place the fly along its path, raising it in front of the fish as it comes within range. Alternatively, allow a leaded pattern to free-fall into the feeding circuit, taking into account the water depth, weight of fly, and speed of the cruising trout. The fly must drop directly ahead of and through the trout's area of vision.

Disguising Your Shape
Minimize your silhouette by crouching (below) *when fishing the margins, which often shelter large trout.*

Primary Requirements
Large trout often prefer the deep, calm margin, so always scan the water near your feet first (above). *You must be accurate in casting and fly presentation at such close range. Beware of alarming the fish.*

Maximum Strain
You may need to kneel to play a large trout. Even on 2.5 kg. (5lb.) tippets, pressure can be brought to bear to counter the fighting fish, so long as the rod is used as a spring (right). *Maintain pressure if the trout is near the bank, as it may panic.*

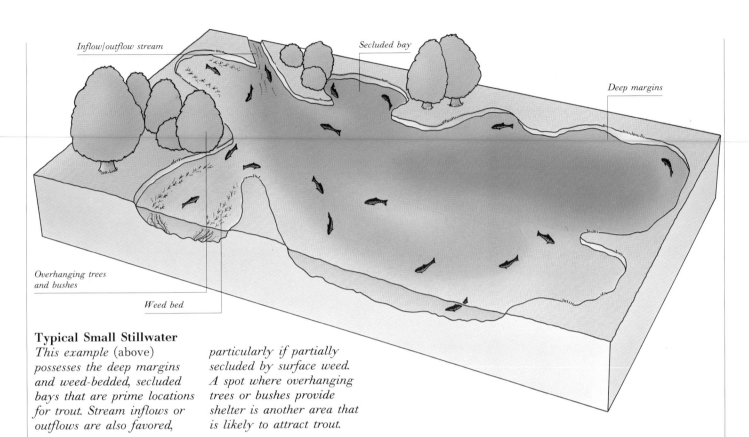

Inflow/outflow stream

Secluded bay

Deep margins

Overhanging trees
and bushes

Weed bed

Typical Small Stillwater
This example (above) *possesses the deep margins and weed-bedded, secluded bays that are prime locations for trout. Stream inflows or outflows are also favored,* *particularly if partially secluded by surface weed. A spot where overhanging trees or bushes provide shelter is another area that is likely to attract trout.*

Rainbow trout in particular may be present in shoals. These groups can include any number of trout, although larger shoals do tend to splinter into smaller groups of five or so. Shoals tend to favor particular places on a lake, such as near a feeder stream, water over a gravel bed or bar, a deep depression, an area of weed beds or, most frequently, curves in the banks.

LOW LIGHT LEVELS

The key to fishing a small stillwater is to take full advantage of its clarity, which enables the constantly moving, vigilant angler to seek out and stalk the quarry. However in low light levels, targeting a particular fish may not be possible, and fishing blind is then the only alternative. If this is the case, select an intermediate or slow-sinking line and choose a "trigger" pattern, such as a tadpole imitation in orange, black, or white. Using this combination of artificial and sink rate in poor light, it is possible to provoke the trout into chasing and taking.

Into The Net
A generous net is a vital piece of equipment (left), *as it protects the trout from unnecessary damage. To harm or even lose a good trout because of the inadequacy of the net is unforgivable.*

Unhooking a Large Trout
The deadly Olive Tadpole pattern is carefully removed from the jaws of the quarry using artery forceps (below).

STRATEGIES

MOST TACTICS FOR small, clear stillwaters require a certain amount of mobility, so comfortable clothing and footwear are essential. Take the minimum of equipment – rod, reel, landing net, the usual accessories, and a few flies. Everything small should fit into a fishing waistcoat. Polarizing sunglasses and a broad-brimmed hat will enable you to see into the depths more clearly and spot patrolling fish. Never become rooted to one spot. You can try to track down specific fish by peering into holes and likely places such as beneath trees, beside rushes, and in deep channels.

Leaded nymphs form the first line of attack. These are generally fished on a leader 3.6-4.9m. (12-16ft.) in length, tapering to between 2.3kg. (5lb.) and 2.7kg. (6lb.) breaking strain. If this system is harnessed to a weight-forward 7 or 8 intermediate, slow-sinking or floating line and a middle- to tip-actioned rod, big fish can be landed with confidence. Remember that even with quite strong tippets of 2.3kg. (5lb.) to 3.2kg. (7lb.) breaking strain the nylon can weaken. After a period of time, be sure to re-knot as you would after having caught a good fish.

LEADED NYMPHS

Using the leaded nymph when stalking or targeting calls for the fly to be cast accurately in front of patrolling trout. This allows sufficient time for the fly to descend to the required taking depth. The take will never be felt – if you do feel anything you will have missed your chance. Try to anticipate where the fly is in relation to the trout. If you see the fish's mouth open, showing a flicker of white, it has taken your fly. If the trout suddenly accelerates forward or feints left or right, your fly has probably been taken. You must strike the instant you see either happen. Of course, as with other forms of fly-fishing, a taut line from rod tip to fly is a essential.

If the free-falling nymph does not work when employing this stalking/ spotting method, try raising the rod tip in conjunction with your left hand and pulling on the line, accelerating the fly away from the trout.

Fishing a Deep Margin
This trout (below) *was seen and then hooked on its patrol route between the overhanging tree to the left and the weed to the right. It is being held hard on a tight line to prevent it from becoming tangled in potential obstacles.*

Fish that are lying motionless either very close to the bottom or near the surface tend not to be interested in artificial flies. Nor do those swimming at high speed, which they often do in pairs. The best target fish are those that saunter along, pausing to take a nymph here and there, or those that seem to be hunting.

INTERMEDIATE LINE AND LONG LEADER

Another tactic that may be useful for small stillwaters, and helpful if you are forced into random fishing, is to use an intermediate or slow-sink line on a fairly long leader of 3.6-5.5m. (12-18ft.), tapering to 2.3-2.7kg. (5-6lb.) breaking-strain. Fish this in conjunction with a good general search pattern such as an Olive Tadpole,

Quiet Backwater
The fly is lowered into the water (below) on a short leader. When the trout takes, it has to be held, as a run would result in line-breakage. The water beneath the tangle of branches is a perfect haven for large trout (right).

Marabou-Tailed Damsel, or similar long-shank nymph or lure. Cast out into a known hot spot or likely area. This may require casts of 23m. (25yd.) or longer. Let the line, leader, and leaded fly settle, then retrieve, using a figure-of-eight style. This kind of retrieve is designed to impart constant movement to the fly.

ROD CONTROL

It is advisable to hold the rod slightly to one side, since, when takes occur, they can be savage, and the spring in the angled rod tip will act as a shock absorber. After ten or so casts, allow the line more time to sink, then retrieve again. Experiment with a few different patterns and then move on to another known area. A systematic approach to retrieve rates, line types, sinking times, coverage and fly choice will help to ensure that you are covering all potential takes.

Ambushing
Careful observation of the quarry is vital before casting. Once cast, the fly is left in position in anticipation of the next take. It is on a trout's patrol route (below). When the trout approaches, lift the fly swiftly off the lake bed.

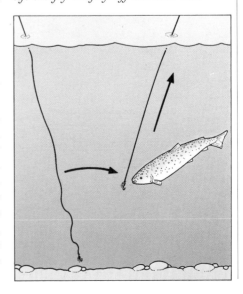

RESERVOIR AREAS

A HUGE RESERVOIR can be very daunting. Trout may be feeding at any depth, from the surface down to 12m. (40ft.) or more, while offering no visible surface indication as to exactly where they are or on what they are feeding.

A reservoir has a great many fish-holding attributes. Below the surface lie many hidden features which attract trout – old roads, ditches, hedgerows, gullies, and plateaus. Above the surface there are the more obvious dam walls, concrete towers, and aerator boils. These are all important features because they offer protection from predators, encouraging food forms to collect around them. The aerator may provide oxygen in hot weather. The sloping banks, which can be either shallow or deep-sided, can give a rough guide to what is happening beneath the water's surface. Mouths of bays, creeks, and peninsulas are also marvelous places for attracting trout.

RESERVOIR TACTICS

Once key trout lies have been established, the next question is which tactics you should employ. Should you choose imitation or attraction? There is no doubt that, on a reservoir, an attractor approach will present fewer problems and initially offer more success than employing an imitative tactic.

Early-season trout can be covered with confidence with a small black lure. Many permutations can be made by altering the depth with various line densities. All you need thereafter are "change" patterns, in which the same pattern is used but in a different color, such as in this case a white or orange version. By methodically trying one depth with one type of fly, another depth with the same fly and then starting again with the same pattern in a different color, you will cover the water effectively.

Boils
In hot weather, boils (above) and oxygenation pipes are prime feeding areas.

Dam and Tower
Towers (right) attract fry, small fish, and insects. The dam is also a hot spot, offering protection from predators.

Sheltered Bays
Bays that are protected and flanked by either grass or trees are favorite trout hiding places (below). The majority of reservoirs have a *steep bank on one side and a shallow bank on the other side, or a deep central channel. Ripples can often encourage trout to feed at or near the water's surface.*

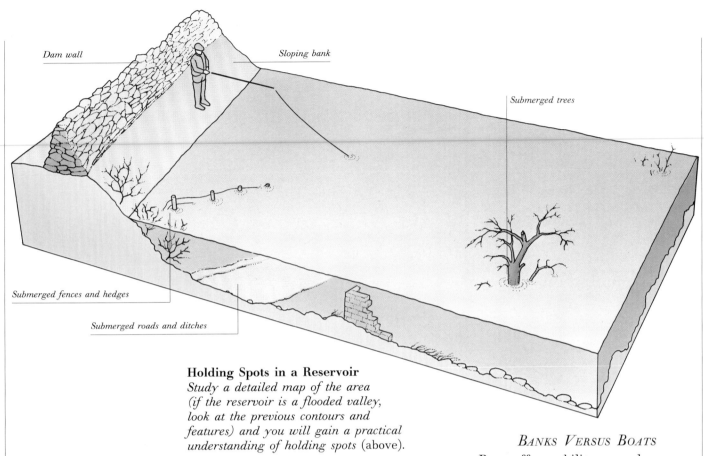

Dam wall

Sloping bank

Submerged trees

Submerged fences and hedges

Submerged roads and ditches

Holding Spots in a Reservoir
*Study a detailed map of the area
(if the reservoir is a flooded valley,
look at the previous contours and
features) and you will gain a practical
understanding of holding spots (above).*

BANKS VERSUS BOATS

Boats offer mobility over a large area of water, but the bank may be preferable during the early to mid-season, when trout can be found in the warmer, shallow water. There is also a stability about bank-fishing that is obviously not found in boats.

It is important that you are properly equipped for a day on the water, and that you know the safety rules for boat fishing. Always fish with a companion, or tell someone where you will be and the time of your return. You should always wear a lifejacket even if you are a strong swimmer, as gusts and squalls can blow up at any time.

Tell-Tale Features
A light ripple is ideal for dry-fly fishing and nymphing near the surface (above). The strip of flat water, flanked by rippling water, also attracts trout.

Boat Fishing
Drifting (right) and, if the wind allows it, hugging the shoreline can be particularly productive. But do not spoil the sport for bank fly-fishers.

BANK-FISHING

BANK-FISHING CAN be divided into nymph and lure styles, each with seasonal variations. For nymph fishing in early season, fish deeper water or shallows that deepen abruptly. In mid-season, insects become more active in the margins. During high season the water is at its warmest and bank-fishing is not productive. The late season is a repetition of the mid-season as trout hunt in the shallows.

For early-season lure fishing, fish deep water with a Hi-D line, short leader, and a buoyant fly. Black lines are best, but it is useful to have a white lure. In mid-season, fish the shallow areas using a floating or slow-sink line. In high season, fish the deepest water using a Hi-D line, short leader, and buoyant fly during the day, and a slow-sink or floating line in the early morning and evening.

Bank-Fishing Lines
The diagram (right) *shows the various types of line used by the bank-fisher:* **A** *Floating line and suspended fly;* **B** *Floating line and long leader;* **C** *Slow-sink line for wind and mid-water trout;* **D** *Hi-D line used with a buoyant fly to avoid bottom obstacles and weeds.*

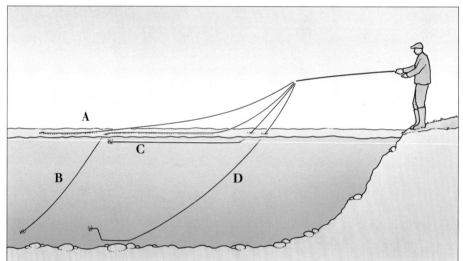

Lure Fishing
Often misinterpreted as being the mindless pulling of large, multicolored flies, lure fishing can be quite sophisticated. Matching the food form is vital when seeking fry-feeding trout. This rainbow (left) *took a Minky fry pattern that resembled the fry on which it had been feeding.*

Cloud Cover
Cloud encourages trout to move nearer to the surface (left). *Choose floating-line tactics.*

Dawn
A floating-fry imitation on a floating line cast along and beside the marginal weed in water no deeper than 0.6-1m. (2-3ft.) accounted for this rainbow (right).

Long Casts
The ability to cast more than 23m. (25yd.) of line (right), may bring you into contact with trout previously frightened by anglers casting much nearer to the shoreline.

Prime Fishing
Dusk encourages trout to come closer to the shoreline. The dam wall, an old fence, and weed-rich shallows (below) are prime hot spots for trout.

Fry Haunts
Harbors and boat stations (above) attract fry, which in turn bring in trout. Fishing around them, using either a floating or medium-sink line with a fry pattern, such as an Appetizer or Minky, can sometimes produce good results (below).

IMITATIVE BANK-FISHING

FLY-FISHING ON reservoirs with imitative patterns requires a thorough understanding of both the relevant insect life and trout behavior. Patience, determination, and familiarity with the area are also assets. You will need a floating line (some anglers prefer double tapers) and perhaps a slow-sink or neutral-density line for windy conditions and flat calms. You should also be able to cast a line up to 27m. (30yd.) with 5.5-8.5m. (18-20ft.) of leader. You will need a few lines, flotant, sinkant, and a net.

Imitative Tactics
The presence of anglers on the bank often pushes trout farther out into the water. In this case, you will require floating lines and long leaders (below).

Loch Tactics
This Scottish loch (left) responds well to bank fishing during early and late season. Employ loch-style boat-fishing tactics rather than imitative reservoir strategies that use insect imitations.

Marrow Spoon
A marrow spoon (below) for examining food recently ingested.

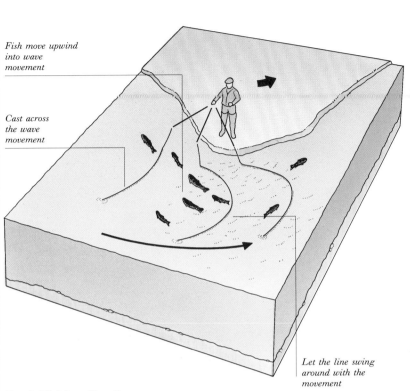

Fish move upwind into wave movement

Cast across the wave movement

Let the line swing around with the movement

Bank-Fishing Hot Spot

A point flanked by a bay (above). After one area has been fished thoroughly (for one-half to one hour), move on a few paces. Repeat the process, moving into the bay itself. If you are a right-handed caster, position yourself so that the wind blows over your left shoulder and vice versa if left-handed. This ensures safe casting by taking the line away from the body.

"Polaroiding"

Thanks to polarizing sunglasses, a high-plateau brown trout comes to the hand from Odells Lagoon, Tasmania (above right). By cutting glare, the glasses allow you to spot individual trout in shallow, weedy areas. Imitative flies and floating line are the main weapons.

Overcoming a Flat Calm

Faced with a flat calm (right), opt for a slow-sink line to minimize disturbance on the surface. You should continue to present flies slowly and imitatively. The stripping basket keeps line from drifting away and sinking. It also prevents line from tangling, allowing longer casts to be made when necessary.

IMITATIVE SEASON

URING EARLY SEASON, deep areas up to 4.5m. (15ft.) can be fished effectively with a floating line. However, it may be necessary to change to line of a different density under certain conditions. In a flat calm it is advisable to use neutral-density line, while in a head-on wind slow-sinking line is preferable. By varying the line density you can cover different levels and so systematically search the whole area.

As a rule the leader should be twice the depth of the water in order to set the fly down to the required depth. When you are fishing in 3m. (10ft.) of water, you will need a 6m. (20ft.) leader. Insect life is slow and somber, therefore your retrieve rates and fly

Perfect Conditions
Cast a long floating line and allow it to bow around (left). Your rate of retrieve should merely keep pace with the drifting bow in the line.

The Nymph-Fisher's Light
Dusk and dawn encourage trout into the margins where ripples disturb the surface vision of the fish (below). In low light, rise forms will be a feature; therefore try to cast your fly in front of the trout.

patterns should echo this. Ultra-slow figure-of-eight retrieves or wind/wave action bowing the line around is all that is required. Patterns should be either tied on a heavy iron hook or leaded to reach the lower water levels. The primary insects to imitate in this case are cased caddis, black, gray, and dark olive midge, and some corixae. The best time is morning to early evening, with the afternoon being particularly good.

INSECT ACTIVITY

Mid-season is the best imitative fly-fishing period. Insects proliferate amid the newly grown weed. Seek any area within 4.5m. (15ft.) of the margins, using floating line and long leaders. There may be trout active from bottom to surface, so be prepared to cover all eventualities. If possible, choose a bank with the wind blowing either onto it or sideways across it. Midge in olive, green, black, and brown predominate, as do cased caddis, shrimp, hoglice, corixae, damsels, and other waterborn creatures. Fish at speeds representative of the natural you are imitating, paying careful attention to surface activity.

When temperatures rise, life can be difficult for the bank-bound imitative fly-fisher. Trout may migrate to the depths, venturing near the bank only at last light and staying there until early morning.

COOLER WATER AND OFFSHORE BREEZES

The best tactic is to seek out cooler water – an offshore breeze can often create this – and fish deep (early-season style) with a long leader and leaded fly. During the evenings and early morning, a dry fly (midge, caddis, or cranefly) cast out and left often works well, especially if there are a few trout rising. Whatever you fish, do so statically or very slowly indeed. Insect life will include orange, red, and olive midge, caddis species, corixae, and shrimp, and there may also be snails and small fish such as fry and sticklebacks.

LATE SEASON

Since the late season echoes the mid-season in terms of insect and trout activity (unless very cold weather kills off hatches), you can use the same line. You should also fish the same areas, but pay particular attention to bays, inlets, and creeks where trout may be harassing corixae and shoals of fry. Be prepared for the sudden feeding on migrating snails that can take place. Species of midge occurring in late season are more likely to be olive, brown, and black. The late season is very much surface-oriented, so it is advisable to carry imitation patterns of caddis, shrimp, olive (pond and lake), and cranefly.

Imitative Fly-Fisher's Prize
A rainbow (above) is deceived by a fly pattern that it mistakes for food.

The Deadly Retrieve
Even in poor light, keep low, using bankside cover, and there is less chance of spooking trout. A slow, figure-of-eight winding movement with the line hand brings a midge pupa through the surface film in a controlled, steady manner (left). This form of retrieve is particularly attractive to trout because it imparts a constant, provocative movement to the nymph.

FLOAT-TUBING

OVER THE LAST ten years, fly-fishing has started to attract a considerable amount of interest, especially in the United States. A float tube or belly boat allows the fly-fisher full freedom of a lake, even making accessible remote areas and places that are normally unfishable from bank or boat.

Nevertheless, open waters such as large lakes and reservoirs demand respect and are certainly no place for a float tube when winds are quite strong. As when wading, safety must take precedence over the attractions of the fishing. I would strongly urge the use of an inflatable lifejacket/waistcoat and suggest that if you are a nonswimmer this method of fly-fishing is not for you.

FLY-FISHING POTENTIAL

However, if sensible precautions are taken, float-tubing can provide enormous enjoyment and, more importantly, open up unexplored areas, many with great fly-fishing potential. When first float-tubing, fish for short periods – at most 1 to 2 hours – until both your experience and paddling strength are sufficient to cope with a longer session.

When the angler is concealed in a tube, trout seem unconcerned, frequently rising extremely close to the inflatable. The belly boat also provides an almost perfect platform for nymph fishing and dry-fly styles (including floating fry) on stillwater. Sunk-line tactics have been developed for float-tubing, but visible floating-line styles are the easier to master in the early stages. Long-range casting is generally not needed.

FLAT CALMS

During flat calms and periods of little ripple, a slow-sink or neutral-density line often helps presentation by removing the surface disturbance made by a floating line. When playing a hooked fish, try to keep the rod arm high, as this will tend to make the trout fight on the surface.

Equipment
Flippers are essential for propulsion and maneuvering. Neoprene waders combat cold water and offer ease of movement (above). Inflate the tube to its maximum size, and make certain that everything you will need is stowed either in the float tube's pockets or in your inflatable waistcoat.

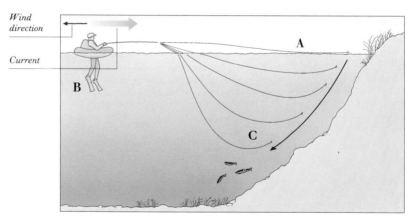

Wind direction

Current

Entering the Water
When wearing flippers (left), it is easier to walk backward. Enter at the "bottom" of the wind, because if a squall gets up you will simply be blown back toward the shore. Choose a place where the water is shallow and has a gradual decline. It is easier to get ashore from a downwind position.

Hot-Weather Tactics
In hot weather fish are usually found at lower levels (above).
A *Cast toward a windward bank or sudden deepening of shallows;*
B *Back paddle upwind, paying out more line and allowing the fly to sink;* **C** *Use a figure-of-eight retrieve to bring the nymph very slowly back to the surface.*

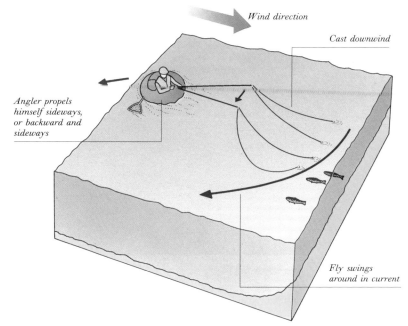

Wind direction

Cast downwind

Angler propels himself sideways, or backward and sideways

Fly swings around in current

The Nymph Swing
Using floating line and a team of nymphs such as midge pupae, make an initial downwind cast of about 12-18m. (40ft.-60ft.), more if possible. Then propel yourself directly sideways or sideways and back to keep control of the line (left).

Float-Tube Tackle
The tackle need not vary greatly from that used for medium river or reservoir fishing (below). For nymph fishing, a 3m. (10ft.) rod, together with a #5 or #6 line, will allow high backcasts and delicate presentations. For sinking-line tactics, a #7 outfit may be better.

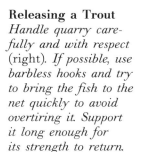

Trout Safely Netted
The short-handled wading style of net (above) is the only viable design for this kind of fly-fishing. It is large enough to hold trout safely as you unhook the fly, using artery forceps.

Releasing a Trout
Handle quarry carefully and with respect (right). If possible, use barbless hooks and try to bring the fish to the net quickly to avoid overtiring it. Support it long enough for its strength to return.

ANCHORING & RUDDER STYLES

DURING THE RECENT increase in popularity of loch-style fishing, the techniques of anchoring and rudder fishing have, sadly, been underused. They remain, however, particularly important weapons in the fly-fisher's armory.

Rudder fishing (or rolling on a long drift) is outlawed on most reservoirs. This is a shame, since its effectiveness in catching mid-water rainbows feeding on daphnia is undisputed. This style has been born out mainly of fishing lead-core lines of 3m. (10ft.) fashioned from trolling line into a shooting head. This line is cast slightly to the side of the boat, which is propelled with the bows downwind, the angler paying out running line while the head sinks. This "pitch-and-pay" method, especially when using tandem lures, is devastatingly effective for brown

Covering Large Waters

Rudder styles can cover large amounts of water effectively at various depths (below). Anchoring enables you to fish the hotspots or locate areas to be fished.

trout and fry-feeding rainbows that are harvesting deep. Many authorities have attributed a decrease in stock (especially of brown trout) to this method, but this is open to conjecture.

ANCHORING

Anchoring is a prime tactic. To say it is a floating casting platform might seem an oversimplification, yet, for all the tactical maneuvers boat fishing offers, this is what it is. A boat on a reservoir enables you to fish out-of-the-way creeks and bays, as well as isolated weedbeds and plateaus where trout often patrol. A knowledge of the water you are to fish — the bottom contours, depth, and features — is a prerequisite . This will aid in selecting tackle and also determine tactics and fly choice.

STATIC BOAT-FISHING

Anchoring is not a chance affair. Success in static boat-fishing depends very much on where the anchor is dropped. Early and indeed late season may require a position just offshore — say 45m. (50yd.) to 70m. (75yd.) — or along the edge of weed beds to intercept fry-feeding trout. Then again, during hot weather, deep-water marks might be the better option, as trout seek the cooler depths of 6-12m. (20-40ft.) or more, feeding

on daphnia, chironomids, or fry. When fishing these depths you need local knowledge of what is occurring below. An old streambed or ditch may provide spectacular fishing if you can get your fly in the vicinity. Anchoring off dam walls, water towers, and other fixtures is also worth trying, and especially advisable if you are using fry patterns and artificials such as booby nymphs.

Trout on reservoirs and lakes are attracted by any features, even submerged trees. By anchoring a

Anchoring
In normal conditions, fix the anchor midships and fish broadside (above).

casting distance away, you can give full range to tactical variations. It is wise to anchor on a shortish rope (twice the water depth) and, after a little time (if fishless), pay out a bit more rope so that fresh water is fished. This works exceptionally well in bays, where great areas of bank can be covered, provided the wind is conducive to this tactic. If you are nymphing across the wind, it is wise to drop anchor with the bow facing into the wind.

An Alternative Method
These anglers have fixed the oars in the rowlocks in order to create the same effect as using a rudder (right). By manipulating either oar, a different angle of drift can be achieved.

No 6. Vekemans RST
A perforated drum-model (above) excellent for shooting-head work, this reel has a wide spool capacity. This feature is advantageous in that troublesome coils do not form in the running line as a result of "coil memory."

Rudder Fishing
The rudder is in position and the boat is set on a drift. The line is a shooting head, the rod rated to #9-#10 (right). By varying line density, an effective search pattern can be used to locate the trout-feeding depth.

THE CATCH

HAT FOLLOWS IS A series of fishing "logs," a record of days in the field, fishing for a variety of trout on widely diverse waters. From catching a rainbow trout to angling techniques on a large manmade reservoir; from a tranquil day's fishing on an enchanting British river to fishing for the mighty steelhead in Oregon with Jim Teeny, fly-fisher *par excellence,* and stalking the European grayling with Roman Moser on the River Traun in Austria.

More often than not when fly-fishing, instinct and experience rather than pure reason suggest tactics and techniques. Why, for example, exchange a successful fly pattern at a certain point in your fishing day? Would it not continue to be productive all day? Why move from what has proved to be a good vantage point? Unless, of course, you are aware that at any moment the sun might catch you as you stand on the bank and cast a terrifying shadow over the trout you are stalking. To become a successful fly-fisher, you must maintain constant vigilance, and be ready to act on the hunches and instinctive reactions which invariably reward the receptive and observant eye. There is no more valuable advice than "in order to catch a trout, first you have to think like one." A sound knowledge and understanding of the world in which the trout moves is an essential part of successful fly-fishing. There is a saying, coined by the late William Lunn, keeper of Hampshire's world-renowned River Test: "The proper fly, properly presented at the proper time, generally brings forth the proper result." Perfectly true, but learning which is the appropriate artificial pattern to use, and how, where and when to cast your line – all this demands patience and application.

RAINBOW

A RAINBOW TROUT FROM any water is a worthy adversary, but combine this trout's sporting qualities with a fast river flow, and you have a fly-fisher's dream. The prospect becomes even more stimulating if the quarry is also educated — by definition, caught and released on a number of occasions, making the trout wary of an artificial fly and all but the most artful presentations. Such trout will not be deceived by any old fly fished in a haphazard, unthinking manner.

Freestone rainbows feed on bottom-dwelling creatures and adult or emerging flies. Since the rainbow trout is generally more ready than the brown trout to feed all through the day, changing depth in the river to do so, you should be prepared to experiment with tactics to suit variations in feeding activity. Even so, river rainbow often prove far more fussy, and so more of a challenge than their stillwater counterparts.

Wading in Fast Water
Felt soles and neoprene waders (above) are indispensable. Carry the rod reversed to protect the fine tip section from damage should you stumble.

Making a Tuck Cast
Stopping the forward-cast hammer-tap abruptly at the 11 o'clock position (below) lets the fly touch the bottom before the line alights on the water.

Fishing a Turbulent Pool
*The conflicting currents produced
by tumbling water often make it very
difficult to get the fly down to trout
that are feeding on the bottom (above).
You can overcome the problem by*
*using a Moser Bottom Bouncer
leaded leader. This allows a small
Baetis nymph on a 0.9m. (3ft.) tippet
to drift realistically in the bottom
layers (above). Cast upstream
and let the fly dead-drift back (right).*

Cork Sight-Bob
*Watch the cork sight-
bob (above) constantly
for a take, striking as
soon as you see
it stop moving on
the water's surface.*

Fine Catch
*A freestone rainbow
(above). The Gold-
Head Pupa's barbless
hook is easily removed,
minimizing any
trauma to the fish.*

RESERVOIR TROUT

T HE STOCKING POLICY operated by many reservoirs favors the rainbow trout. Recent years have seen a tremendous growth in competition marinas, where boat anglers concentrate particularly on rainbows. Rules outlaw leaded flies and restrict pattern size, making the angler dependent on sound tactics.

A detailed knowledge of the water and of the various presentations of artficial flies on lines of different densities is critical. The ability to switch in a matter of seconds from a Hi-D line and a team of buzzers to a floating line and a dry fly is the key to reservoir success.

Floating Line and Buzzers
Line and fly (above) *are retrieved slowly figure-of-eight style, subsurface.*

The Competitive Spirit
Tension mounts as anglers (below) *prepare for 9 hours afloat.*

Apart from the difficultly of locating the trout, which is often a challenge on a large water, the rainbow's grouping instinct may necessitate repeated excursions over shoals. This makes the trout nervous.

Small, somber flies and light leaders are often most successful. This approach is particularly advisable in calm conditions, when a mirror-like surface tends to make the presentation more suspect to the educated fish. Where conditions allow, drifting along a shoreline can produce excellent results. To cover the water better, particularly in a competition, fish from opposite sides of the boat when weather permits.

Heading for the Drift

Often, clues exist, such as wind or calm lanes, or markers such as buoys (right). Always be alert to the possibility of rising trout. If a drift does not produce after an hour of fishing with a variety of tactics, change and search for another. Repeat this procedure until fish are located.

Changeable Weather

You might go out in a flat calm and two hours later be fishing in driving rain and a Force 5-6. These anglers (left) have switched to sunk line in order to overcome the wave action. Often a neutral or intermediate will work when a floater has failed.

The Prize Reservoir

The bloom (silver rays in the fins), that indicates peak condition, runs into the tail. Trout such as this (above) can strip a great deal of line from a reel in one run. One of the hardest-fighting fish in the angling world, they are worthy adversaries.

BROWN TROUT

SLEEPY IT MAY seem, but an idyllic chalk stream is invariably the scene of many an epic battle with the most sophisticated quarry of all, the native brown trout. The brown trout's loathing of anything discordant or unnatural has been the undoing of many a chalk stream angler. The first task, therefore, is to find out on what the trout are feeding, and then fish imitatively, often matching the hatch as accurately as possible. Terminal tackle and presentation are equally important. When a variety of insect species hatch simultaneously in a compound hatch, trout often favor one type. At such times, close scrutiny of the water surface and an analysis of rise forms is essential. If in doubt, it is advisable to opt for a smaller fly than the one that appears to match the natural, since its smaller size makes the trout less suspicious. If a brown trout constantly refuses an offering, a lighter tippet may be what is needed to offer a more natural presentation.

The shape and silhouette of the pattern is also particularly crucial in dry-fly fishing. If artificials carry too much hackle to appear realistic, it is advisable to trim the underside of the hackle into a V-shape on the bankside. This tactic has outwitted many a wily chalk stream brownie. Yet, for all the attentions lavished on chalk stream fly patterns and imitations, it is the angler's cautious approach and accurate fly presentation that are crucial to success.

The wild brown trout is a particularly valuable asset, threatened as it is by pollution and water abstraction. It should therefore always be released back into the river to ensure the continuance of the species.

River Maintenance
The Itchen (above) in southern England is unusual in that most stretches of this highly productive chalk stream are keepered full-time.

Stalking a Fish
If you creep along the bank in somber clothing and in a semi-crouched position (left), you may spot a trout on the inside line, rising close to the bank. Hold loops of line to dispatch an immediate cast. Stealth, accuracy and delicacy are the watchwords to bear in mind while executing this delicate maneuver.

Precise Delivery
A trout is spotted rising immediately behind the fallen willow branches on the opposite river bank (above), a prime lie for any fish. Make a long, tight loop delivery, aiming above the target. The key is to be accurate while remaining undercover. This demands practice in a garden or on an open playing field with fly rod and target.

Netting a Fish
As the played-out fish (left) comes to the net, sink the net and bring the trout to it. By staying low and out of sight, you will avoid frightening the trout further.

Conservation of Stocks
This peak-condition chalk stream fish (below) is returned to the water unharmed but perhaps a little wiser.

Protecting the Line
When the trout is on, the fly-line is wound onto the reel, away from bankside hazards (above). The rod is held high in order to protect the fragile tippet from sudden shocks caused by a fighting fish.

Reading the Water
Dusk brings out Baetis *spinners and blue-winged olive duns (above). Careful observation reveals that the trout have switched from spinners to the larger blue-winged olive duns.*

STEELHEAD

JIM TEENY'S KNOWLEDGE of steelhead, their behavior, and the appropriate tactics and flies is masterly. To many fly-fishers, these fish present the ultimate challenge. The sea-run rainbow trout's fighting qualities are second to none. It has suffered over the last century from pollution and exploitation, but the indigenous population has been helped by the introduction of hatchery-bred fish. Steelhead fishing often calls for rods capable of casting lines between #7 and #10. Floating line is widely used. Jim Teeny designed his own extra-fast sinking tip to overcome fast currents. Tactics are similar to those used in other forms of freestone fly-fishing – upstream, dead drift, dry fly and nymph for slow water and low summer levels; across-and-down styles with either floating or sunk line interspersed to arrest fly movement and speed. Above all, the steelhead fly-fisher must adapt in order to cope with this unpredictable quarry.

Shoal of Steelhead
You will rarely be lucky enough to find a large school of steelhead (above). When rivers drop down, becoming low and clear, these fish will often stack up in the deeper pools. You may find it difficult to get steelhead to bite. Sometimes longer and lighter leaders are required, along with smaller flies. Careful, quiet wading, and a gentle approach are vital. Keep tackle to a minimum, since steelheading involves stealth and often a great deal of walking.

Spotting Your Fish
Jim Teeny scans the surface (below) for traces of steelhead. He designed polarized glasses for this important function. The rocky margins demonstrate exactly why resilient tackle is essential and caution a priority when steelheading in this kind of terrain. A dislodged rock may spook the quarry, making successful steelheading still more demanding. Jim's essential tackle is contained in a short waistcoat that allows for deep wading, should this be necessary.

Hooking and Fighting Steelhead

Jim exerts maximum pressure (right) *over the blistering first run of a fresh steelhead. A firm strike sets the hook, and, held correctly, the rod will absorb some of the pressure. Holding the rod near to the butt ring will absorb more pressure. If you are wading when a large fish is hooked, try, where possible, to reach the bank, since by standing on firm ground you will achieve more control.*

Superb Specimen

This fabulous steelhead (below) *measures 95cm. (37^1/2in.) in length and has a girth of 45cm. (17^1/2in.). It weighs about 8kg. (18lb.). If you hold the fish by its tail and under its belly, you can provide good support.*

Releasing the Catch

By gently supporting the fish's head (left) *and directing it into the current to refresh it in flowing water, you can return a prize steelhead unharmed to the shallows of the river.*

Teeny Nymph

A general pheasant-tail pattern (left) *to carry in a range of colors. Good in low water and bright conditions with light line and small-fly tactics.*

GRAYLING

GRAYLING DIFFER FROM trout in their feeding behavior and reactions to freestone fly patterns. Having been hooked, say, eight times, rainbow trout become largely uncatchable; grayling, on the other hand, may be caught and released up to ten times, even in one season.

Their habitat is similar to the trout's, as is their diet. However, whereas rainbows or brown trout operate at most levels in the river system, the grayling tends to favor either bottom-feeding nymphs, caddis grubs or larvae and shrimps, or surface feeding. When feeding on floating flies, grayling tend to lie in holding areas on the bottom where current diversions among rocks and stones afford an easier lifestyle.

RESPONSE TO THE ARTIFICIAL

The grayling's area of vision, encompassing the surface, can trigger a response, in which they glide up from considerable depths to intercept a floating offering. Thus the dry fly is accepted by the grayling in a near-vertical position, unlike the trout.

In general, their acceptance of imitations is very much quicker than that of the trout, calling for a faster sinking action. While the grayling's rapid, angled rise often causes it to miss the artificial, it will rise again to a carefully re-cast fly. Grayling have softer mouths than trout and demand a gentler strike.

EUROPE AND NORTH AMERICA

The challenge posed by the European grayling (*Thymallus thymallus*) has led to the proliferation of specific tactics and fly patterns. The North American form, *Thymallus arcticus*, is far less common and, perhaps because of this, is highly prized for its silvery beauty. It is found in both lakes and rivers and is often fished for with the fly.

Preliminary Investigations
Start the day (above) *by searching the areas nearest the bank (tranquil water and pockets). It is here that fish may be feeding on female caddis that have died following the egg-laying exertions of the previous evening.*

The Switch Cast
Where vegetation prohibits back-casting, use a shooting roll cast or switch cast (below) to reach the middle. Let the fly dead drift until a surface blip reveals that a grayling has taken.

Applying Tension
A hooked grayling will often use the resistance to the current of its large, sail-like dorsal fin to help it fight (left). However, by creating slack line and holding the rod high, you can force the fish to the surface. Here it may jump spectacularly again, causing problems if it lands on the 1.5kg. (3lb.) tippet. Give slack at this point if possible. Slowly, relentless rod tension tells, and the grayling comes to the hand. The deer-hair adult caddis can be seen in the top jaw.

Shortening the Fight
If you apply as much pressure as possible to the grayling while playing it, bringing the fight to a speedy conclusion, the fish will be less stressed (below). Nets are useful but seldom necessary when wading and releasing fish.

A Flexible Response
A Traun grayling weighing 1.5kg. (3lb.) is returned (below). When grayling are feeding on a specific insect, use the corresponding artificial.

SMALL STILLWATER TROUT

————◆————

STALKING TROUT IN small, clear waters is not to everyone's taste. Some fly-fishers are openly hostile to the idea of catching large trout from such places, claiming they are too easily caught on the fly. But trout introduced into small stillwaters learn quickly, and there is an art in persuading these trout to accept your artificial fly. This skill can be acquired only by careful study of clear water and a detailed familiarity with the patrol routes, favored hiding places, and foibles of large stillwater trout.

Time spent in reconnaissance of the stillwater you intend to fish is seldom time wasted. As essential as the technique of spotting the fish is the fly-fisher's ability to cast a fly accurately to its feeding area.

Stealth and Camouflage
Wearing drab colors and using bankside cover, where available, to break up your silhouette, enables you to scrutinize the lake's deep margins carefully (left). Given a fair depth of water, patrolling trout come very close to the bank. The fly rod is permanently at the ready, so a quick and accurate cast can be made with ease. Sufficient line looped in the left hand will allow any distant fish to be covered.

Improving Observation
Crystal-clear, chalk-filtered water (above) allows you to observe prospective trout at close quarters and even stalk them individually, usually with weighted nymph patterns. To aid your observation, wide-brimmed hats and polarized glasses are essential. The trick of seeing trout underwater, sometimes at considerable depths, is to peer through and beneath the surface rather than regard it as an impenetrable barrier.

Using Side Strain
A fish hooked at close range
(below) *makes a run toward*
the bushes. By using side
strain (holding the rod
parallel to the water), you
can turn the trout, forcing
it to fight on the surface. At
this point, the rod is brought
upright to counter pressure
on the fragile leader and act
as a shock absorber.

The Critical Moment
Bend down to avoid fright-
ening the trout (right), *for at*
this time it may well panic.
The net is sunk, ready to
accept the quarry. The rod
is now upright, not only
guiding the trout to the net
rim, but ready to act as a
shock absorber in case of
any desperate last-minute
bid for freedom.

Landing a Fish
A trout of about 2kg. (6lb.)
is enmeshed and ready to
be brought in (below). *With*
trout of this size, never lift
the net, but slide it toward
you with the rim just above
the surface, then grasp the
rim and lift vertically.
Avoid using the handle.
Once ashore, remove the
hook with forceps and either
return the fish to the water
immediately or kill it
promptly, using a priest
in the correct manner.

Cockwill's Hare's-Ear
This shrimp pattern (left)
suits all fly-fishing methods.

You will r
a bobbin l
a dubbing
A whip-fi
the thread

Starting
can be dor
with a to
method o
consists of
turns of
itself. Thi:
and secure
and firmly
whicheve
However,
hand, forr
around yo

1 Whip-fin
about four i
shank to tie

4 Rotate you
four or five
thread again

FLY-TYING

HERE IS LITTLE that can beat the satisfaction of catching a fish on a fly that you have tied, perhaps even invented, yourself. However, there are other advantages to tying your own flies. You are able to make a pattern look exactly as you think it should, imitating the precise shade and shape of the natural you have observed as you fish. You can also tie a fly that takes account of local conditions and variations.

All that is needed is a small work area, a good light, a few items of equipment, and a basic selection of materials. In the past, flies were tied using a range of natural materials — feather and fur — some of which are not available today because they come from protected species. Fortunately, substitute materials have been produced, and new artificial materials for fly-tying are being created all the time. These factors have greatly increased the variety and styles of pattern that can be tied.

Flies are made by winding on one material after another to create tail, body, wings, and hackles. These are all held in place by a continuous piece of tying thread which is tied off

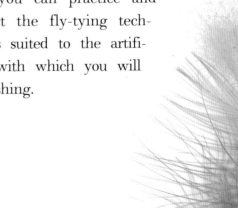

when the fly is complete. There are many different techniques for creating bodies, wings, and hackles, depending on the natural you are imitating and the materials you are using. Once you have grasped these basic techniques, you will be in a position to tackle any type of pattern and even to develop your own. To begin with, it is advisable to tie up simple patterns in order to get used to handling the materials you use. It is a good idea to tie a few examples of each pattern so that you can practice and perfect the fly-tying techniques suited to the artificials with which you will be fishing.

WEIGHTING & WING CASES

A SIMPLE WAY to add weight to a fly, and an alternative to the lead eyes on p.234, is to wind some lead-wire beneath the dressing. This is known as weighting or leading. Folded wing-cases, made of feather fiber, are used to imitate the nymphal stage, in which the insect's wings are inside its body. A simple-hackle wet fly is tied by first creating a body, then tying in a collar hackle and whip-finishing.

1 Take a short piece of lead-wire the same thickness as the hook shank.

2 Make a few turns of the wire in the center of the hook shank. Trim.

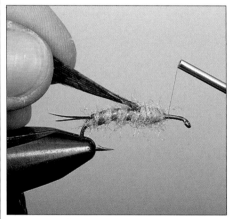

1 Double wing case Tie in feather fibers to body and build the thorax (see Dubbing a Body, p.229).

2 Fold the doubled feather slip over the thorax and tie it down.

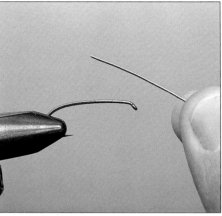

3 Repeat to create two stepped wing-cases, then whip-finish.

Hare's-Ear Nymph
Incorporating a wound, weighted body (above) and folded wing case.

1 Single wing case Tie in a feather slip for the wing case after forming the body.

2 Create the thorax, then fold the feather over it. Tie down and trim off the excess material.

You will need a sharp pair of scissors, a bobbin holder for the tying thread, a dubbing needle, and hackle pliers. A whip-finish tool is useful for tying the thread off when the fly is complete.

Starting off and whip-finishing can be done as effectively by hand as with a tool. The whip-finish is a method of finishing off the fly. It consists of a wrapping of at least three turns of tying thread wound into itself. This forms the head of the fly and secures the tying thread neatly and firmly. The steps are the same whichever method you choose. However, when whip-finishing by hand, form the loop in the thread around your first two fingers.

OFFERING THE THREAD TO THE HOOK

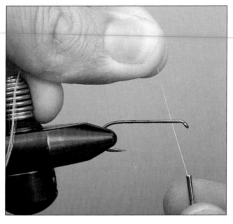

1 Place the thread taut against the hook shank. Hold the free end steady.

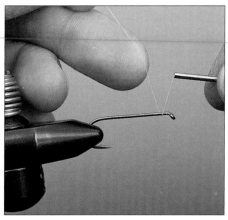

2 Take the thread around the shank, catching the free end as you go.

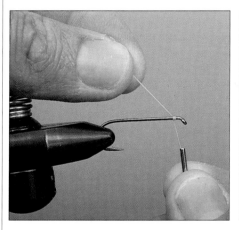

1 Whip-finishing by hand Make about four turns around the hook shank to tie down the free end firmly.

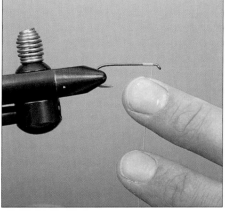

2 Keeping the thread taut, place two fingers against the thread with the back of the hand facing you.

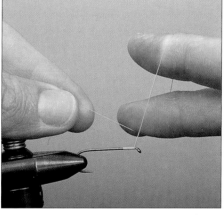

3 To form a loop swing your hand through 180°, catching the thread against the bottom finger.

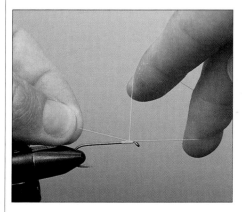

4 Rotate your hand around the shank four or five times, trapping the tying thread against the shank.

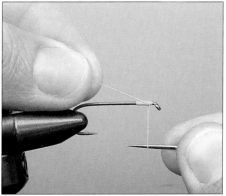

5 Use a dubbing needle to keep the loop taut as you pull the thread tight, and trim off.

Hairy Prince
This pattern (above) *incorporates a neat head that has been varnished for protection and allure.*

TAILS

TAILS ARE TIED in at the bend of the hook. The most difficult part is positioning them to lie straight on top of the hook shank. This is achieved by using the pinch-and-loop method, as follows: as you bring the tying thread up, catch it against the side of the hook with your thumb. Letting the thread loop above the hook, pinch it against the other side of the hook as you wind round. Still pinching the thread against the hook, pull the loop down tight on top of the tail material and hook. This method is also used for attaching wings that have to sit parallel to the hook.

Many materials are used for bodies (see Fly Dressings, pp.240-77 for each fly's component parts). These include floss silk, hair, flat tinsel, peacock or ostrich herl, and artificial materials such as Antron, Lurex, polythene, polypropylene, latex, Haretron, and Plastazote.

Today, flosses may be made from silk, but artificial flosses are also available. Whatever the material used, the body is formed by winding it on in layers along the hook shank to build up an even shape. It is important to remember to leave sufficient room at the eye for the hackle and head.

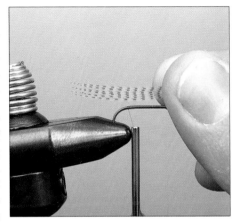

1 The tail must lie on top of the hook shank, directly in line with it, so it extends straight out behind the hook.

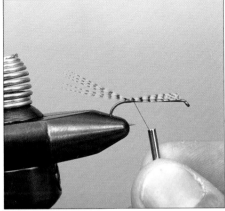

2 Hold the tail material at the bend of the hook. Make four or five pinch-and-loop turns to secure it. Trim off.

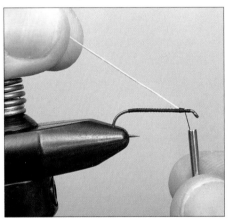

1 Winding on a body Wind a layer of tying thread toward the eye. Tie floss in with a few turns of thread.

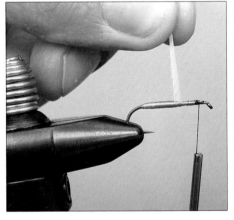

2 Wind on the body material carefully, spreading it out evenly as you go to create a smooth shape.

GE Nymph
A wound feather-fiber body (above).

3 Secure the end of the body material with a few turns of tying thread, and trim off any excess material.

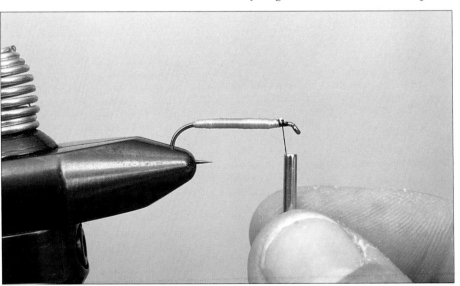

BODIES

HAIR BODIES ARE created using a method called dubbing. This is necessary because hair fibers are too short to wind on as they are.

The methods for dubbing a body are as follows: take a bunch of hair and roll it into a ball. Next, tease out the fibers and twist them into a rope. Alternatively, the bunch of fibers can be twisted evenly and smoothly onto the tying thread before being wound on. Choose the method you find achieves the best result for you.

A thorax is formed in the same way, but extra material should be dubbed onto the thread (see p.236) to create more volume. Very short fibers can be applied using a dubbing loop (see p.231).

The most important point to bear in mind when using flat materials such as latex or tinsel to create a body is that it must be wound on in even turns that overlap each other only very slightly. This is essential, as only the smoothest of finishes will create a realistic fly, which imitates the appropriate natural so closely that it will deceive the most seasoned and wily of trout.

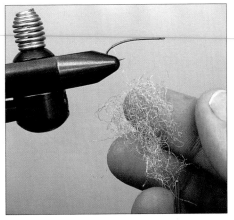

1 Take a small bunch of hair and tease out the dubbing material with your fingers.

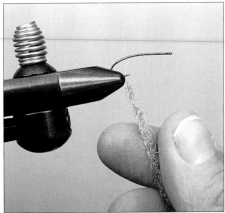

2 Roll the dubbing material between your thumb and forefinger in one direction only to form an even thread.

3 Wind the dubbing around the hook shank. A dubbed body should not be too bulky or hairy, so take care not to use too much material. If you wind on ribbing, you can use a dubbing needle to tease out some of the fibers.

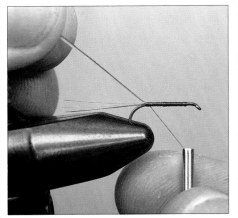

1 Flat materials Tie in the piece of body material at the tail, so the first turn butts up against the tail fibers.

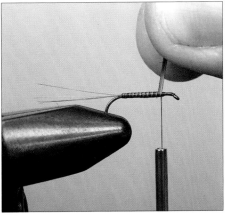

2 Wind on in turns that just overlap. Stop just short of the eye and tie off. Trim away any excess material.

Sedge Pupa
A rope-dubbed body (above) *using irise-dub, an Antron mix.*

HACKLES

ACKLES IMITATE THE legs of a fly, or the legs and wings in action together. They are tied from a variety of different materials, although hackle feathers are the most commonly used. Dry-fly hackles are formed from stiff cock hackles that help the fly pattern float on the water's surface. The hackle of a wet fly, however, must not prevent it sinking, and must move well when wet. In order to achieve this effect, wet-fly hackles are tied generally from less buoyant soft hen hackles or fur.

To match the size of a hackle to the appropriate hook size, the length of the fibers of the hackle should equal twice the width of the gape of the hook. When you have tied in a hackle, hold it at right angles to the hook with the top side of the feather facing toward the head of the fly. Hold the hook firmly and keep it in this position as you wind it on. If it twists, remove it, select another and start again.

Simple dry- and wet-fly hackles are tied using the collar method, the hackle being wound on with a couple of turns and then securely tied off again. A false hackle is a hackle on the underside of the fly only; the top part of the hackle can be trimmed off after tying.

FORMING A NYMPH HACKLE

1 After creating the body, attach a slip of feather, which will form the wing-case. Then tie in the hackle.

2 Add dubbing for the thorax. Pull hackle stem over thorax and tie in. To finish, see Wing-Cases, p.236.

A SIMPLE DRY-FLY HACKLE

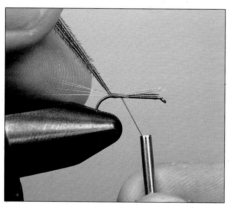 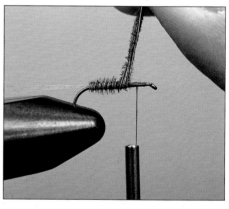

1 A tail is tied in at the bend. Feather fibers are attached in the same place.

2 The feather-fiber body is wound on with even turns. Finish the body a little way short of the eye.

3 Remove the fibers from the base of the hackle and tie it in next to the body with a few turns of the thread.

4 Gripping the hackle with the hackle pliers, make two or three turns around the hook shank.

5 Wind the tying thread through the hackle fibers, tie down the tip and trim. Whip-finish for a neat head.

Using a Dubbing Loop to Form a False Hackle

1 Form a loop in the tying thread and trap the fur fibers inside it.

2 Twist the loop of thread so that the fibers are held tightly. A dubbing twister can be used for this.

3 Make two or three turns around the hook shank and tie off. Trim away the hackle-top to create a thorax.

PALMERING

A PALMERED HACKLE extends along the length of the whole body of the fly to give it bulk. It is used in wet- and dry-fly patterns. In wet flies it imparts extra movement and liveliness, and in dry flies it provides buoyancy and improves their capacity to float.

The hackle is chosen in the same way as for other hackles (see opposite) and prepared by stripping fibers away from the base of the quill to make it easier to tie in.

Tying a Palmered Hackle

1 Tie in a length of body material and tinsel or wire at the tail.

2 Wind the body material and tying thread back toward the eye and tie in a hackle.

3 Wind the hackle along the hook to the tail with evenly spaced turns. It is important to keep the tension on it.

4 The wire/tinsel ties down the hackle at the tail and is wound back up the hook through the hackle fibers.

5 The wire/tinsel holds the hackle securely in place along the body. Any excess material is trimmed off.

WINGS

THERE ARE MANY different ways of tying wings on to imitate the different stages in a natural's life cycle. In some patterns, such as lures, the purpose of wings is to give an illusion of movement and life to the fly as it moves through the water. Different materials are used for creating wings, including feather slips, hackle points, hackle fibers, and hair, in addition to the many and various artificial materials now available that enable the fly-tier to create still more convincing artificials.

Adams
A hackle-point dry fly (above) *with a dubbed body.*

FEATHER-FIBER WINGS

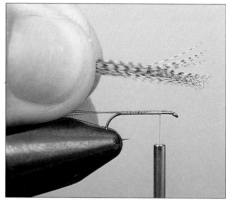

1 Tear a bunch of fibers from a hackle feather. Position it to extend a little beyond the hook bend.

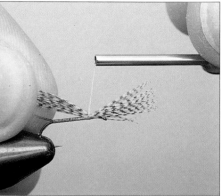

2 Attach the fibers to the hook near the eye with some tight turns of the tying thread.

3 Divide the bunch of fibers into two. Wind the thread around them in a figure-of-eight pattern.

4 The figure-of-eight tying has created a traditional V-wing fly.

HACKLE-POINT WINGS

1 Lay matching feathers side by side on the shank. Make three turns with tying thread.

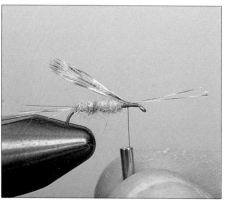

2 Make figure-of-eight turns with the thread around the hackles to separate them and make them stand up.

3 The finished hackle-point wings.

DRY-FLY WINGS

FEATHER FIBER IS used in small patterns, and can be tied in a V pattern or as a roof wing, when the dry-fly wings lie on top of the hook shank. Soft hen-hackle points are used to tie mayfly spinners, as these must float in the surface film.

Hair wings are used in many patterns as they give the fly good buoyancy and therefore aid flotation. The bunch of hair must be cut off straight so that all of the fibers are the same length.

Polypropylene is a popular artificial material. It is a transparent yarn that is used to tie no-hackle spinners, and is a buoyant material that lies in the surface film.

Depending on the appearance of the natural being imitated, dry-fly wings can be attached in a variety of positions. An upright position is achieved by winding on thread both in front of and behind the wing slips; a semi-upright position is achieved by winding the thread in a figure-of-eight pattern; a horizontal position, which imitates a spent fly, is also tied by using a figure-of-eight pattern.

1 The fibers should project in front of the eye by about two-thirds the length of the hook shank. Tie in.

2 Make a few turns in front of the fibers to make them stand up. Divide thread in figure-of-eight tyings.

3 A body and hackle have been added to complete the fly.

Gulper Adams
A parachute version (above) *of the Adams, using a polypropylene wing.*

1 Start by building the body. Then offer up the piece of polypropylene yarn next to it.

2 Trap the yarn on the hook with a turn of the thread. Make figure-of-eight turns to secure it.

3 Trim the wings to the correct length and then spread out the wing fibers with a dubbing needle.

LEAD EYES & LURES

L EAD EYES COME in different sizes
and provide a convenient way of
adding weight to a fly. Marabou is a
very soft feather that comes from
turkey legs. It has great mobility and
creates a pulsating movement in the
water, which attracts the trout. Its
fluorescent colors are highly visible,
and lures tied with it are popular on
stillwaters. Hair wings are preferable
in fast water, as they move with the
water better than marabou.

ATTACHING LEAD EYES

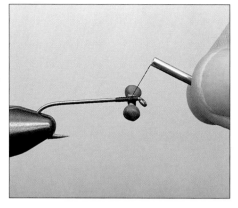

1 Hold the pair of eyes below the
hook shank. Secure it in position with
figure-of-eight turns of the thread.

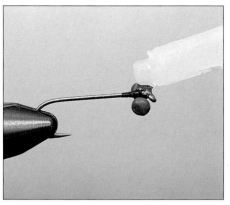

2 Adding a little glue will make the
tying extra firm.

1 Marabou wing Tear a bunch of
fibers from a marabou plume.

2 When held in position, the length
of the wing should match the end of
the tail.

3 Make a few tight turns with the
tying thread. Trim off any excess
marabou with an angled cut.

HAIR WING (LOCKING TURN)

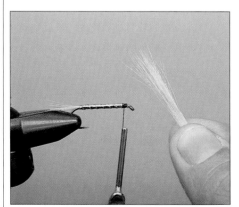

1 Match the ends of the fibers and
offer to the hook. The wing should
extend to the hook bend.

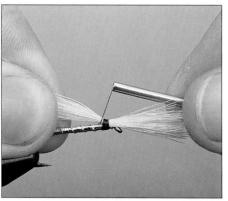

2 Tie in with several turns of the
thread, then take turns under and
over the wing, locking in place.

3 Trim off any excess material with
an angled cut. Cover with several
turns of thread.

QUILL-SEGMENT WING

MANY TYPES OF hair are available for the tying of fly patterns. In addition, the bleaching and dyeing of squirrel hair has created an impressive range of bright colors. The wider the variety of colors available, the more accurate the resulting artificial will be. For further examples of materials and their use in the tying of particular fly patterns, see Fly Dressings, pp.240-77.

When removing a bunch of fibers, take great care to cut them off straight so that they are even in length. Any irregularity in the artificial's silhouette could alert the trout to danger, so it is important to trim the fibers precisely.

The fly-tying method given here is for forming a quill-segment wing for a wet fly. Each of the wing slips should be cut from two exactly matching feathers so that the wings of the artificial are identical in size, shape and color.

Paired slips are used with the undersides of the feathers facing each other when tying wet flies. When held correctly in position, the curve of the slips keeps the wings' tips together. The wings are positioned so that they sit low on the shank.

1 Cut two identical slips from two matching wing feathers.

2 Held in position on top of the hook, the wing slips should extend just beyond the end of the hook shank.

3 The slips should match each other in size and shape exactly.

4 Hold the slips in place. Make a few turns using the pinch-and-loop method (see Tails, p.228).

5 Whip-finish, either by hand or with the whip-finish tool, to create a head.

6 Matched concave slips make a wet fly (*above*); matched convex slips make a dry fly.

WEIGHTING & WING CASES

A SIMPLE WAY to add weight to a fly, and an alternative to the lead eyes on p.234, is to wind some lead-wire beneath the dressing. This is known as weighting or leading. Folded wing-cases, made of feather fiber, are used to imitate the nymphal stage, in which the insect's wings are inside its body. A simple-hackle wet fly is tied by first creating a body, then tying in a collar hackle and whip-finishing.

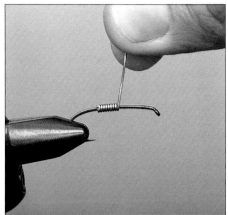

1 Take a short piece of lead-wire the same thickness as the hook shank.

2 Make a few turns of the wire in the center of the hook shank. Trim.

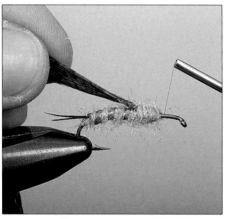

1 Double wing case Tie in feather fibers to body and build the thorax (see Dubbing a Body, p.229).

2 Fold the doubled feather slip over the thorax and tie it down.

3 Repeat to create two stepped wing-cases, then whip-finish.

Hare's-Ear Nymph
Incorporating a wound, weighted body (above) *and folded wing case.*

1 Single wing case Tie in a feather slip for the wing case after forming the body.

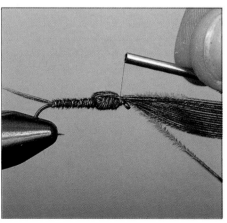

2 Create the thorax, then fold the feather over it. Tie down and trim off the excess material.

SIMPLE WET FLY

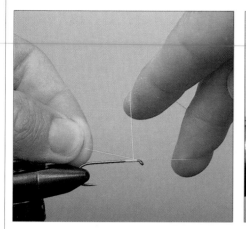

1 Make a few turns of the tying thread to start the fly off.

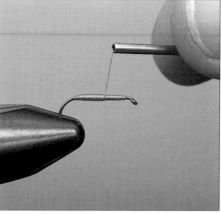

2 Form a body that extends from the eye to the bend.

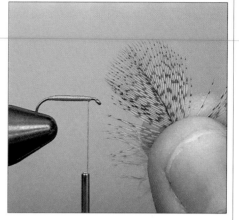

3 Take a soft hen hackle and stroke the fibers so that they lie at right angles to the quill.

4 Tie in the hackle at the eye.

6 Build a head (*above*) to finish.

5 Make two or three turns round the shank with the hackle. Tie off with the tying thread. Trim away surplus.

Partridge and Orange
A simple wet fly (above) *best tied sparsely.*

Cove Black Spider
Simple midge species imitation (above), *using black silk body and hen hackle.*

MATUKA WINGS & MUDDLER HEAD

THE MATUKA METHOD is so-named after the New Zealand bird whose feathers were used for this style of tying originally. This wing type can be finished with a collar hackle and whip-finish head.

Spun deer-hair, for the muddler head, is a hollow and buoyant fly-tying material. It can be fashioned to the exact shape required.

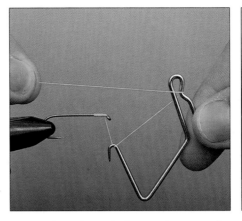

1 Matuka wings A fly can be started off either by using a whip-finish tool or by hand (see p.227).

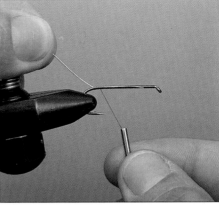

2 Take the thread to the bend and catch in body material and ribbing. Take the thread back to the eye.

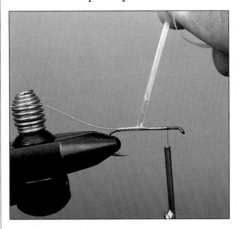

3 Build up the body, leaving the ribbing free.

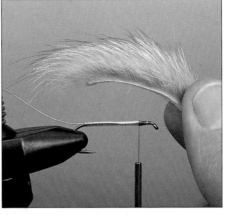

4 Take a rabbit's-fur strip wide enough to encompass half the hook width and half the shank length.

5 Tie in the wing at the eye, making sure it is firmly held in place.

Mink Zonker
This is a fur-bodied, Matuka-style fly pattern (above).

6 Hold the end of the wing firmly between your finger and thumb so it rests along the body. Begin to wind the ribbing back along the hook through the wing fibers with evenly spaced-out turns.

7 Separate the fibers with your spare hand. Make about six or seven turns along the length of the body to hold the wing firmly in place. Tie off the ribbing securely and trim away any spare material.

1 Muddler head Take a small bunch of deer-hair and make sure that the ends align.

2 Attach at the eye with two loose turns of the tying thead.

3 Make a few more loose turns, and then pull the thread tight downward to make the hair flare outward.

4 Hold the hair back and make a few turns to secure it in place. Push back against the body.

5 Keep adding bunches of hair to fill the gap between the body and the eye of the hook. Whip-finish.

6 Trim the hair with sharp scissors, leaving some hair extending back over the body.

Woolhead Sculpin
Substitute lambswool for deer-hair to form a dense silhouette (above).

7 The larger the spun deer-hair head, the better it will float, so when tying dry patterns do not cut the hair too short. However, always trim the hair very short for wet-fly patterns that need to perform sub-surface.

DIRECTORY OF FLY DRESSINGS

HE ART OF fly-tying is a fast-growing area of fly-fishing. This once minority interest has become almost an art form. Throughout the world have sprung up organizations and clubs solely dedicated to the pursuit, and some truly startling innovations have resulted.

One of the most researched areas is the accurate interpretation of food forms. At some stage, every fly-tyer wants to re-create a natural in minute detail. As a result, the search for suitably imitative materials knows no bounds. However, it is worth noting that for all the realism that can be suggested, it is often the ragged flies that seem to work best. Putting the fly in a sink full of water will give you an approximate idea of how it will behave in a stream or lake. Colors generally darken when immersed in water; hackles and other materials sometimes fold flat, thereby altering the silhouette. Very few materials are actually required for fly-tying, but in practice it is difficult to resist the variety now available. In years gone by, feathers from bustard eagles, condors, owls, and other rare species were used. Seal's-fur was used for bodies; bear-hair for wings. Substitutes for the natural materials are now widely available. The demands of conservation are leading to the discovery of new materials all the time: seal's-fur substitute; Antron, a tri-lobal nylon fiber which traps air bubbles and imitates a breathing form; microcellular foam gives necessary buoyancy. The secret of successful fly-tying is to experiment with as wide a variety of pattern types as possible, once the ground rules have been firmly established. The high point of fly-fishing will always be a trout deceived by your own pattern, created from an array of materials with a vise, a few basic implements and an enquiring mind.

SEE PAGES
80-81

Steelhead
Classic

Fly Name	Hook	Silk	Tail	Rib	Body	Wing	Hackle
Spruce	LS 4 x long 4 to 12	Black	Peacock-sword fibers	None	Red floss or yarn; peacock herl	Matching badger hackles	Badger collar
Orange Comet	Wilson salmon dry fly 4 to 10	Black	Orange buck tail	None	Gold oval tinsel with two silver bead eyes	None	Long orange cock hackle
Mickey Finn	LS 4 to 12	Black	None	None	Silver Mylar tube	Yellow and red buck tail	None
Burlap	LS 4 to 10	Black	Gray/brown buck tail	None	Burlap wound tightly or cream dubbing, as substitute	None	Long grizzly
Grizzly King	Low-water salmon 4 to 12	Black	Red fox squirrel fibers	Oval gold tinsel	Black floss	Brown buck tail	Long grizzly
Silver Hilton	Low-water salmon 4 to 12	Black	Silver mallard	Oval silver tinsel	Black chenille	Grizzly hackles	Long grizzly
Black Ghost	LS 4 x 4 to 12	Black	Yellow cock hackle	Flat silver Mylar	Black floss	White cock hackles	Yellow cock hackle
Parmachene Belle	Low-water salmon 4 to 12	Black	White and red feather	Silver tinsel	Yellow mohair or floss	Matched quill	None

Fly Name	Hook	Silk	Tail	Rib	Body	Wing	Hackle
Flash Fly	Low-water salmon 2 to 12	Black	Silver Flashabou	None	Oval silver tinsel	Pink marabou	Red cock
Ferry Canyon	Low-water salmon 4 to 12	Black	Fluorescent red yarn or floss	Oval silver tinsel	Black chenille	Purple marabou	Black hen
Flamingo Zonker	O'Shaughnessy 2 to 6	Red	Mylar strands	None	Silver Mylar tube	Pink rabbit's-fur	None
Bomber (Finland)	Wilson salmon dry fly 6 to 14	Cream	White calf tail	Palmered blue dun hackle	Cream seal's-fur or substitute	Polar bear or substitute	Grizzly
Popsicle	Low-water salmon 4 to 12	Fluorescent red	None	Fluorescent orange chenille	Fluorescent orange chenille	Orange marabou	Spun purple rabbit
Bear-Hair Bugger	LS x 4 4 to 12 (weighted)	Black	Brown/black bear-hair	Oval silver tinsel	Black chenille	None	Long black cock
Teeny Nymph	Low-water salmon 4 to 14	To match body	None	Optional copper wire	Pheasant-tail fibers	None	Pheasant-tail fiber ends
Flesh Fly	O'Shaughnessy 2 to 6	Cream	None	Silver tinsel	White floss	None	None
Egg-Sucking Leech	LS x 4 long nickel 2 to 10	Orange	None	Silver tinsel	Optional pearl flat Mylar	Natural rabbit	Orange cock
Woolly Bugger (Original)	LS x 4 Long 2 to 6	Black	Plume of black marabou	Palmered black cock	Black chenille	None	None
Magic Sam	Low-water salmon 2 to 8	Black	Red gill plastic formed	None	As tail	White and yellow marabou	Yellow cock
Muskrat Strip	LS 2 to 10 x 4 long	Black	None	Oval silver tinsel	Pearl flat Mylar	Muskrat tied as zonker	Red floss
Purple Woolly Bugger/ Egg-Sucking Leech	LS 4 x long 2 to 6	Black	Purple marabou	Palmered black cock hackle	Dark purple chenille	None	None
Mouse	Bass stingerhook size 2	Any color; strong	Thin strip chamois leather	None	Bunches long-fibered deer-body hair	None	None

SEE PAGES
84-5

Steelhead
Egg Flies & Dry Flies

FLY NAME	HOOK	SILK	TAIL	RIB	BODY	WING	HACKLE
Rusty Bomber	Wilson salmon dry fly 6 to 10	Black	Red fox squirrel	Ginger cree cock	Rust spun deer-hair	Fox squirrel fibers	None
Oversize Troth Elk Hair Caddis	Wilson salmon dry fly 8 to 12	Cream	None	Palmered furnace cock	Green Haretron	Elk body hair	None
Steelhead Caddis	Wilson salmon dry fly 6 to 10	Black or hot orange	None	None	Orange/rust Antron	Oak turkey	None
Grease-Liner	Low-water or Wilson salmon dry fly 4 to 10	Black or hot orange	Deer-hair fiber	Palmered ginger cree	Rust Antron or Poly II	Elk body or deer-hair	As wing
Water-Walker	Wilson salmon dry fly 6 to 10	Black	Black deer-hair fiber	None	Spun deer-hair	Calf tail	Deer-hair
Egg Fly	Mustad ring eye egg 2 to 8	Hot orange	None	None	Orange, white or chartreuse tow wool	None	None
Fall Favourite	Low-water salmon 4 to 12 or Wilson	Fluorescent red	None	Oval silver tinsel	Silver flat nylon	Orange squirrel	Red or orange cock
Egg-Roe Cluster	Low-water salmon 4 to 8	Fluorescent red	None	Oval silver tinsel	Flame chenille	Peach/egg tow wool	Pearl Flashabou
Polar Shrimp	Low-water salmon 4 to 10	Red	Red/orange cock hackle	Oval silver tinsel	Orange chenille	Polar bear hair or calf tail	Red cock hackle
Father's Bright Roe	Low-water salmon	Fluorescent red	Plume of white marabou	None	Red and white chenille	Peach/light roe tow wool	None
Green Roe	Low-water salmon 4 to 8	Red	None	Oval silver tinsel	Chartreuse chenille	Chartreuse tow wool	Pearl Flashabou
Pink Deviant	Low-water salmon 4 to 10	Fluorescent red	Cerise/magenta yarn	Oval silver tinsel	White chenille	Fluorescent pink squirrel	Red cock hackle
Skykomish Sunrise	Low-water salmon 4 to 12	Fluorescent red	Red and yellow cock hackle	Oval silver tinsel	Flame chenille	White buck tail or calf tail	Red/orange cock
Babine Special	Low-water salmon 6 to 10	Black	Red cock hackle	Oval silver tinsel	Red floss silk	White buck tail or calf tail	Red cock hackle
Umpqua Special	Low-water salmon 4 to 12	Red	White cock hackle	Oval silver tinsel	Yellow and red floss silk	Red over white buck tail	Furnace as collar
Admiral	Low-water salmon 4 to 12	Black	Red cock hackle	Oval silver tinsel	Red floss silk	White buck tail or calf tail	Red cock
Alaska Alexander	Low-water salmon 4 to 8	Fluorescent red	Polar bear or substitute	None	Red and white chenille	Fluorescent Lureflash	Around hook

FLY NAME	HOOK	SILK	TAIL	RIB	BODY	WING	HACKLE
Black Spider	WG 10 to 14	Black	None	Fine silver wire	Black silk	None	Black hen
Ivens' Brown-and-Green Nymph	6 to 10	Brown	4 strands of peacock herl	Oval gold tinsel	Green dyed and brown dyed ostrich herl with peacock herl strands on top and along length of body	None	Peacock herl head
Midge Pupa	10 to 16	Black	*See* hackle	White cock-hackle stalk	Black feather fibers, or black tying silk; thorax of bronze peacock herl. (Other colors: red-olive-orange)	None	White cock
Black-and-Peacock Spider	6 to 12	Black	None	Dark silk floss	Dark silk floss under body with 3 or 4 strands of bronze peacock herl twisted together and wound over underbody	None	Black hen
Amber Nymph	10 to 14	Black	None	Optional rib of tying thread	Amber floss silk or amber yellow seal's-fur tied thickly with brown seal's-fur thorax	Gray brown feather for wing-case	Honey hen
Ombudsman	LS 8 to 10	Brown	None	Fine copper wire	Bronze peacock herl with an overbody of dark mottled hen-wing feather partly encasing body	None	Brown cock or hen
Jersey Herd	LS 6 to 12	Brown	Bronze peacock herl	None	Wide copper-colored tinsel to form cigar shape under 12 strands of bronze peacock herl	None	Peacock herl
Grenadier	12 to 16	Red	None	Oval gold tinsel	Hot orange floss or seal's-fur	None	Furnace cock
Chomper (Series)	10 to 12	Brown	None	None	3 or 4 strands of white ostrich herl under a wing-case of brown Raffene	None	None
Cove's Pheasant Tail	WG 8 to 12	Brown	None	Fine copper wire	10 or 12 fibers from a cock pheasant's center tail feather, with a thorax of blue underfur from a wild rabbit	None	None
Collyer's Brown Nymph	10 to 12	Brown	Tips of cock-pheasant fiber	Oval gold tinsel	Cock-pheasant fibers from center tail feather with a thorax of chestnut-dyed ostrich herl	Cock pheasant; ostrich flue	None
Buzzer	10 to 12	Black	None	Flat gold	Black yarn tapered	Bunch of white floss silk	None
Baby Doll	LS 6 to 10	Black	Yarn from body	None	White fluorescent yarn to form back, body, and tail	None	Black tying silk head
Sweeney Todd	LS 6 to 14	Black	None	Flat silver tinsel	Black floss	Black squirrel tail	Crimson hackle fibers
Appetizer	LS 6	Black	Cock-hackle and mallard breast feathers	Fine oval silver	White chenille	White marabou; gray squirrel	Beard hackle as for tail
Black-and-Orange Marabou	LS 8	Black	Hot orange cock-hackle fibers	Oval gold tinsel	Flat gold tinsel	Black marabou; jungle cock	As for tail
Muddler Minnow	6 to 12	Brown	Oak turkey slips	Oval gold tinsel	Flat gold tinsel	Squirrel; oak turkey	Deer-hair collar

SEE PAGES
90-91

Reservoir
Bottom Nymphs

FLY NAME	HOOK	SILK	TAIL	RIB	BODY	WING	HACKLE
Reed Nymph	LS 10 to 12	Brown	Honey badger cock-hackle fibers	Fine copper wire	Weighted underbody. Overbody of peacock herl with a shell-back of pheasant tail	None	Furnace or honey badger
Bead-Eyed Montana	6 to 10	Black	Bunch of black marabou	Oval silver tinsel	Black chenille for $2/5$ with fluorescent yellow chenille for $1/5$	None	Silver bead or chain eye
Harris Stick	LS 10 to 12	Buff	Black marabou	Fine oval gold tinsel	Underbody of lead-wire, varnished. Overbody of natural hare's-body fur	None	Red cock; amber rabbit's-fur
Stick Fly	LS 8 to 10	Black	None	Copper or gold wire	Pheasant-tail fiber; olive swan herls; green peacock herl. Thorax: yellow floss silk	None	Pale ginger cock
Green-Butt Tadpole	WG 6 to 8	Black	Black marabou fibers	Oval silver tinsel	Fluorescent green chenille butt; remainder black chenille. Weighted and underweighted versions possible	None	None
Minky	Capt. Hamilton 6	Brown	Green floss; pearl Flashabou	Oval gold tinsel	Mixed hare's-mask fur	Mink fur tied Matuka style	Hackle tied front of wing
Short Green-Tag Stick	WG 10 to 16	Brown	None	Fine brass wire	Cock-pheasant tail fibers	None	Brown cock hackle
Bewick's Booby	WG 10	Black	Bunch of black marabou	Oval silver tinsel	Short butt of fluorescent yellow floss; spun black marabou fibers; other colors: orange, yellow and white	None	Plastazote balls in nylon
Woolly Worm	8 to 12	Black	Tuft of red fluorescent floss or yarn	Oval silver	Black chenille; peacock herl back	None	Grizzle hackle palmered
Hoglouse	10 to 12	Brown	Partridge fibers	None	Hare's-mask fur with a shell-back made of epoxied oak turkey feather tied in 3 doubled sections	None	Brown partridge
Randall's Dragon	LS 4 to 12	Olive	Dyed olive goose biots	Clear flat mono-filament	Mixture of 40% olive rabbit and 60% insect-green seal's fur, clipped short after ribbing. Same for thorax	Olive duck quill wing-case	Goose biot legs
Deep Pupa	Midge hook 10 to 14	Black	Scarlet butt of DFM floss	Floss rib as for butt	Black seal's-fur body and thorax	Wing-cover of pearl Flashabou	Head: rabbit underfur
Hot-Spot Pheasant Tail	LS 8 to 14	Black	Pheasant-tail fiber tips	Fine copper wire	Pheasant-tail feather fibers with a thorax of yellow seal's-fur and pheasant-tail fibers over	None	Pheasant-tail fibers as legs
Hairy Prince Green Butt	Tiemco larval hook 8 to 16	Brown	Brown goose biot; green butt optional	Flat gold	Mixed hare's-mask	White goose biots	Furnace
Fraser Booby Nymph	8 to 10	Brown	White marabou plume	Oval silver tinsel	Hare's-face fur and guard hairs picked out	None	Nylon Plastazote balls
Eyed Damsel II	LS 8 to 12	Olive	Olive hackle points	Copper wire	Green seal's-fur or dubbed marabou; thorax: red and olive seal's-fur	Green raffia wing-case	Olive mallard breast
Corixa	10 to 12	Brown	None	Fine silver wire	White floss silk	Hen wing quill slip	Head: lemon dots

Fly Name	Hook	Silk	Tail	Rib	Body	Wing	Hackle
Filoplume Damsel	Tiemco larval hook LS 8 to 10	Olive	Plume of olive marabou	Silver wire	Olive marabou fibers wrapped along hook shank with a thorax of a filoplume of dyed olive	None	Badger; peacock herl
Long-Shank Hare's Ear	10 to 14	Brown	Fluorescent white floss	Flat medium gold tinsel	Mixed furs from hare's-mask, dubbed and well picked out	None	None
Gold-Ribbed Hare's Ear	LS 10 to 14	Brown	Bunch of guard hair	Fine flat gold	Hare's-ear, all shades	None	Furnace hen
Butcher Nymph	10 to 12	Black	Dyed red fibers	Flat medium silver tinsel	Black seal's-fur body and thorax	Brown mallard wing-case	Red hackle
Diawl Bach	LS 12	Brown	Brown cock-hackle fibers	None	Peacock herl	None	Brown hen hackle
GE Nymph	LW 12 to 14	Olive	Brown mallard fibers	Fine gold wire	Olive feather fiber with a thorax of dyed olive rabbit's-fur	Wing-case of dyed olive hen fibers	Throat hackle as tail
Yellow Olive	12 to 14	Olive	Golden-pheasant crest feather	Fine gold wire	Wound phosphor-yellow floss	Dark feather wing-case	Olive throat hackle
Green-Eared Pheasant Tail	10 to 12	Brown	Pheasant-tail fibers	Copper wire	Pheasant-tail fibers with 2 ears of fluorescent green floss. Thorax of peacock herl	Wing-case of pheasant-tail fibers	None
Mason's Pheasant Tail	MW 10 to 14	Brown	Pheasant-tail fibers	Oval gold tinsel	Pheasant-tail fibers with a thorax and wing case of same	None	Badger throat hackle
White-Hackle Pheasant Tail	10 to 16	Brown	Pheasant-tail fibers	Fine gold wire	Pheasant-tail fibers with a green seal's-fur thorax	None	White hen hackle
Lurex Spider	WG 10 to 14	Black	None	Fine silver wire	Black silk floss	None	Black hen
BP Buzzer	12 to 14	Black	None	Fine silver wire	Black seal's-fur, picked out	Wing-case of pheasant-tail fibers	None
Carnhill Poly-Rib Buzzer	Midge hook 12 to 14	Claret	None	Clear polythene rib	Claret swan's feather fibers; white goose biots; thorax of claret seal's-fur	Swan feather fiber wing-case	White wool filaments
Deer-Hair Midge	10 to 14	Black	None	Fine silver wire	Black seal's-fur picked out	None	None
Cove's Sedge Pupa	WG 10 to 14	Olive	None	Fine flat gold	Back of pheasant-tail fibers with a body of pale green seal's-fur and a thorax of wild rabbit underfur	None	None
Fraser Sedge Pupa	10 to 12	Brown	None	Open turns of yellow floss silk	Rear body of tapered amber seal's-fur merging to yellow at thorax	Hen pheasant wing-cover	None
Jorgensen Fur Caddis Pupa	10 to 12	Brown	None	None	Brown fur dubbed tightly; thorax as for body but well picked out	Tied mallard slips	Partridge breast

Reservoir Emergers

Fly Name	Hook	Silk	Tail	Rib	Body	Wing	Hackle
Deer-Hair Emerger	LS 12	Brown	None	None	Cock-pheasant center tail fibers	None	Red game or cree
Grafham Muddled Emerger	10 to 14	Black	None	None	Black dyed goose fibers with a black Ethafoam thorax	Gray duck	Black cock
Jardine Emerger	12 to 16	Black	None	None	Blue rabbit underfur	None	Well-marked badger
Timberline Emerger	10 to 14	Red	None	None	Orange seal's-fur or substitute	None	Cree
Sparkle Pupa	12 to 16	Olive	None	None	Dark olive seal's-fur or substitute	*Cul-de-canard* feather	White cock
Sienna Sedge	12 to 16	Primrose	Light furnace cock-hackle fibers	Fine gold wire	Primrose floss silk waxed to darken it to near olive	Gray mallard	Greenwell or light furnace
Invicta	10 to 14	Orange	None	Flat gold tinsel	Arc chrome butt with ginger seal's-fur or substitute	White goose-wing slips	Ginger cree
Olive Seal's-Fur Nymph	10 to 16	Brown	None	None	Dark olive seal's-fur or substitute to match the hatch	None	Furnace
Suspender Midge Pupa	10 to 14	Black	None	None	Black seal's-fur, well picked out	White Antron fibers	None
Pike's Suspender	10 to 16	Black	Butt of silver Mylar	Polythene strip	Black seal's-fur or substitute	*Cul-de-canard* feather	Black cock
Carnhill Adult Buzzer	10 to 18	Brown	Butt of fluorescent red seal's-fur	None	Hare's-ear fur, dubbed and well picked out	Blue dun cock hackle	Cree cock hackle
Bristol Emerger	12 to 20	Black	None	Fine polythene strip	Black seal's-fur or substitute; Ethafoam head	Tan elk-hair fibers	Natural black cock
Brown Emerger	10 to 20	Brown	None	None	Hare's-ear fur dubbed and ends cut to form head; yellow spot butt of floss silk	None	Palmered furnace
Wadham's Hare's Ear	8 to 10	Green	None	None	Natural deer-hair, cut to shape; underbody of dark green seal's-fur or substitute	Woodcock body fibers	Rusty dun cock
Chironomid Pupa	8 to 12	Brown	None	Arc chrome nylon floss	Cinnamon ostrich herl	Partridge flank feathers	Palmered ginger cock
Orange JC	10 to 18	Brown	None	Brown cock hackle	Brown dubbing of Haretron or Poly II	None	Furnace cock tippets
Deer-Hair Hatching Buzzer	10 to 18	Brown	None	Brown cock hackle	Brown (tan) dubbing of Haretron or Poly II	Cree cock-hackle tips	*See* rib

Fly Name	Hook	Silk	Tail	Rib	Body	Wing	Hackle
Daddy-Longlegs	LS 8 to 12	Brown	None	Tying thread	Buff to ginger feather fibers or similar color Antron fibers	2 furnace hackle points	Furnace; pheasant-tail
Hawthorn	UE 10	Black	None	Very fine silver wire	Peacock herl	Blue dun hackle point tied in a V	Black cock; black swan
Grey Duster	12 to 14	Brown	None	None	Wild rabbit brown fur mixed with blue underfur to give gray mixture	None	Badger
Grafham Hopper	10 to 14	Scarlet	None	None	Scarlet seal's-fur	Pheasant-tail fiber legs	Furnace hackle
Lake/Pond Olive Dun	12 to 16	Brown	Gray/brown mallard feather fibers	Very fine gold wire	Pale gray condor herl, lightly stained with picric acid	Blue-gray water hen feathers	Pale honey dun
Greenwell's Glory	10 to 14	Yellow	None	Fine gold wire	Yellow floss silk	Blackbird, starling or mallard slips	Coch-y-Bondhu
Bristol Hopper	10 to 12	Red	Arc chrome yellow butt	Flat copper-colored tinsel	Ginger to amber seal's-fur	None	Honey cock; red head
Bob's Bits	FW 10 to 14	Black	None	None	Olive seal's-fur	White goose or swan fiber wing	Furnace hackle
Black Bob	10 to 12	Black	None	None	Black Haretron fibers, well teased out	None	None
Para Midge	12 to 18	Black	None	Silver tinsel	Flat silver tinsel around the bend of hook. Black seal's-fur level with the point of the hook to eye	*Cul-de-canard* tied in upright	Black cock
Hare's-Face Midge	10 to 14	Brown	None	Fine brass wire	A tip of fluorescent red floss and the remainder of the body of dubbed hare's-mask	*Cul-de-canard*	Furnace cock hackle
Realistic Dry Midge	12 to 18	Black	None	Polythene	Black seal's-fur or Haretron with a cover of black Plastazote	Blue dun cock-hackle tips	Black cock hackle
Elk-Hair Caddis	8 to 10	Brown	Fluorescent yellow butt	None	Olive synthetic dubbing	Natural elk-hair	Brown palmered cock
Goddard and Henry Sedge	LS 8 to 12	Green	None	None	Deer-hair spun on shank and clipped to shape; lower body: dark green seal's-fur	None	2 rusty dun cock hackles
Saville's Super Sedge	8 to 12	Brown	None	Arc yellow DRF nylon floss	Ostrich herl dyed cinnamon with a palmered ginger cock hackle	Hen-pheasant wing slips	As body
Grouse-Wing	10 to 18	Brown	None	None	Brown Haretron (other colors to imitate various species)	Brown partridge feathers	Palmered furnace hackle
Spent Caddis	10 to 12	Brown	None	None	Brown/gray seal's-fur	Golden pheasant	Ginger hackle

SEE PAGES
98-9

Reservoir
Innovations

Fly Name	Hook	Silk	Tail	Rib	Body	Wing	Hackle
St Clements	LS 10	Yellow	Mixed orange and yellow marabou	Oval silver wire	Twisted strands of orange and yellow chenille	Orange and yellow marabou	Palmered saddle hackles
Flat Roach	LS 12	White	Squirrel; orange cock; Flashabou	None	White deer-hair spun and trimmed to flat fish shape; body marking with felt-tip Pantone pen	None	None
Concrete Bowl	LS 6 to 10	Black	Plume of black marabou	Oval silver tinsel	Wound butt ends of tail	None	Phosphor-yellow chenille
Grizzly Nobbler	Dog-nobbler	White	White marabou	Fine oval silver tinsel	Pearl yarn	None	Grizzle cock hackle
Carnhill Nobbler	6 to 10	Orange	Plume of orange marabou	Fine oval gold	Orange chenille (also black and green and white and green)	None	Hot orange cock
Pink Panther	LS 6 to 10	White	Plume of shocking-pink DF marabou	Medium flat silver tinsel	Shocking-pink DF seal's-fur	None	None
Cat's Whisker	LS 6	Black	Plume of white marabou	Fine oval silver	Yellow fluorescent chenille	Plume of white marabou	Bead-chain eyes; black head
Datchet Razzler	LS 6 to 10	Yellow	Yellow marabou	None	Yellow Ethafoam glued to shank and trimmed to fish shape	None	Deer-hair collar and head
Rabbit Zonker	LS 6 to 10	Red	Frayed end of body material	None	Broad pearl Mylar tube	Wild rabbit tied in at tail and head	None
Shipman's Buzzer	10 to 14	Brown	Fluorescent white nylon	Pearl Mylar	Fiery brown seal's-fur or substitute	None	Filaments as for tail
Green-Butt Griddle Bug	LS 6 to 12	Black	White living rubber leg material	Small flat silver	Black chenille with a butt of green DF chenille over a lead-weighted body	None	Legs and horns as for tail
Mink Spuddler	LS 4 to 10	White	None	Oval silver	White Haretron	White mink fur strip tied Matuka style	Colored deer-hair
Oakham Orange (Pearl)	10 to 14	Hot orange	Fluorescent orange floss	Fine gold wire	Flat gold tinsel	None	Hot orange cock hackle
Bewl Green	WG 8 to 10	Olive	Dark olive cock-hackle fibers	Heavy copper wire	Dubbed, dark olive seal's-fur or substitute	None	Palmered light olive hackle
Fiery Grenadier	10 to 14	White	Fluorescent hot orange floss	Fine gold wire	Hot orange seal's-fur or substitute	None	Palmered natural red game cock
Flashback Nymph	10 to 18	Brown	Brown hackle fibers	Gold wire	Arctic or natural brown hare's-fur with a shell-back and thorax of pearl Flashabou	None	Partridge throat hackle
Fidget	LS 12	White	As for hackle	None	Pearl Phildar Sunset yarn	Buck tail; Plastazote	Cock hackle

Reservoir Lures & Attractors

SEE PAGES **100-101**

FLY NAME	HOOK	SILK	TAIL	RIB	BODY	WING	HACKLE
The Waggy	LS 6 to 8	Black	Black rubber waggy tail	Flat silver tinsel	Black chenille	Black marabou	Black cock; green feathers
Black Chenille	LS 6 to 10	Black	Black hackle fibers	Flat silver tinsel	Black chenille	Matching black cock hackle	Black hackle fibers
Appetizer	LS 6 to 10 in tandem	Black	Orange and green hackle fibers	Flat silver tinsel	White chenille	Squirrel and marabou	Throat as for tail
Rabbit Viva	LS 6 to 10	Black	Green fluorescent floss tail	Flat silver tinsel	Black chenille	Rabbit's-fur tied Matuka style	Black hen saddle
Goldie	LS 10 in tandem	Black	Yellow hackle fibers	Gold wire	Flat gold tinsel	Yellow and black goat hair	Yellow saddle hackle
Rasputin	LS 6 to 8	Brown	Part of body back	None	Back and tail: bunch of brown mottled turkey fibers. Body: Plastazote foam cut and glued to hook shank	None	Ginger saddle hackle
Whiskey Fly	LS 6 to 10	Orange	Tag of fluorescent orange	*See* body	Flat silver tinsel with a fluorescent orange silk floss rib; all varnished	Calf tail; Flashabou horns	Hot orange hackle
Muddlerine	Waddington shank with treble hook	Red	Pearl crystal hair on the treble	None	Gold Mylar tube	Gray squirrel-tail	Collar of clipped deer-hair
Jack Frost	LS 6 to 10	White	Crimson yarn	None	White fluorescent yarn covered with polythene strip	Plume of white marabou	White and red saddle hackles
Minnow Streamer (Male)	LS 6 to 10	Olive	Blue dun hackle fibers	Oval silver tinsel	Fluorescent white floss silk	Olive cock hackles tied back-to-back	Red fiber throat hackle
Floating Fry	LS 6 to 10	White	Ethafoam cut to fish-tail shape	None	Pearl Mylar tube over Ethafoam underbody	None	Black head; white eyes
Leprechaun	LS 6 to 10	Black	Green hackle fibers	Flat gold tinsel	Fluorescent lime green chenille	Green cock hackles tied back-to-back	Green throat hackle
Sinfoil's Fry	LS 8 to 12	Black	None	None	Underbody: flat silver tinsel. Overbody: polythene strip built up to cigar shape; collar of scarlet floss silk	Back: brown mallard feather	Black head; white eyes
Missionary	LS 10	Black	Red cock-hackle fibers	Flat silver tinsel	White chenille	Gray mallard or teal breast feather	Throat hackle as for tail

SEE PAGES
102-3

Reservoir
Competition Wet Flies

Fly Name	Hook	Silk	Tail	Rib	Body	Wing	Hackle
Toffee-Paper Wickham	10 to 14	Brown	None	Fine, green copper wire	Green Lurex or similar	None	Palmered red game
Pearly Wickham	10 to 14	White	Red game cock fibers	Fine silver wire	Pearl Flashabou or similar	None	Palmered light red game
Red-Arsed Wickham	10 to 14	Brown	Fluorescent red floss	Fine gold wire	Flat gold tinsel	None	Palmered light red game
Annabelle	10 to 16	Yellow	Fluorescent yellow floss	Fine gold wire	Body flat gold	None	Red cock; grizzle head
White Palmer	10 to 14	White	Pearl crystal hair fibers	Fine silver wire	Fluorescent white floss	None	Red cock; grizzle head
JC Viva	LS 6 to 10	Black	Green fluorescent yarn	Fine silver tinsel	Black chenille	Marabou; black squirrel	Furnace or game hackle
Peach Booby	WG 8 to 12	Red	Part of body material	None	Peach yarn wound around shank and along and over back	None	Varnished black head
Killer	S or LS 10 to 12	Brown or olive	Olive cock-hackle points	Fine copper wire	Olive green seal's-fur or substitute	None	Head: polythene balls
Vindaloo	10 to 14	Hot orange	Dyed hot orange tippet	Fine gold wire	Fluorescent scarlet seal's-fur or substitute	None	Olive partridge breast
Toogood's White	LS 8 to 12	Red	Fluorescent red floss	Fine oval silver	White chenille	White marabou	Palmered hot orange cock
Light Bulb	LS 6 to 10	Black	Bright yellow hackle fibers	None	White chenille	Marabou and buck wings	Fluorescent red throat
Orange Wiggler	10 to 12	Orange	Hot orange marabou	Wide flat gold	Butts of marabou tail to form body	None	Yellow head with red eyes
Mini Appetizer	LS 6 to 8	Black	Orange and green hackle; mallard fibers	Oval silver tinsel	White fluorescent chenille	White marabou and squirrel	None
Pearly Hare's Ear	10 to 14	Red	Red floss; white marabou	Fine silver wire	Dubbed hare's-ear	Brown feather fiber wing-case	Throat hackle as tail
Orange Priest	10 to 14	Hot orange	Fluorescent hot orange floss	Gold wire rib optional	Flat gold tinsel	None	Sparse hot orange hen hackle
Fluorescent Red Palmer	10 to 14	Red	Dyed fluorescent red hair fibers	Fine gold wire	Fluorescent red seal's-fur or substitute	None	Palmered furnace cock
Peach Doll	10 to 12	Black	As for body	None	Peach-colored yarn tied along and over the back	None	Black head

Small Stillwater
Large Nymph

FLY NAME	HOOK	SILK	TAIL	RIB	BODY	WING	HACKLE
Mayfly Nymph	LS 8 to 12	Brown	Brown pheasant-tail	Pheasant-tail fibers	Angora yarn	Pheasant-tail fibers	Pheasant-tail fibers
Fluorescent-Green Montana	LS 6 to 14	Black	Cock-hackle fibers	None	Black chenille	Black chenille	Black cock
Game Pie	LS 8 to 14	Brown	Short orange marabou	Oval gold tinsel	Gray squirrel	Pheasant-tail fibers	Brown partridge
Rabbit-Strip Damsel (Zonker)	Standard shank 8 to 10	Olive	Olive rabbit	None	Silver Mylar; olive seal's-fur or substitute	Olive Swiss straw	Olive partridge
Pulling Damsel	LS 8 to 12	Black or olive	Dark olive marabou	Flat gold tinsel	Dark green seal's-fur or substitute	Pheasant-tail	None
Lambswool Damsel	LS 8 to 12	Olive or brown	Olive goose-feather fiber	Orange rod-tying thread	Blue and orange yarn	None	Olive partridge
Blue Damsel	LS 8 to 14	Blue or black	None	None	Blue ostrich and seal's-fur	None	None
Alder Larva	LS 8 to 12	Dark brown	White marabou	Fine gold wire; white marabou	Hare's-ear and rust Antron	Brown/olive seal's-fur	Brown partridge
Yellow Ears	LS 10 to 12	Tan, cream or yellow	Yellow marabou	Flat pearl Mylar tinsel	Yellow seal's-fur or substitute	Yellow pheasant-tail	Yellow cock hackle

Small Stillwater
Nymphs & Small Attractors

SEE PAGES
106-7

FLY NAME	HOOK	SILK	TAIL	RIB	BODY	WING	HACKLE
Brown Nobbler	10 to 12	Brown	Plume of brown marabou	Flat gold	Brown chenille	None	Ginger cock
Orange Tadpole	8 to 12	Orange	Plume of hot orange marabou	Flat silver tinsel	Hot orange chenille overweighted body	None	Orange saddle
Hern Worm	10 to 12	Brown	3 or 4 pheasant-tail fibers	Fine copper wire	Remainder of pheasant-tail fibers used for tail	None	Weighted head
Yellow Nobbler	8 to 12	Black	Arc chrome yellow marabou	Oval gold	Yellow chenille	None	Ginger and white hen
Pink Lady	8 to 12	Black	Plume of black marabou	None	Black chenille with red/pink chenille thorax	None	None
Wiggle-Tail Hare's-Ear	10 to 12	Red	Small plume of orange/red marabou	Flat medium gold	Mixed hare's-mask fibers, well picked out	None	None
Orange Cut-Down	10 to 12	Orange	Small plume of orange marabou	Tying silk	Rest of marabou tail feathers wound around shank	None	Weighted head
Wobble Worm	Grub 10 to 14	Black	Plume of black marabou	None	Underbody of flat silver tinsel with black seal's-fur sparsely dubbed over	None	Yellow weighted head
Viva Tadpole	LS 8 to 10	Black	Plume of black marabou	Oval silver tinsel	Black chenille with green chenille head	None	None
Patterson Red Spot	10 to 14	Olive	None	Gold wire	Underbody: fine lead-wire; olive mohair, seal's-fur and strands of red DFM yarn tied and clipped	Clear plastic strip overall	None
Phantom Pupa	10 to 14	White	None	Silver wire	Silver wire	None	White hen saddle
Damp Crane Fly	LS 10 to 12	Brown	None	Fine brass wire	Fibers from cock-pheasant center tail	Cree hackle point	Furnace cock
Yellow Corixa	12 to 14	White	Optional white feather fiber	Silver wire	White floss silk covered with clear polythene and amber seal's-fur thorax	None	Badger hackle
Lead Speck	12 to 14	Brown	Fibers of dyed yellow hen hackle	None	Fine lead-wire varnished with dyed yellow rabbit's-fur thorax	None	None
Cockwill's Hare's-Ear Shrimp	10 to 14	Brown	None	Fine oval silver	Hare's-mask fur mixture, picked out after ribbing	None	None
Lead Bug	10 to 12	Yellow	Yellow floss silk	None	Lead-wire body, varnished	None	None
Green-Waisted White	10 to 14	Red	White marabou	Flat silver	White chenille with middle segment of yellow chenille	None	White hen saddle

Small Stillwater
Formative Patterns & Oddities

See pages 108-9

Fly Name	Hook	Silk	Tail	Rib	Body	Wing	Hackle
Voss Bark Nymph	10 to 12	Brown	Cream cock-hackle fibers	None	Olive seal's-fur with thorax of brown/claret seal's-fur	None	Red cock
Short DFM Green Partridge	12 to 14	Yellow	None	None	Yellow DFM floss silk	None	Partridge
Brassy Pheasant Tail	Roman Moser bead on WG 10 to 12	Gray	Points from pheasant tail	Copper wire	Pheasant-tail fibers. Thorax (bead) cover of pheasant-tail fibers	None	White hen
Orange Shrimp	Grub 10 to 12	Brown	None	Oval silver wire	Hot orange seal's-fur with a polythene strip back over weighted body	None	None
BW or Barrie Welham Nymph	10 to 14	Black	Red and yellow fluorescent hair	Fine oval gold	Brown yarn	None	Hen hackle
Olive Dog-Nobbler	LS 10 to 12	Olive	Olive marabou	None	Olive seal's-fur or dubbed olive marabou	None	None
Original Mayfly Nymph	LS 10 to 12	Brown	Pheasant-tail fibers	None	White ostrich herl with 2 bands of tying silk level with and above the bite of the hook	None	None
Red Diddy or Rubber-Band Fly	Capt. Hamilton 8	Red	Part of a red rubber band	Fine gold wire	Crimson floss silk or seal's-fur, picked out	Pheasant-tail fibers	Partridge
Hinged Damsel	Rear LS 12 Front standard double 10 tied in tandem	Olive	Olive cock-hackle points	Copper wire	Rear hook: olive marabou or ostrich herl; front hook same, but with a thorax cover of pheasant-tail fibers	None	Orange cock
Orange Twinkle Nymph	8 to 12	Orange	Hot orange cock-hackle fibers	Oval gold tinsel	Orange twinkle; thorax cover of pheasant-tail fibers; weighted body	None	Partridge
Twinkle Damsel	8 to 12	Olive	Olive cock-hackle fibers	Oval gold tinsel	Olive twinkle	None	None
Fuzzy Crawler	LS 8 to 12	Brown	Natural hare fibers	Flattened monofilament	Brown Haretron; body should be wider than thorax and flattened; legs of pheasant tail	None	None
Dragonfly Nymph	4 to 8 weighted and flattened rear half only	Brown	Brown marabou tied short	Fine copper wire	Brown Haretron	None	None
Peachy	10 to 12	Black	Bunch of hot orange floss	None	Peach floss with a cover of hot orange floss	Marabou	*See* body
Montana Wasp	10 to 12	Fluorescent yellow	Bunch of orange floss	None	Yellow and black chenille with a thorax cover of black chenille and a black cock hackle	None	Black cock
Montana Cat's Whisker	10 to 12	Red	Lime green fluorescent marabou	Fine silver wire optional	White chenille with a fluorescent green chenille thorax and black chenille cover	None	Black cock
Poppet	10 to 12	Black	Yellow floss butt	None	Black yarn	None	Black cock

SEE PAGES
112-13

Chalk/Limestone Classics

Fly Name	Hook	Silk	Tail	Rib	Body	Wing	Hackle
American Black Gnat	12 to 18	Black	Black hackle fibers	None	Black yarn	Gray mallard wing slips	Black cock
Grannom	12 to 16	Black	None	None	Green fluorescent floss; natural mole	Hen-pheasant wing slips	Ginger cock
Iron Blue Dun	12 to 16	Black	Blue dun cock-hackle fibers	None	Red rayon tip; natural mole	Gray mallard slips	Iron blue cock
Sherry Spinner	14	Sherry	Fibers of rusty pheasant tail	Fine gold wire	Orange rayon floss	Spent blue dun hackle	Light ginger cock
Tup's Indispensable	14 to 18	Yellow	Blue dun and brown cock-hackle	None	Yellow floss and light pink floss	White calf body hair	Blue dun cock
Lunn's Caperer	14 to 18	Crimson	None	None	Marabou herls and yellow swan fibers	None	Rhode Island Red cock
Lunn's Yellow Boy	12 to 14	Pale orange	Pale buff cock-hackle fibers	Yellow silk	Yellow hackle stalk or yellow seal's-fur	Pale pink buff cock hackle	Pale pink cock
Houghton Ruby	14 to 18	Crimson	3 blue dun cock-hackle fibers	None	Rhode Island Red hackle stalk dyed crimson	2 light blue dun hackle tips	Rhode Island Red cock
Red Spinner	14 to 16	Claret	Brown hackle fiber	Oval gold wire	Bright red or claret seal's-fur	2 blue dun or rusty dun hackles	Natural red cock
Light Cahill	14 to 16	Yellow	Cream or light ginger cock fibers	None	Creamy fox or seal's-fur	Barred wood duck breast feather	Cream cock
Pale Morning Dun Thorax	12 to 14	Yellow	White cock-hackle fibers	None	Sulphur Haretron	Blue dun goose fibers bunched	Pale cream cock
Red Sedge	10 to 12	Red	None	Silver wire	Gray rabbit's-fur	Gray mallard wing slips	Red cock
Pale Watery	14 to 16	Yellow	Pale blue dun cock-hackle fibers	None	Pale yellow rabbit's-fur	Pale blue dun hen hackle points	Pale blue dun cock
Greenwell's Glory	12 to 16	Yellow	Light furnace cock fibers	Gold wire	Yellow well-waxed tying thread	Mallard or starling wing	Ginger/black furnace
Blue-Winged Olive UK	14 to 18	Black	Red game cock	Fine gold wire	Gray rabbit's-fur	2 hackle points of blue dun	Red game cock
Lunn's Particular	14 to 16	Crimson	Rhode Island Red game cock hackle	None	Undyed cock-hackle stalk from Rhode Island Red cock hackle	Spent blue dun tips	Medium Rhode Island
Ginger Quill	14 to 16	Black	Natural red cock fibers	None	Stripped peacock-eye quill	Starling or mallard	Natural red cock

FLY NAME	HOOK	SILK	TAIL	RIB	BODY	WING	HACKLE
Emerger	LS 12 to 14	Brown	Cock-pheasant-tail fibers	Brown tying silk	Cream/light brown rabbit's-fur; dubbed deer-hair; black deer-hair fibers	Spectraflash thorax; deer-hair	None
Lough Arrow	8 to 10	Brown	Cock-pheasant-tail fibers	Gold wire	Golden olive seal's-fur	None	Orange cock/gray mallard
Stillborn	LS 8 to 12	Brown	Hare fibers	Brown floss	Cream Antron with a thorax cover of deer-hair	None	None
Straddle Bug	LS 10 to 12	Brown	Brown mallard fibers	Fine gold wire	Natural raffia with peacock herl	None	Summer duck
Gosling	8 to 10	Yellow	Cock-pheasant-tail fibers	Gold wire	Golden olive seal's-fur substitute	None	Orange cock/gray mallard
Floating Nymph	12 to 14	Brown	Wood-duck fibers	White parcel string	Olive seal's-fur and Antron mix	None	Golden olive cock
Maitland's Hatching Mayfly	LS 10 to 12	Brown	Pheasant-tail fibers	Copper wire	Rear: pheasant-tail fibers; Front: yellow olive seal's-fur or substitute	Roe deer-hair	Pale ginger
Drowned May	LS 10 to 12	Black	Brown goose quill fibers	None	White floss silk; badger hackle	None	Guinea fowl breast feather
French Partridge	LS 12	Brown	Cock-pheasant-tail fibers	Gold wire	Natural raffia with palmered olive cock	None	Partridge
Nevamis	LS FW 8	Yellow	Cock-pheasant-tail fibers	Oval gold	Cream seal's-fur or substitute	Pale blue dun cock	Honey cock
Shadow Mayfly	LS 10 to 12	Black	None	None	As for hackle	Ginger hackle	Grizzle
Lively Mayfly	Grub 10	Crimson	Pheasant-tail fibre	Tying silk along body	Detached body of white deer hair fibers; cream seal's-fur thorax	Wood duck	Badger or grizzle
Grey Wulff	8 to 14	Black	Natural deer hair	None	Muskrat or substitute	Deer-hair	Dun cock
Fly-line Mayfly	10 to 12	Olive	Light brown hackle stalk	Tying silk along body	White floating flyline ribbed with tying silk	Hen badger	Grizzle
Silhouette or Thorax Dry Mayfly Dun	LS 8 to 12	Black	Moose fiber	Black floss	Light brown Haretron	Blue goose shoulder	Grizzle
Green Drake Wulff	10 to 12	Black	Roe-deer fibers	Yellow floss	Olive Antron	Roe deer-hair	Olive-dyed cock
Lunn's Spent Gnat	LS 10 to 12	Brown	Brown hen quill fibers	Fine gold wire	White floss or natural sheep's-wool	White hen feathers	Partridge or cock

SEE PAGES
116-17

Chalk/Limestone
Nymphs

FLY NAME	HOOK	SILK	TAIL	RIB	BODY	WING	HACKLE
Killer Bug	10 to 16	None	None	None	Underbody of fine lead-wire overlaid with beige darning yarn to form cigar shape; fine copper wire to tie off	None	None
Shrimper	10 to 14	Olive	None	Fine gold wire	Olive and claret seal's-fur or substitute; polythene shell-back; weighted body	None	Olive palmered
Sawyer's Pheasant-Tail	12 to 16	Fine copper wire	Cock-pheasant-tail fibers	None	Underbody: copper wire with a hump for the thorax; overbody: pheasant-tail fibers with copper wire tied at thorax	Wing-case: pheasant-tail fibers	None
Pink Shrimp	10 to 14	Orange	Gray mallard fibers	None	Mixture of pink and gray seal's- or rabbit's-fur well picked out	None	None
Hoglouse	10 to 12	Olive	Brown mallard/wood duck	Fine gold wire	Hare's-face mask fur	Oak turkey	None
Troth Pheasant-Tail	10 to 20	Black	Brown mallard fibers	Fine gold wire	Pheasant tail; pheasant-tail wing-case; peacock herl thorax	None	None
Gerr-off	10 to 14	Brown	None	None	Mixed olive/brown and pink seal's-fur; clear polythene strip	None	None
Blue-Winged Olive Nymph	LS 10 to 14	Brown	Olive-dyed brown mallard fibers	Brown tying silk	Medium olive rabbit's-fur with a few mallard fibers as legs	None	None
Squirrel Nymph	10 to 14	Brown	Brown feather fibers	Copper wire	Squirrel's-fur dubbed and well picked out	None	None
Grey Goose	12 to 16	None	Golden-pheasant tippets	Copper wire	Underbody of copper wire; overbody gray goose fibers wound with copper wire	Goose-fiber thorax	None
GE Nymph	12 to 14	Brown	French partridge breast feather	Copper wire	Olive feather fiber; black feather thorax; olive mole fur	None	None
Green Squirrel	12 to 14	Olive	Brown feather fibers	None	Olive squirrel body fur	Pheasant tail; thorax: squirrel	None
PVC	10 to 14	Brown	Golden-pheasant tippets	None	PVC strip wound over olive feather fiber	Pheasant tail; feather thorax	None
Hatching Buzzer	10 to 16	Brown	None	Red/orange floss; silver wire	Feather fiber of appropriate shade; black/olive thorax cover; wild rabbit's-fur	None	Black head hackle
Bow-Tie Buzzer	12 to 16	Brown	Pheasant-tail fibers	Silver Lurex rib	Underbody of gold-colored copper wire; overlaid with flat silver tinsel; overbody of pheasant-tail fibers	White yarn	None
Gold-Ribbed Hare's-Ear	12 to 16	Brown	Mallard breast feather fibers	Fine flat gold	Hare's-mask; thorax cover of pheasant tail	None	None
Poly-Rib Buzzer	10 to 14	Brown	None	See body	Bronze peacock herl; polypropylene thorax and white Antron dubbing	None	None

FLY NAME	HOOK	SILK	TAIL	RIB	BODY	WING	HACKLE
Grey Suspender Pupa	LS 10 to 14	Black	Grizzle hackle fibers	Black tying silk	Gray rabbit underfur with thorax of olive fur	None	None
March Brown Floating Nymph	10 to 14	Brown	Lemon wood duck	None	Hare's-fur with Antron fur loop	As for tail	None
Moser Emerging Caddis/Sedge	RM Barbless 10 to 12	Brown	None	Fine silver	Olive, orange and brown seal's-fur	*Cul-de-canard* with Antron loop	*Cul-de-canard*
Cream Suspender	12 to 18	White	White or cream hackle fibers	None	Antron or seal's-fur	Polyball	None
Stillborn Olive	12 to 18	Olive	White or cream goose quill fibers	None	Light olive seal's-fur; extension body tied "wonderwing" fashion	White/cream quill fibers	None
Red Sedge Emerger	12 to 14	Brown	None	Fine gold wire	Dark brown rabbit's-fur	Thorax: rabbit's-fur; mallard wing	None
Floating Nymph (Jardine)	14	Brown	Wood-duck fibers	Fibers of white string	Dark olive Antron	None	Golden olive cock
Kaufmann Floating Nymph	12 to 20	Color of body	Split dark dun hackle fibers	Contrasting tying silk	Antron floss	Dun poly wing-case	None
Emerger II (Jardine)	12 to 20	Brown	Light blue dun hackle fibers	None	Olive brown seal's-fur	None	Light blue dun hen
Last Light Special	12 to 20	Brown	None	None	Olive brown dyed rabbit with yellow Antron floss	None	Ginger cock
Goddard's Suspender Pupa	12 to 16	Brown	White floss as breathing filaments	Fine flat silver tinsel	Olive brown dyed seal's-fur; bronze peacock herl thorax	None	None
Emerging March Brown	12 to 14	Brown	A few deer-hair fibers	Fine gold wire	Dubbed deer-hair	Antron floss wing	None
Collyer Deer-Hair Midge Pupa	12 to 14	Brown	White yarn as breathing filaments	Medium flat silver	Orange brown ostrich herl	None	None
Carnhill's Adult Buzzer	12 to 16	Brown	None	Flat clear mono-filament	Dark olive seal's-fur with thorax	Gray mallard wing	Olive green hackle
Muskrat Emerger	12 to 14	Brown	Honey-colored hair or hackle	None	Muskrat	*Cul-de-canard*	None
Raider	12 to 14	Olive	White silk floss	None	Muskrat	None	Ginger saddle
Little Green Midge	14 to 20	Olive	None	None	Light olive seal's-fur tied thinly	*Cul-de-canard*	Light olive

SEE PAGES **120-21**

Chalk/Limestone
Floating Adults

Fly Name	Hook	Silk	Tail	Rib	Body	Wing	Hackle
Gulper Adams	12 to 18	Black	Mixed grizzle and brown hackle fibers	None	Blue rabbit's or muskrat underfur	White polypropylene	Grizzle
Sparkler	14 to 18	Black	Fibers of blue dun cock hackle	None	Light gray or light olive rabbit's-fur	Sparkle yarn	Blue fur
Loop-Wing Adams	12 to 18	Black	Light brown and grizzle hackle fibers	None	Gray Poly II or blue rabbit's underfur	Two silver mallard feathers	Grizzle hackle
Mill Evening Dun	14 to 18	Black	Badger hackle fibers	None	Deer-hair; fine gold tinsel	Starling wing slips divided	Grizzle hackle
Funnel Dun	12 to 18	Olive	Brown cock fibers tied on bend	None	Light olive seal's-fur or substitute with darker fur around thorax	None	Cock hackle
Adams	14 to 22	Gray	Mixed grizzle and brown hackle fibers	None	Muskrat or blue-gray poly equivalent	Grizzle hackle tips	Grizzle/ brown cock
Beacon Beige	14 to 18	Brown	Plymouth cock fibers	None	Peacock-eye quill	None	Plymouth/ Indian cock
Sparkle Dun	12 to 20	Olive	Sparkle yarn	None	Light olive seal or rabbit's-fur	Light brown deer-body hair fibers	None
Harrop Dun	12 to 20	Olive	Brown cock fibers	None	Light olive fur	Spun light brown deer-body hair	Light brown cock hackle
Duck's Dun	14 to 22	Brown	Badger cock-hackle fibers	None	Light olive fur	Bunch of *cul-de-canard* fibers	Gray cock-hackle horns
Micro Caddis	18 to 24	Brown	None	None	Gray rabbit dubbed fine	Partridge fibers	Brown cock fibers
Upside-Down Dun	UE 14 to 20	Olive	Long gray or iron-blue cock fibers	None	Olive Haretron	*Cul-de-canard* feathers	Olive cock hackle
Kite's Imperial	14 to 18	Purple	Gray or brown hackle fibers	Fine sold wire	Natural heron or substitute with thorax behind hackle	None	Brown or honey hackle
Fluttering Caddis	12 to 16	Gray	None	None	Muskrat or substitute fur	Blue dun; mink-tail hairs	Light blue dun
No-Hackle Dun	12 to 22	Olive	Clear micro-fibelts divided	None	Olive poly dubbing	Gray mallard wing slips	None
Para Dun	16 to 20	Light brown	Clear micro-fibelts divided	None	Two-thirds gray dubbing; rest light-yellow dubbing at thorax	*Cul-de-canard* fibers bunched	Iron blue tied para fashion
Tent-Wing Caddis	12 to 18	Brown	None	None	Light gray or white seal's-fur	Hen pheasant slip	Brown cock

Fly Name	Hook	Silk	Tail	Rib	Body	Wing	Hackle
Richard Walker's Sedge	10 to 12	Chestnut	Butt of DFM orange yarn	Fine gold wire	Chestnut rabbit's-belly fur or ostrich herl	Red game cock	Brown cock hackle
Polywing Spinner	12 to 16	Cream	Cream hackle fibers	Tying silk rib	Seal's-fur	Polythene fiber wing	None
Brown Miller	10 to 16	Brown	None	None	Golden calf tail	None	*See* body
Terry's Terror	10 to 16	Brown	Red and yellow buck tail	Copper Lurex	Peacock herl	None	Red game cock
Fallen Spinner	14 to 18	Brown	Cream hackle fibers	Tying silk rib	Dark brown Poly II	None	White hen hackle
Depositing Caddis	LS 12 to 14	Brown	None	Tying silk	Olive green seal's-fur	Hen-pheasant quill	Palmered ginger cock
Sunset Spinner	14 to 18	Maroon	White bristles	Lurex	Rust/red/brown Poly II	Blue dun cock hackles	*See* wing
Patterson Sunk Spinner	12 to 16	Crimson	Hare's whiskers or horse-hair	Hare's-whisker	Copper wire underbody and nylon monofilaments	Badger hackle	*See* wing
Jardine's Sunk Spinner	12 to 14	Olive	White bristles	None	Olive seal's-fur	None	Badger saddle
Rust Spinner	18 to 24	Orange	White cock-hackle fibers	None	Rust rabbit's-fur	White cock hackle	None
Caenis Fallen Spinner	20 to 24	Brown	White bristles	None	Gray rabbit's-fur	Crystal hair	Blue dun cock
Sparkle Spinner	12 to 14	Brown	Sparkle yarn	None	Red rabbit's-fur dubbing	Black marabou	Black cock
White Wing (Black)	18 to 22	Black	Black cock fibers	Tying silk	White polypropylene dubbing	White floss	Blue dun
Poly Caenis	18 to 24	White	White hackle fibers	None	Brown dubbing fur	Blue dun fibers	Cream full hackle
Baetis Spinner	14 to 18	White	White buck tail	None	Cream herl	Cream fibers	Grizzle
Angler's Curse	18 to 24	Black	White hackle fibers	None	Brown and grizzle hackle	Grizzle hackle point	Brown/grizzle
Adams Midge	16 to 20	Black	Brown cock grizzle fibers	None	Muskrat	Grizzle hackle tips	Brown/grizzle

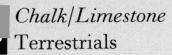

Chalk/Limestone
Terrestrials

Fly Name	Hook	Silk	Tail	Rib	Body	Wing	Hackle
Hawthorn Fly	12 to 14	Black	None	None	Black tying silk; black pheasant-tail fibers	White hackle	Black cock
Black Spider	12 to 16	Claret	None	None	Claret tying silk	None	Black cock
Halford Black Gnat	14 to 22	Black	None	None	Black tying silk	Gray mallard	Black cock
Letort Cricket	10 to 12	Black	None	None	Black wool or rabbit	Goose quill	None
Black Ant	12 to 26	Black	None	None	Black polypropylene	None	*See* body
Black Beetle	12 to 20	Black	None	None	Peacock herl; mallard quill	None	Black cock
Soldier Beetle	12 to 14	Red	Red game cock	None	Orange/red seal's-fur	None	Game cock
Ladybird	14 to 16	Black	None	None	Bronze peacock herl	Pheasant tail	Black cock
Black Midge	18 to 26	Black	Black hackle fibers	None	Black rabbit's-fur	None	Black cock
Inchworm	10 to 12	Insect green	*See* body	Insect-green tying thread	Insect-green deer-hair	None	None
Brown Ant	12 to 20	Brown	None	None	Brown rabbit's-fur	Mallard	*See* body
Brown Midge	18 to 26	Brown	Brown hackle fibers	None	Brown rabbit's-fur	None	Ginger cock
Crowe Beetle	10 to 14	Black	None	None	Black deer-hair	None	None
McMurray Ant	14 to 22	Black	None	None	Balsa wood and monofilament	None	Black/red cock
Black Emerger	12 to 18	Black	None	Fine silver wire	Black seal's-fur	Elk hair	None
Flying Ant	12 to 18	Black	None	None	Black seal's-fur; black deer-hair	Mallard	Black cock
Ethafoam Beetle	WG 12 to 14	Black	None	None	Black seal's-fur; black Ethafoam	None	Black cock

Rain-fed / Freestone Classics

SEE PAGES **128-9**

FLY NAME	HOOK	SILK	TAIL	RIB	BODY	WING	HACKLE
Adams Irresistible	12 to 16	Black	Moose mane fibers	None	Clipped natural deer-hair	Grizzle hackle	Brown and grizzle
Renegade	12 to 16	Black	Small butt of gold Lurex	None	Peacock herl	None	Brown/ white cock
Wickham's Fancy	12 to 16	Brown	Ginger game cock-hackle fibers	Gold wire	Flat gold Lurex or Mylar	Starling or mallard	Ginger red/red game
Grey Wulff	12 to 16	Black	Roe deer fibers	None	Gray rabbit's-fur	Roe-deer fibers	Gray cock
Black Gnat	12 to 16	Black	None	Fine silver wire	Black floss silk	Starling or mallard	Black cock
Coch-Y-Bondhu	10 to 12	Black	Strands of black deer-hair	None	Small butt of flat gold tinsel and bronze peacock herl	None	Coch-y-Bondhu hackle
Bi-Visible	10 to 14	Black	None	None	*See* hackle	None	Black cock
Alder	10 to 16	Black	None	None	Magenta peacock herl	Brown hen	Black cock
Coachman	10 to 14	Black	Brown partridge	None	Peacock herl	White goose	Red game cock
March brown	12 to 16	Brown	None	Yellow floss and fine gold wire	Gray rabbit; red and yellow rayon floss	Hen pheasant	Brown partridge
Partridge & Orange	12 to 16	Black	None	None	Orange floss silk	None	Brown partridge
Greenwell's Glory	10 to 16	Yellow waxed	Brown partridge	Gold wire	Yellow waxed silk	Blackbird	Light furnace
Silver March Brown	12 to 16	Brown	None	Oval silver	Flat silver	Hen pheasant	Brown partridge
Hare's Lug	12 to 16	Brown	None	Fine gold wire	Hare's-ear fur	None	Golden plover
Snipe & Purple	12 to 16	Purple	None	None	Purple tying silk	None	Snipe breast feather
Black Spider	12 to 16	Crimson	None	None	Crimson floss silk	None	Black hen hackle
Red Tag	10 to 16	Brown	Red yarn	None	Peacock herl	None	Game cock

SEE PAGES
130-31

Rain-fed / Freestone
Small Nymphs

Fly Name	Hook	Silk	Tail	Rib	Body	Wing	Hackle
Small Green Caddis	12 to 14	Brown	None	Fine gold wire	Insect-green rabbit's-fur; thorax light brown rabbit's-fur	Mallard	Brown partridge
Amber Longhorn Pupa (Emergent)	10 to 18	Brown	None	Flat orange or red Lurex	Amber/orange seal's-fur	Partridge	Brown partridge
Traun Red-Spot Shrimp (Scud)	Sedge 8 to 14	Olive	Picked out body fur	Gold wire	Lead-wire underbody with olive mohair and seal's-fur	None	Body fur on underside
Traun Pupa	Sedge 8 to 14	Black	None	None	Yellow seal's-fur; thorax of dark red seal's fur	Printed wing	None
Glitter Pupa	Sedge 10 to 14	Brown	None	Gold wire; Flashabou rib	Cream Antron	None	None
Straw Shrimp	Sedge 10 to 12	Olive	Olive hackle	Gold oval wire	Fine lead-wire underbody	None	Palmered olive cock
Deep Olive Pupa	12 to 20	Olive	None	None	Olive and rust seal's-fur underbody; olive Antron overbody	Light deer-hair	None
Muskrat (Pellis)	10 to 12	Brown	Brown cock hackle	Fine silver wire	Brown muskrat or rabbit substitute	None	Brown hen hackle
All-Purpose Dark (Orvis)	LS 8 to 12	Brown	Cock-pheasant hackle	Fine gold wire	Medium brown rabbit's-fur	Pheasant-tail fibers	Grouse hackle
Hendrickson	10 to 12	White	Brown partridge	Brown rayon floss	Brown and pink rabbit's-fur	Partridge-feather fibers	Partridge
Marabou Nymph	LS 8 to 12	Black	Moose mane	Fine gold wire	Black marabou	Moose mane	None
Mahogany Nymph	10 to 12	Brown	Cock pheasant	Brown rayon floss	Mahogany seal's-fur	Partridge-feather fibers	None
Light Cahill	FW 10 to 14	White	Mandarin duck	None	Pale cream/gray yarn	None	Mandarin duck breast
Filoplume Mayfly Nymph	10 to 12	Brown	Cock pheasant	Fine gold wire	Olive marabou	Olive marabou filoplume	None
Copper Nymph	10 to 12	Brown	Golden pheasant	None	Copper wire body; brown seal's-fur head	None	None
Adams Flashback	10 to 12	Brown	Grizzle hackle	Fine silver wire	Dark brown fur	None	Blue dun head hackle
March Brown	16 to 20	Brown	Pheasant-tail fibers	Fine gold wire	Pheasant-tail fibers; hare's-mask fur	Brown turkey wing	Brown partridge

Fly Name	Hook	Silk	Tail	Rib	Body	Wing	Hackle
Tellico Nymph	LS 8 to 16	Black	Natural guinea-fowl hackle	Peacock herl	Lead-wire underbody; yellow rayon overbody	None	Brown cock hackle
Bread Crust	LS 10 to 12	Orange	None	Silver Lurex and Swanundaze	Fine lead-wire underbody; bright orange yarn overbody	None	Hen grizzle
Montana Nymph	LS 8 to 12	Black	Black hackle tips	None	Black chenille; yellow chenille thorax	Black chenille wing-case	None
Prince	LS 10 to 12	Brown	Brown goose biots	Gold Lurex	Peacock herl; white goose biots	None	Brown hen hackle
Zug Bug	LS 10 to 12	Red	Peacock sword-feather fibers	Gold Lurex	Weighted body; bronze peacock herl	Lemon mallard slips	Brown cock hackle
Large Black Stone	LS 10 to 12	Brown	Goose biots	Clear mono-filament	Black seal's-fur; white-tipped turkey tails	None	None
Girdle Bug	LS 6 to 10	Black	Black or white rubber strips	None	Black chenille; white rubber legs and antennae	None	None
Ted's Stonefly	LS 4 to 10	Brown	Brown goose biots	None	Brown chenille; orange chenille thorax with black hackle wound through	None	None
Bottom-Scratcher	LS 14 to 16	Black or yellow	Black marabou plume	None	Hare's-mask fur; thorax of tan dubbed deer-hair	None	Gold head
Cream Crawler	LS 4	Yellow or cream	None	Clear mono-filament	Cream ostrich herl and seal's-fur	Goose quill slips	None
Dave's Stonefly Nymph	4 to 14	Black	Dyed goose biots	Yellow mono-filament	Antron; yellow seal's-fur	Hen pheasant	As wing
Casual Dress	6 to 12	Brown	Brown stripped goose	None	Muskrat fur	Black ostrich herl	Muskrat
Kaufmann Stone	2 to 10	Black	Black goose biots	Dark brown mono-filament	Dark brown seal and rabbit; thorax as for body; brown stripped goose antennae	Mottled turkey wing-case	None
Box Canyon Stone	2 to 8	Brown	Goose biots	None	Weighted underbody; black yarn body; palmered cock hackle	Mottled turkey wing-case	Ostrich herl
Golden Stone Nymph	LS 2 to 10	Cream or white	Oak turkey	Tan silk	Cream yarn underbody; oak turkey shell back	Pheasant-tail fiber	Oak turkey
Orvis Stone	LS 2 to 10	Black, brown or olive	Brown partridge	Tan silk	Tan, mid-brown or olive Haretron	Brown Swiss straw	Ring-neck pheasant
Early Brown Stone	LS 10 to 16	Cream	Brown partridge	Clear mono-filament	Brown and gray hare's-fur	Turkey tail	Brown hackle

SEE PAGES
134-5

Rain-fed / Freestone
Streamers

Fly Name	Hook	Silk	Tail	Rib	Body	Wing	Hackle
Colorado Gold Muddlerbou	2 to 8	Brown	None	None	Orange/yellow seal's-fur; deer-hair spun and clipped; white deer-hair under	Orange/ brown marabou	None
White Marabou Muddler	4 to 10	Gray	Red hackle fibers	None	Flat silver tinsel with head of natural deer-hair	White marabou	None
Belgian Sculpin	4 to 10	Brown	2 cree hackles	Oval gold tinsel	Buff seal's-fur; spun deer-hair head	Brown partridge	None
Muddled Black Mink Zonker	4 to 10	Black	None	None	Black Antron; head of clipped deer-hair	Natural mink	None
Troth Bullhead	2 to 8	Brown	White deer-hair; black marabou	None	Weighted underbody; white deer-hair with black marabou back; head of spun deer-hair	*See* body	None
Black Zonker	LS 6 to 12	Black	Mylar body end fibers	None	Black Mylar	Black rabbit	None
Pulsata	6 to 10	Brown	None	None	Natural rabbit's-fur; head of spun deer-hair	Natural rabbit	None
Woolly Worm (Brown)	LS 8 to 12	Brown	Scarlet hackle fibers	None	Brown chenille	None	Palmered ginger cock
Woolly Bugger	LS 6 to 12	Crimson	Black marabou fibers	None	Black chenille	None	Palmered black cock
Threadfin Shad	6 to 10	White	*See* body	None	Silver Mylar tube body; brown marabou; white head and painted eye	None	None
Furnace Matuka Variant	6 to 10	Black	Furnace hackles	Flat silver tinsel	$^2/_3$ red, $^1/_3$ green floss silk	*See* tail	Deer-hair
Olive Matuka	6 to 10	Black	Golden olive hackles	Oval gold	Olive yarn or seal's-fur	*See* tail	Golden olive hen
Royal Coachman Bucktail Streamer	8 to 10	Black	Golden-pheasant tippets	None	Butt of bronze peacock herl; red silk floss thorax	White hair	Natural red cock
Silver Darter	4 to 10	Black	None	None	Silver Mylar body with small red butt	Badger hackle	Peacock sword fibers

FLY NAME	HOOK	SILK	TAIL	RIB	BODY	WING	HACKLE
Sofa Pillow	6 to 8	Tan	Orange elk hair	None	Orange polypropylene yarn	Elk hair	Ginger hackle
White Wulff	10 to 16	White	White calf tail	None	White rabbit's-fur	White calf tail or body hair	Badger cock
Stonefly Roger	10 to 12	Olive	None	Yellow rayon floss	Olive seal's-fur	Grizzle hackle	Badger cock
Grizzly Wulff	10 to 16	Brown	Natural roe hair	None	Yellow rayon floss	Natural roe hair	Brown and grizzle
Royal Wulff	10 to 16	Brown	Natural elk hair	None	⅔ peacock herl; ⅓ rayon floss	White calf tail	Brown cock
Golden Stone	10 to 12	Brown	Elk hair	None	Yellow rayon floss	Elk hair	Palmered cree hackle
Yellow Humpy or Goofus Bug	8 to 20	Brown	Elk hair	None	Yellow rayon floss	Elk hair	Brown and grizzle
Rat-Faced McDougal	10 to 16	Gray	Red game cock	None	Natural deer-hair, spun and clipped	Red game hackle	Red game hackle
Irresistible Wulff	10 to 16	Brown	Red game cock	None	Clipped deer-hair	White calf tail	Red game cock
Fluttering Caddis	10 to 16	Brown	None	Fine gold wire	Cock-pheasant tail	Brown cock hackle	Brown cock
March Brown (Dry)	10 to 16	Brown	Cock hackle and partridge	None	Brown and gray hare underfur	Hen pheasant	Brown cock
Goddard Caddis	LS 8 to 12	Green	None	None	Spun deer-hair	None	Rusty dun cock hackles
Henryville Special	10 to 12	Brown	None	None	Green rayon floss	Mallard	Grizzle cock
Olive Dun	12 to 16	Olive	Olive dun hackle fibers	Fine copper wire	Medium olive seal's- or mole's-fur	Starling, blackbird or mallard	Olive cock
Troth Elk-Hair Caddis	10 to 18	Brown	None	None	Hare's-mask fur	Tan elk hair	Brown palmered hackle
Coachman	10 to 16	Black	None	None	Peacock herl	None	White and red cock
Badger Hackle	10 to 16	Black	Ginger cock hackle	None	Flat silver tinsel	None	Badger cock

SEE PAGES
138-9

Rain-fed / Freestone
Large Dry Flies & Nymphs

Fly Name	Hook	Silk	Tail	Rib	Body	Wing	Hackle
Goddard Caddis	4 to 10	Brown	None	None	Natural deer-hair; dubbed green seal's-fur	None	Red game cock hackle
Henry's Fork Hopper	8 to 12	Yellow waxed	None	None	Cream elk-rump fibers	Deer-hair and hen wing	None
Daddy-Longlegs	LS 12 to 14	Brown	None	None	Natural raffia body wrapped in polythene strip	Cree hackle points	Brown cock
Moser's Adult Stone	LS 6 to 10	Brown	None	None	Brown and dark brown deer-hair	Printed wing; goose biot	None
Joe's Hopper	LS 10 to 12	Brown	Red cock hackle	None	Yellow deer-hair, clipped	White-tipped turkey	Grizzle and brown cock
Extended-Body Daddy-Longlegs	LS 12 to 14	Brown	None	None	Brown deer-hair; brown tying silk; red painted head	Furnace hackle point	Red game cock
Yellow Stone	LS 6 to 10	Yellow	None	None	Yellow seal's-fur; brown elk hair; enamel yellow body	Printed wing	None
Dave's Hopper	LS 10 to 12	Dark brown	Bright red buck tail	*See* hackle	Dark yellow yarn; olive deer-hair head; cock-pheasant tail fibers	White-tipped turkey	Brown palmered hackle
Hoolet	6 to 10	Black	None	Fine copper wire	Peacock herl body	Dark brown hen quill	Dark red game cock
Stimulator	6 to 16	Re-waxed orange	Deer-body hair	None	Orange polypropylene; dark orange rabbit's-fur thorax	None	Ginger hackle
Simulator	4 to 10	Color to match body	Goose quill	Copper wire	Angora goat and Haretron colors	Light elk	Saddle hackle
Fluttering Golden Stone	6 to 8	Yellow waxed	None	None	Yellow polyester yarn	Gray/black hen hackle	Ginger saddle hackle
Little Black Stonefly	10 to 18	Black	Black mink	None	Black mink dubbing fur	Gray hen hackle	Black hackle
Bitch Creek	4 to 8	Black	White rubber filaments	*See* body	Weighted underbody; black chenille overbody with green and orange chenille	None	Ginger cock
MacSalmon	2 to 8	Brown	None	None	Orange macramé yarn; dark brown deer-hair head	White horse-hair	None
Caterpillar	10 to 16	Olive	None	Fine silver wire	Green silk floss underbody; peacock herl	None	Ginger hackle
Black Stone	4 to 10	Brown	Brown goose biots	Matching Swanundaze	Black Haretron; turkey wing; goose quill antennae	None	None

Flies Around the World
Australia & New Zealand

SEE PAGES **140-41**

FLY NAME	HOOK	SILK	TAIL	RIB	BODY	WING	HACKLE
Black Matuka	4 to 8	Black	Fibers from red cock saddle hackle	Oval silver tinsel	Black chenille	Black hen hackles tied Matuka style	Black hen
Rabbit	6 to 10	Black	None	Oval gold	Black chenille	Gray/white rabbit zonker strip	None
Hare & Copper	10 to 14	Black	Hare fibers	Copper wire	Weighted underbody; hare's-fur dubbed and picked out	Bunch of hare's-fur fibers	None
Cordallid	6 to 10	Brown	None	None	Brown deer-hair cut and shaped to form body and head	Brown deer-hair fibers	None
Mrs Simpson	4 to 10	Black	Black squirrel-tail fibers	None	Black chenille	Cock-pheasant feathers	None
Governor Nymph	10 to 12	Black	Red game cock-hackle fibers	None	Red floss silk with peacock herl	Wing-case of hen pheasant	Throat hackle as for tail
Horned Caddis	10 to 12	Black	None	Silver wire	Gray rabbit's-fun with white rabbit's-fur thorax	None	None
Parson's Glory	8 to 10	Black	Two cree hackle points	Oval silver tinsel	Orange chenille	Cock hackles, Matuka style	Light cree

Flies Around the World
Germany & Austria

Fly Name	Hook	Silk	Tail	Rib	Body	Wing	Hackle
Woelfle Emergent Caddis	10 to 16	Brown	None	Pearlescent Spectraflash	Olive Haretron abdomen; brown marabou thorax	Traun River sedge wing cut to shape	None
Deer-Hair Emerger	RM barbless 10 to 14	Brown	None	None	Deer-hair with a bunch of polyester yarn fibers tied as a wing; all fibers well picked out	None	None
Gold-Head Pupa	WG 10 to 18	Brown	None	None	Irise-dub body with over turn of deer-hair dubbing behind gold bead	*See* body	None
Moser Sedge Pupa	10 to 14	Brown	None	None	Amber Irise-dub abdomen; tan Irise-dub thorax	None	Ginger cree
Female Caddis	10 to 16	Brown	None	None	Gray body-gill with a thorax cover of polycelon foam doubled	None	None
Gold-Head Pupa II	WG 10 to 18	Olive	None	None	Dark olive Irise-dub with a thorax of mixed olive deer-hair body fibers	Brown deer-hair dressed forward	None
Balloon Caddis	10 to 16	Yellow	None	None	Brown Antron with a head of yellow polycelon foam	None	None
Dark Caddis	LS 10 to 14	Black	None	None	Mixed gray including dark gray deer-hair body fibers dubbed	Brown deer-body hair	As for body, well picked out
Light Caddis	LS 10 to 14	Brown	None	None	Mixed light and dark brown deer-hair body fibers	Swiss straw marked with gray pen	As for body, well picked out
Chironomid Pupa	RM arrowpoint 12 to 18	Black	None	Split white raffine	Black raffine; light and dark gray/brown deer-body hair thorax	Swiss straw marked with Pantone pen	None
Grayling No. 1	16 to 20	White	None	None	Amber Antron	Two stubs white raffine	Cream cock hackle (small)
Traun-Wing Caddis	Jardine 12 to 20	Brown	None	None	Brown Haretron palmered with light brown cock hackle	Pearlescent Flashabou	As for body
Sparkle (Baetis/Ephemerella) Nymph	RM arrowpoint 14 to 20	Brown	3 to 4 fibers jungle cock spade feather	None	Brown olive Haretron abdomen; dark brown Irise-dub thorax	None	None
"F" Fly	14 to 20	Olive	None	None	Bronze peacock herl	*Cul-de-canard* feather	None
Gammerus	Jardine living nymph hook 12 to 20	Brown	None	Brown mono	Fine gray deer-hair and cream seal's-fur or substitute; shellback of olive Swiss straw	None	None
Numiades Nymph	12 to 14	Black	2 to 3 pheasant-tail fibers	None	Numaides quill or substitute; mixed yellow and green ostrich herl thorax	None	None
Antron Dry Emerger	10 to 18	Olive	None	None	Mixed olive and dark gray Antron	Gray polypropylene	Grizzle cock

FLY NAME	HOOK	SILK	TAIL	RIB	BODY	WING	HACKLE
Cocchetto Nymph	14 to 16	Black	None	Natural red hackle	Moth cocoon dubbing	None	Unclipped hackle
Précieuse	12 to 18	Gray or black	Gray hackle fibers	Silver tinsel	Gray poly dubbing	None	Short fibered ash gray
Pallaretta	12	Black or brown	None	Black silk	Yellow silk varnished	None	Dark blue dun
Ossolina Emerger	14 to 16	Black	None	None	None	None	Pale ginger hackle
The Dormouse Nymph	10 to 14	Black	Dormouse tail fibers	None	Dormouse tail fur	None	None
Mave	12 to 14	Pale yellow	None	Primrose	Purple	None	Mottled spade hackle
Valsesiana	16 to 18	Purple	None	None	Purple	None	Black hen
Bartellini Spider	16 to 20	Red	None	None	Red fluorescent silk	None	White hen
La Rue	16 to 18	Brown	None	Brown silk	Light olive silk	One only, mottled brown/gray	Short brown hackle
"F" Fly	10 to 18	Black, gray, olive or yellow	None	None	Tying thread or heron herl	Small duck-gland feather	As wing
Verano Amarillo	12 to 14	Primrose	Medium blue dun	None	Yellow goose/swan fiber; green fiber	None	Medium blue dun
Oliva	12 to 14	Primrose	None	None	Olive fur or synthetic dubbing	None	Soft grizzle hen
Hoz Seca	14	Light brown	Medium blue dun	Fine copper wire	Olive synthetic fur	Gray polypropy-lene	Blue and light red dun
Moustique 1	14 to 16	Black or brown	Blue dun hackle fibers	None	Yellow floss silk	Blue dun hackle tips	Green duck feather
Ucero	10 to 12	Red	Polypropy-lene yarn	Brown thread	Cinnamon polypropylene dubbing	None	Poly yarn, sloping backward
Tajo	14 to 16	Primrose	Medium blue dun	None	Varnished orange silk	Gray polypropylene	Blue dun
Universal Caddis	10 to 12	Black	None	None	Light-green PVC strip	Pheasant-wing quill	Natural red cock

SEE PAGES
146-7

Flies Around the World
Scandinavia

Fly Name	Hook	Silk	Tail	Rib	Body	Wing	Hackle
Rhyacophila Pupa	Grub hook 12	Brown	None	3.6kg. (8lb.) olive mono-filament	Olive Antron dubbing well brushed out	None	Grouse hackle
Nalle Puh/Stone (Dark)	Standard 12	Black	None	None	Wound black polypropylene yarn, with palmered natural black cock hackle	Polar or brown bear	Black cock
Orange Pupa	LS 8 to 10	Brown	None	Fine gold wire	Optional lead underbody; rear 3/4 peachy-orange Antron, dubbed	None	None
Rhyacophila Larva	LS 12	Brown	None	1.8kg. (4lb.) yellow mono-filament	Clear PVC strip over back of olive Antron-dubbed body	Mottled feather wing-case	None
Nelson Caddis	LS 14	Brown	None	None	Dubbed cinnamon polypropylene	Natural grizzled deer-hair tips	Red game cock
Green-Antron Pupa	LS 10	Brown	None	3.6kg. (8lb.) olive mono-filament	Light olive green Antron dubbed and well brushed out	None	Grouse ostrich marabou
Nalle Puh	LS 6	Orange	None	None	Wound orange polypropylene yarn, palmered with medium red game cock	Brown-dyed polar bear hair	Red cock
VA-Sedge	LS 14	Brown	None	None	Wound dark brown herl over cigar-shaped underbody	Synthetic caddis wings	Dark red game cock
Rackelhane	Standard 10	Dark brown	None	None	Dubbed medium olive seal's-fur or substitute	Yellow and brown polar bear	None
Dragonfly Nymph	LS 12	Olive	Olive marabou tips	Clear mono-filament	Wound olive marabou	Cock-pheasant tail	None
Grouse-Wing Sculpin	LS 1 to 2	Olive	Ends of 2 grouse feathers	Tinsel; 2.7kg. (6lb.) mono-filament	Mixed dirty yellow and orange mohair or seal substitute, applied with dubbing loop	Grouse-tail feathers	Grouse clipped
Mysis Relicta	Tiemco swimming nymph hook (400 T) 12	White	White marabou tips	Pearl Mylar	Wound white marabou	None	White cock
Stonefly Nymph	LS 12	Olive	2 dark feather-fiber tips	Silver wire	Yellow floss and orange thread; dark feather fiber bound along top of body	Layered dark feather fibers	None
Flat-Head Sculpin	LS (6x) 2 to 4	Brown	Ends of 2 grouse feathers	Silver wire	Polypropylene dubbing (dubbing loop) 3/5 mud brown, 1/5 orange, 1/5 scarlet	Grouse fibers, Matuka style	Grouse feathers
Paraleptophlebia Nymph	LS 12	Brown	Cock-pheasant-tail fibers	Fine silver wire	Gray marabou or ostrich herl; mottled hen pheasant or turkey, bound along top of body with ribbing	Feather fiber wing-case	None
Muskrat Muddled Zonker	LS (6x) 2 to 4	Brown	End of muskrat zonker strip	Heavy silver wire	Soft tanned strip of muskrat bound along top of body with ribbing wire, Matuka style	Red floss	Red floss
Perch Fly	LS (6x) 2 to 4	Gray	Scarlet cock-hackle fibers	Oval gold tinsel	Gray marabou or aftershaft wound in a dubbing loop	Rabbit strip	Scarlet cock

FLY NAME	HOOK	SILK	TAIL	RIB	BODY	WING	HACKLE
Dog's Body	12 to 16	Brown	Cock-pheasant tail fibers	Oval gold	Camel-colored dog's-hair	None	Plymouth Rock and red cock
Daiwl Bach	10 to 12	Black	Brown fibers	None	Peacock herl	None	Hen hackle
Conway Red	LS 6 to 10	Black	None	Red floss or flat red tinsel	Black floss	Badger back hairs	Blue dun cock
Herefordshire Alder	12 to 14	Black	Blue dun fibers	None	Pheasant-tail fibers	None	Honey dun
Harry Tom	8 to 10	Brown	Honey dun fibers	Silver wire	Natural rabbit's-fur	Mallard	Black throat hackle
Moc's Cert	LS 6 to 10	Black	None	Oval silver	Flat silver tinsel	Black squirrel or jungle cock cheeks	Black hen hackle
Williams' Favourite	12 to 14	Black	Black whiskers	Silver wire	Black floss silk	None	Cock-pheasant feather
Haul-A-Gwynt	12 to 14	Black	None	None	Black ostrich herl	Black crow or substitute	Honey dun
Dai Ben	6 to 10	Black	Honey dun fibers	Flat silver tinsel	Rabbit's-fur	None	Furnace cock
Teifi Terror	8 to 10	Black	Furnace hackle	Gold wire	Black floss	None	Coch-y-Bondhu
Coch-Y-Bondhu	12 to 14	Crimson	None	None	Bronze peacock herl	None	Partridge; claret cock
Welsh Partridge	12 to 16	Black	Brown partridge	Oval gold tinsel	Claret seal's-fur	None	Red cock hackle
Red Tag	10 to 12	Black	Red yarn tag	Gold wire	Peacock herl; optional gold wire tip	None	Blue dun hen
Lewis' Grannom	14 to 18	Green	None	None	Olive mole	None	Gray partridge neck
Kell's Blue	12 to 14	Purple	Blue dun cock	Oval silver tinsel	Heron herl or substitute	None	Coch-y-Bondhu
Yorke's Favourite	10 to 14	Black	Red swan/ goose quill	None	Peacock herl	None	Well-marked badger
Grey Duster	12 to 16	Brown	None	None	Natural rabbit's-fur with blue underfur	None	None

Flies Around the World
Sea Trout

SEE PAGES 150-51

FLY NAME	HOOK	SILK	TAIL	RIB	BODY	WING	HACKLE
Blackie (Waddington)	Waddington	Black	None	None	Silver Mylar tube; black buck tail	None	None
Surface Lure	4 to 10	Black	Extension of body material	None	Ethafoam; black peacock herl with blue buck tail tied over	None	None
Ruane's Fancy	ED 8 to 14 treble	Black	None	None	None	Midnight blue GP tippet	None
Terror	Two 10s tied tandem	Black	Red ibis substitute on rear fly	None	Flat silver tinsel	Blue swan with teal cheeks	None
Goldie	LS 6 to 10	Black	Yellow hackle fibers	Gold wire	Flat gold tinsel	Yellow and black goat's-hair	Yellow cock fibers
Peter Ross	Rear hook 8 to 10 Front hook 6 to 8	Black	GP tippets	Oval silver wire on front fly	Rear fly flat silver tinsel; front fly red seal's-fur substitute	Grizzle hackle points	Black hen hackle
Headley's Speck	Size 14 to 18 treble	Red	None	None	None	None	Black cock hackle
Medicine (Mallard)	4 to 6	Red	None	Optional oval silver tinsel	Flat silver tinsel	Dark brown mallard	Light blue cock
Wickham's Fancy	12 to 16	Brown	Ginger cock-hackle fibers	Oval gold tinsel	Flat gold tinsel	Gray duck	Ginger or light red cock
BA Pretty	12 to 14	Black	Light blue dun fibers	None	Flat gold	None	Blue dun
Flashabou Alexandra	8 to 12	Black	Pearly Flashabou strips	Oval silver tinsel	Flat silver tinsel	Peacock sword, ibis, jungle cock	Black cock or hen
Bloody Butcher	8 to 14	Black	Red ibis or substitute	None	Flat silver tinsel	Blue mallard-feather slips	Red cock
Loch Ordie (Dapping)	10 to 12	Black	None	None	None	None	Game-cock hackles
Silver Invicta	10 to 14	Black	GP crest feather	None	Flat silver tinsel	Hen pheasant	None
Red Stuart	10 to 12	Black	Red cock-hackle fibers	None	Flat gold tinsel	Dyed red goat hair	Dyed red palmered cock
Red Palmer (Dapping)	10 to 14	Black	None	Gold wire	Red yarn or red seal's-fur	None	Palmered game cock

Fly Name	Hook	Silk	Tail	Rib	Body	Wing	Hackle
Doobry	10 to 12	Black	Red fluorescent floss	Fine gold wire	Flat brassy gold	None	Palmered black cock
Loch Ordie	10 to 12	Black	None	None	*See* hackle	None	Hen hackles
Kate McLaren	10 to 12	Brown	Golden-pheasant breast feather	Oval silver tinsel	Black dubbing fur	None	Black cock
Clan Chief	10 to 12	Black	Red and yellow floss tag	Oval silver tinsel	Black dubbing fur	None	Crimson and black cock
Ke-He	10 to 12	Black	Red yarn with pheasant tippets	Gold wire	Bronze peacock herl	None	Red hen
Zulu	10 to 12	Black	Tag of red yarn	Flat silver or gold tinsel	Black fur dubbing	None	Black cock
Goat's Toe	10 to 12	Black	Flat gold butt with tag of red yarn	Flat gold	Bronze peacock herl	None	Blue peacock
Black Ke-He	10 to 12	Black	Red yarn with pheasant tippets	Gold wire	Bronze peacock herl	None	Black hen
Blue-Tag Red Palmer	10 to 12	Scarlet	Cambridge blue tag	Oval gold tinsel	Red seal's-fur	None	Ginger cock
Heckham Peckham	10 to 12	Black	Golden-pheasant tippets	Oval gold tinsel	Red seal's-fur	Mallard	Black cock
Black Pennell	10 to 12	Black	Golden-pheasant tippets	Oval silver tinsel	Tip of oval silver tinsel; black floss silk	None	Black cock
Machair Claret	10 to 12	Black	Golden-pheasant tippets	Gold wire	Black and claret floss silk	None	Black cock
McLeod's Olive	10 to 14	Olive	Gold tag; olive hen-hackle fibers	None	Olive seal's-fur	Blae	Olive hen
Malloch's Favourite	10 to 14	Brown	Silver tag; gray-partridge fibers	None	Stripped quill	Wood cock	Blue dun hen
White-Hackled Invicta	10 to 14	Brown	Golden-pheasant crest feather	Gold wire	Yellow seal's-fur	Hen pheasant	Red brown cock
Burleigh	10 to 14	Brown	Ginger hen-hackle fibers	Gold wire	Waxed yellow floss silk	Blae	Ginger hen
Yellow Owl	10 to 16	Black	Hen pheasant	Black floss silk	Yellow floss silk	Hen pheasant	Brown partridge

SEE PAGES
154-5

Flies Around the World
Ireland

Fly Name	Hook	Silk	Tail	Rib	Body	Wing	Hackle
Gosling (Sam Anderson)	8 to 12	Yellow	Cock-pheasant tail fibers	Gold wire	Golden olive or yellow seal's-fur	None	Orange cock
Green Peter	8 to 12	Olive	None	Fine oval gold tinsel	Pea-green rabbit's-fur	Hen pheasant	Olive hen
Olive Bumble	10 to 12	Yellow	Golden-pheasant tail fibers	Gold Lurex	Golden olive seal's-fur	None	Olive cock
Mayfly Nymph	10 to 12	Olive	Cock-pheasant tail fibers	Silver wire	Flat silver tinsel	None	Light brown cock
Bibio	10 to 14	Black	None	Fine flat silver tinsel	Black seal's-fur	None	Black cock
Claret Bumble	10 to 12	Claret	Golden-pheasant tippet fibers	Oval gold tinsel	Claret seal's-fur	None	Claret and black cock
Murrough	10 to 12	Black	None	Fine gold wire	Claret seal's-fur	White-tipped turkey tail	Brown cock
Melvin Bumbling Bibio	8 to 14	None	None	Fine silver oval	Silver Mylar; red and black seal's-fur	None	Black cock and hen
Connemara & Black	6 to 12	Black	Golden-pheasant tippets	Fine silver wire	Black seal's-fur	Bronze mallard	Black cock; blue jay throat
Melvin Olive	8 to 12	Black	Golden-pheasant tippets	Oval gold	Olive seal's-fur	Gray duck	Golden olive cock
Balinderry Olive	6 to 12	Brown	Golden-pheasant tippets	Flat gold closely ribbed	Golden olive seal's-fur	Red swan; mallard	Ginger or honey badger
Fiery Brown	8 to 12	Brown	Red game cock	Oval gold tinsel	Fiery brown seal's-fur	Bronze mallard	Red game cock
Kingsmill	8 to 12	Brown	Golden-pheasant crest feather	Silver wire	Green fluorescent floss; ostrich herl	Swan tail	Black hen
Irish Mallard & Claret	6 to 12	Claret	Golden-pheasant tippets	Oval gold	Claret seal's-fur	Wood duck	Claret
Sooty Olive	10 to 12	Olive	Golden-pheasant tippets	Oval gold	Dark olive seal's-fur	Bronze mallard	Dark olive
Melvin or Rogan's Extractor	8 to 10	Brown	Red golden-pheasant fibers	Gold wire	Flat gold tinsel	Speckled mallard	Lemon yellow cock
Hare's Ear	10 to 12	Brown	Hare's-mask guard fibers	Oval gold tinsel	Hare's-mask fur	Gray mallard	As for tail

Fly Name	Hook	Silk	Tail	Rib	Body	Wing	Hackle
White Marabou Muddler	4 to 8	Black	Red cock and twinkle	None	Flat silver tinsel with brown deer-hair spun and clipped for the head	White marabou plume	None
Royal Coachman	8 to 14	Black	GP tippets	None	Bronze peacock herl with red floss silk center	White goose	Natural red cock or hen
Grey Ghost	4 to 10	Black	None	Flat silver tinsel	Orange floss silk	Gray cock hackles; white buck tail	White buck tail
Thunder Creek	6 to 12	White	*See* wing	None	Embossed silver tinsel	Brown buck tail	None
Royal Coachman Trude	10 to 18	Black	GP tippets	None	Peacock herl divided by a band of red floss silk	White calf tail	Brown cock
Zonker Sculpin	2 to 6	Black	Strands of pearl Flashabou	Gold wire	Weighted underbody of black seal's-fur or substitute	Black rabbit zonker strip	None
Dave's Chamois Leech	Low-water salmon 2 to 10	Olive	Oval olive strip of chamois	None	Olive Haretron; olive chamois	None	Long-fibered partridge
Dark Hendrickson	10 to 16	Black	Wood duck	None	Muskrat dubbing fur	Wood-duck feather fibers	Medium bronze dun
Light Cahill	10 to 18	Yellow	Wood duck	None	Cream fur dubbed	Wood-duck feather fibers	Light ginger hen
Filoplume Mayfly Emerger	WG 14 to 16	Black	Wood duck	None	Rabbit underfur and gray fox squirrel body fur	Gray pheasant	Brown partridge hackle
Cut-Wing Dun	12 to 16	Black	Cock-hackle fiber	None	Olive hare's-fur or Antron	None	Blue dun
Carey Special	4 to 12	Black	Ringneck pheasant breast fibers	Fine flat silver tinsel	Brown chenille	None	Ringneck pheasant
Brooks' Stonefly	2 to 8 4 x L	Black	Crow quill fiber	Copper wire	Black seal's-fur or substitute	None	Grizzle over ostrich
Polywing Spinner	14 to 16	Black	Magic spinner tails widely spaced	None	Rusty poly dubbing	Pale gray or white poly yarn	None
Muskrat-Wiggle Nymph	Rear 12 to 16 ring eye. Front down-eye 12 to 18	Gray	Wood duck	Copper or gold wire	Muskrat dubbing body fur	Mallard-wing quill	Wood duck
Quill Gordon	14 to 18	Primrose	Blue dun	None	Peacock-eye quill	Wood-duck feather fibers	Blue dun cock
Foam Ant	10 to 14	Black	None	None	Black Ethafoam cut to shape	None	Black hen

KNOTS

1 NEEDLE KNOT For joining backing (mono) and leader butt sections

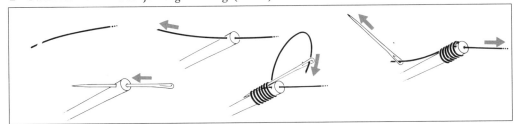

2 COVE, WATER OR SURGEON'S KNOT For joining together two sections of nylon

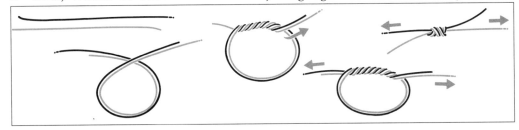

3 DOUBLE GRINNER KNOT For joining together two sections of nylon

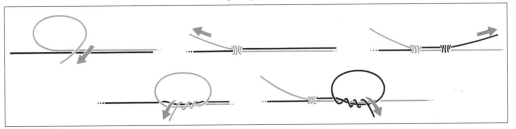

4 TURLE KNOT For joining fly to tippet

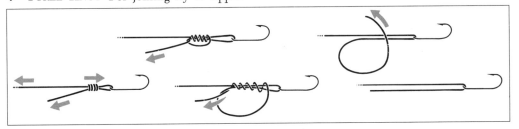

5 GRINNER KNOT For joining fly to tippet and/or leader

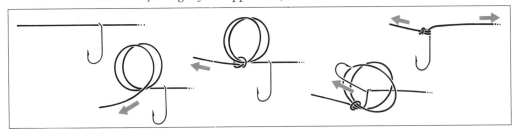

GAZETTEER

ADDRESSES

This is a personal selection of fly-fishing locations worldwide.

ENGLAND

Rivers:
River Avon, Wiltshire
River Eden, Cumbria
River Itchen, Hampshire
River Test, Hampshire
River Wharfe, West Yorkshire
River Wye, Derbyshire

Reservoirs/Lakes:
Avington, Hampshire
Chew and Blagdon, Avon
Dever Springs, Hampshire
Grafham Water, Cambridgeshire
Rockbourne, Hampshire/Wiltshire
Rutland Water, Leicestershire

WALES.

Rivers:
Llyn Brenig, Clwyd
River Conway, Gwywedd
River Dee, Clwyd
River Mownow, Hereford/Gwent
River Vrynway, Powys
River Usk, Gwent/Powys

SCOTLAND

Rivers:
River Don, Aberdeenshire
River Tweed, Borders

Lochs:
Loch Assynt, Sundertherland
Loch Harray & Swaney, Orkney
Loch Levan, Kinross
Loch St. John's, Caithness

IRELAND

Loughs:
Lough Carra, Co. Mayo
Lough Melvin, Co. Leitrim
Lough Corrib, Co. Galway

Lough Derg, Co. Clare
Lough Arrow, Co. Sligo
Lough Sheelin, Co. Cavan

AUSTRIA

River Erlauf, Bavaria
River Lammer, Salzburg
River Traun, Gmunden River
Salza, Salzburg

GERMANY

River Berbach, Black Forest
River Isar, Bavaria
River Kinzig, Black Forest
River Traun, Bavaria
River Wiesont, Bavaria
River Wolf, Black Forest

FRANCE

The Cure, Avallon
River Lot, Lozere
Gave d'Osseau, Pyrenees
Gave d'Oloran, above Pont-de-Dognen, Western Pyrenees

ITALY

Bolzano District
Dolomite Region
Trentino District

SPAIN

Rio Durro (upper) Area
Rio Ebro Area
Rio Narcea Area
Rio Navia (upper) Area
Rio Segura Area
Rio Sil (upper) Area

FINLAND

River Tenojoki, Finnish Borders
Kuusamo Region
Hossa and Kylmaluoma Region
Prurajarvi Fishery Area
Saarharvi Region

NORWAY

River Andselven, Voss
River Kistefoss, Voss
River Voss, Voss
River Vosso & tributaries
Lakes Drammen, Vikersund
Lake Mjosa & Gjovik

YUGOSLAVIA

River Soca, Bovec
Focamea, Drina Area
Konjic, Neretva Area
Licko Lesce, Gacha Area
Urosevac/Brezdvica Area

AUSTRALIA

Lake Eucumbene, NSW
Little Pine Lagoon, Tasmania
Lake Peddar, Tasmania
Yarra River, Victoria

NEW ZEALAND

Motu River, North Island
Ruakituri, North Island
Rotarua Area, North Island
Matuura, South Island
Ben Avon Lagoons, South Island
Waitaki River, South Island

CANADA

Bow River, Calgary, Alberta
Kamloops District, Brit. Columbia
Blackwater River, Brit. Columbia
God's River, Manitoba
Throughout Newfoundland & Labrador.

USA

Frying Pan River, Colorado
Rivers Beaverkill and Catskills, New York State
Yellowstone Park, Montana
Hat Creek, California
Silver Creek, Idaho
Lake Ausable, Michigan

ALASKA

Allagwak, Kenai Peninsur
Kenai River, Skilak Lake
Talarik Creek, Iliamna
Naknek River, Sitka
Port Banks, Eva Creek, Sitka

The following is a list of addresses for suppliers and useful fly-fishing associations:

American Rivers, 801 Pennsylvania Avenue SE, Suite 303, Washington D. C. 20003, USA

Association of Professional Game Angling Instructors (Donald Downs, Secretary), The Mead, Hosey, Westerham, Kent, TN16 1TA, England

Bob Church, 16, Lorne Road, Northampton, NW1 3RN, Eng.

Farlows of Pall Mall, 5, Pall Mall, London, SW1, England

Federation of Fly-fishers, 1088 West Yellowstone, Montana, 59758, USA

Fly Dressers' Guild, E. A. Walling, 29 Windmill Hill, Ruislip, Middlesex, HA4 8PY, England

House of Hardy Ltd., 61, Pall Mall, London, SW1 5JA, England

Lureflash, 10, Adwick Road, Mexborough, South Yorkshire, S64 0BZ, England

The National Federation of Anglers, Haig House, 87 Green Lane, Derby, England

The Orvis Co. Inc., The Mill, Nether Wallop, Stockbridge, Hampshire SO20 8ES, England

The Orvis Co. Inc., Historic Route 7A, Manchester, Vermont, USA

Salmon and Trout Association Fishmongers Hall, London, EC4R 9EL, England

Trout Unlimited, 501 Church Street NE Vienna, Virginia 22180

GLOSSARY

Acid/alkaline water The acidity or alkalinity of water is measured on a scale from 0 to 14 known as the pH scale. The pH value of pure water is 7. Values below this figure indicate progressively greater acidity, and those above it indicate progressively greater alkalinity. The best trout water is alkaline; acid water is less favorable, since it reduces the quantity of organisms on which trout feed.

Action The way in which a rod is designed to perform, particularly during casting. A tip-action rod is most flexible near the tip, while a through-action rod is flexible from the middle to the handle. Medium-action rods are considered middle to tip.

AFTM The Association of Fishing Tackle Manufacturers. The AFTM scale assigns a weight rating to fly-lines, enabling them to be matched to the rod. In the US the same scale is sometimes referred to as the AFTMA (American Fishing Tackle Manufacturers Association) scale.

Attractor An artificial fly designed to provoke a fish to take through aggression rather than to imitate a natural insect.

Backing line Nylon monofilament, braided Dacron or similar 6.8-9kg. (15-20lb.) b.s. which bulks out a fly reel spool, under the fly-line, and prevents line twists and tight coils. Backing is also advantageous when a large fish is hooked and makes a long run, tailing out the entire fly-line.

Bag limit The maximum number or weight of fish permitted by the regulations governing a water.

Bob fly The uppermost fly in a team of wet flies. Its position causes it to bob or dance on the surface. Also known as the top dropper.

Boobying Fishing a buoyant fly on a short leader and Hi-D extra fast-sinking line, then "inching" it along the bottom. A stillwater tactic.

Breaking strain The manufacturer's estimate of the strength of a line when it is dry. A line is weaker when wet or knotted.

Butt This term can refer to the bottom section of a rod where the line rating and manufacturer's name is shown; or to the thick part of a leader, the first section having been joined to the fly-line. This normally consists of 9-10 kg. (18-20 lb.) b.s. mono, but can be braided mono section.

Chalk stream A stream or river rising from a spring in chalk hills. The water, which is clear and rich in life forms, usually including trout, runs steadily and at a consistent level since it is only slightly affected by rainfall.

Check A ratchet or other system in a reel, used to vary the line's resistance to being pulled off by a running fish.

Colored water Water, particularly in a river or stream, agitated by rain to the extent that bottom material is stirred up, clouding it.

Compara dun An imitation dry fly devised by Al Caucci and Bob Nastasi. It relies on a fan-shaped hair wing for flotation and incorporates a dubbed body using primary colors.

Dapping A technique in which the wind is used to billow the line out in front of the angler, causing the fly to bounce lightly over the water.

Dead drift Method of fishing the fly in which the current alone is used to carry it along without any additional movement being imparted to it by the angler. Used in both dry- and wet-fly fishing tactics.

Deceiver An artificial fly tied as a near copy of a particular insect species.

Disturbance pattern A dry or wet fly which attracts fish by disturbing the water surface during a retrieve or swinging movement across the current.

Dog days A period during the season when trout succumb to spiraling water temperatures and seek cooler depths, becoming torpid and uninterested in feeding. Fishing deep and slow is usually the only way to succeed in such periods.

Double-taper A fly-line that tapers from the middle to both ends and can therefore be reversed when the fishing end begins to show signs of wear.

Drag A V-shaped ripple caused by a dry fly that moves unnaturally across the surface of the water rather than drifting with the current. Trout are usually discouraged from taking by this form of presentation.

Drift fishing Method of boat fishing in which the boat is allowed to drift with the wind. See Loch-style.

Drogue This acts as an underwater parachute, slowing down the boat when necessary. Used when loch-fishing, it is held by a cord and fixed amidships.

Drop-off fishing A sudden change of depth on a stillwater, ie. an expanse of 1m. (3ft.) deep shallows which abruptly descends to 3-4m. (10-15ft.). During early season this is an ideal spot for fishing.

Dropper A short length of line carrying a wet fly and joined to the leader between the end, or point, fly and the fly-line. Some leaders are made with droppers attached, but the latter may be tied to a plain leader by means of a blood knot. One, two, or three droppers may be used.

Dry fly An artificial fly designed to be fished on the surface of the water.

Dubbing Binding fur (seal's-fur substitute, animal body, manmade silk, Antron) to the tying silk before winding around to form an artificial fly body.

Dun Sub-imago or imperfect fly of an ephemerid (mayfly) family that has just hatched on the water surface from the nymphal stage. The name refers to its drab color scheme in both wings and body.

Eclosion Insect emergence from a pupa case or of larva from an egg.

Eddy Water less turbulent than the surrounding water, at the current's edge or where two streams meet.

Emerger pattern An artifical dry fly that imitates a hatching insect.

Entry The way an artificial fly alights on or passes through the water.

False cast Casting technique in which more line can be extended with each forward cast without touching the water until the fish can be reached.

Figure-of-eighting A method of imparting a steady, provocative movement to the fly on the retrieve by winding bunches of line into the palm of the line hand.

Fishing the rise Technique in which casts are made to spots where a fish rises to feed at the surface.

Flash An artificial fly's tinsel body or Flashabou wing-strip that attracts trout. Also the reflection and fish-scaring properties of a highly varnished rod or the surface of certain glossy fly-lines and leaders.

Floating line A fly-line lighter than water that floats on the surface. It is used to present a dry fly or a sub-surface pattern.

Float tube An inflatable boat used for fishing on lakes and rivers.

Flotant A substance, usually grease or silicone, used to make dry flies, lines, and leaders float better.

Forward taper A fly-line in which weight is concentrated in the forward section. Also known as a weight-forward or torpedo-head line.

Foul-hook To hook a fish anywhere but in the mouth.

Freestone river A river which tends to some acidity and contains a stony/rocky river bed with few weeds. Generally found in mountain/hilly areas, they rely on precipitation to form the sometimes considerable flows.

Gape The distance between the point of a hook and the shank.

Ghillie A British term for a companion or keeper on a river system who knows the water intimately and instructs on how to achieve best results. Familiar throughout Scotland, especially on salmon rivers.

Guide Similar to a ghillie, though the name tends to be associated with trout and steelhead fishing. A guide's advice on unknown waters is invaluable on unfamiliar territory.

Hackle A long, pointed cock or hen feather bound around the shank of a fly-hook to represent the legs and thorax of a natural insect. Cock feathers are used in dry flies since their stiff tips assist floatation. Hen feathers are softer and so are used to create the hackle in wet flies.

Hackle pliers Pliers that hold the hackle securely by the tip in fly-tying.

Hackle points The stiff hackles made from cock feathers and used to represent the wings of a natural insect.

Hatch The simultaneous surfacing of a large number of flies of the same species. To "match the hatch" is to imitate the hatching species as closely as possible at each stage.

Hauling Technique used in casting in which the line is accelerated during the forward and backward casts by being pulled hard by the line hand.

Head-and-tail rise A rise by a trout to a nearly mature or mature fly in or just under the water's surface.

Humping The action by which a surface-feeding trout's dorsal fin and back disturb the surface of the water. The "bulge" produced in this way suggests a nymphing trout.

Ice-off The time when rivers flow again, having been covered by snow and ice.

Imago A mature upwing fly. Also known as a spinner or perfect fly.

Imitator An artificial fly tied to imitate a natural food form.

Induced take The slow raising of the rod to bring an artificial fly toward the surface.

Jigging A technique in which a weighted fly is repeatedly allowed to sink below the rod tip and then raised in front of a trout, inducing it to take.

Landing Bringing a trout into a net or the hand after playing.

Larva The subaquatic form of some insect species.

Leader A length of nylon that can either be tapered mechanically,

stepped down in sections using various diameters, or on straight nylon length, which forms the junction between fly-line and fly. It creates less disturbance than the bulky fly-line, so delicate presentation can be made. By lengthening a leader, when using floating line, greater water depths can be overcome.

Level line A fly-line that is of the same diameter throughout its length.

Lie The place that a trout occupies in the water system, ie. a resting lie – cover from predators; a feeding lie – little cover but a good supply of food forms; a prime lie – a place offering both good food and cover.

Loch-style Boat-fishing technique for lochs and large stillwaters. The boat is taken upwind and then, starting from a position broadside-on to it, allowed to drift downwind while (usually) two anglers fish teams of wet flies by casting short distances downwind of the boat. In strong winds a drogue can slow the movement.

Long lining A method of broadside drift fishing in a boat on large stillwaters – a phrase coined by Bristol fly-fishers who fish floating lines, long leaders, and nymph patterns to such deadly effect that the method has become used widely.

Lure A large wet fly designed to suggest the fry of various small fish species on which trout feed, or to attract trout by the boldness of its shape and/or color.

Marrow spoon A long spoon passed down a dead fish's gullet to remove the stomach contents for examination. A stomach pump works in a similar way but allows live trout to be returned unharmed.

Mend Casting a curve in the line without disturbing the fly or leader to enable a slower-drift, upstream mend or faster-drift downstream mend; or a downstream mend that is thrown when nymph fishing. When the floating loop of line straightens, a trout has taken and you should strike.

Mending the line Technique used to control the speed at which a fly fishes on a river. After the fly has alighted, additional line is flicked up

or downstream onto the water, preferably without jerking the fly. An upstream mend tends to produce slack line, so that the fly fishes more slowly; a downstream mend increases the speed of the fly.

Meniscus The slight concavity in the surface film of still water.

Nether-Avon style An alternative name for the Sawyer nymph method of fishing a weighted nymph upstream of a trout, sometimes used in conjunction with the induced take.

Northampton style Also known as "side-swiping" or "rudder-fishing." In this method of boat fishing the boat drifts sharp end down-the-wind (bow first) while the angler(s) cast at right angles to the craft, allowing the line to prescribe a wide arc, finishing back from the stern, where it is retrieved. Used with most lines, especially lead-core, on calm days floating or neutral densities with imitative patterns.

Nymph General term for an insect between the egg stage and hatching, when the insect lives underwater. Also describes patterns that imitate this stage and are fished below the surface.

Nymph and hang This recent diversion in loch-style fishing (broadside drifting) employs a team of two or three midge pupae, with or without an attractor pattern on the top dropper, on a Hi-D line. A slow retrieve imitates the ascending naturals and is good during dry bright weather and cold weather.

Odging A reservoir bank-fishing term which describes how, during flat calm conditions, an angler may cast out a longish length of floating line 20-30m. (20-30yd.), then walk along the bank manufacturing a large bow or bend in the line, then retrieve.

Oviposit To lay eggs upon, above, or below the water surface.

Palmered hackle A method of winding a cock hackle (usually) down a hook shank in open turns, then either "trapping it down" by reverse windings of tinsel, or leaving it in order to create a "buzz" of fibers.

Parachute fly A dry fly in which the hackle is tied so that the fly lies

parallel to the water's surface and appears natural when seen from below.

Playing Containing and subduing a fish sufficiently to land it safely.

Point Thin terminal section of a leader, often knotted to it and usually 30-45cm. (12-18in.) long, to which the fly is tied. Also known as a tippet.

Point fly The bottom fly in a team of flies. Also known as the tail fly.

Polaroiding An Australian expression which describes a style of fishing, usually in shallow water, when trout are stalked before being cast to.

Pool A wider, rounded area of the river that usually occurs just below narrow, fast runs. Since food from upstream gathers there, it is often a haunt of feeding fish and a place to rest from the current.

Priest A short, weighted club used to administer a sharp blow (the "last rites," hence the name) to the back of a fish's head, just behind the eyes.

Pupa The inactive stage of winged insect species development, occurring between the larval stage and maturity.

Put-and-take fishery A commercial trout fishery that is regularly stocked and otherwise managed in order to maintain a population and size of fish that will provide good sport.

Put down To frighten a feeding fish by making a noise, casting a shadow on the water or other means.

Rainfed rivers Also refers to "spate" rivers. See Freestone.

Reach mend A casting term that involves moving the rod briskly to the right or left while it is traveling forward through the air, creating a bend or bow.

Resting a fish Temporarily ignoring a fish that has been put down until it regains its confidence and resumes feeding.

Retrieve Fishing a dry fly, nymph, or lure back to the angler so that it can be "picked off" the water and recast. When a dry or sub-surface fly is used, the line is retrieved either by being pulled by the forefinger and thumb of the line hand through a gap formed by the rod-hand's forefinger resting on the rod handle, or by figure-of-eighting. Nymphs and lures are retrieved by pulls of variable speed with pauses of variable duration.

Reversed wings Artificial wings tied to lie forward of the head, pointing away from the hook – Mole fly and Wulff series.

Riffle-hitch Popular with steelhead and salmon fly-fishers, this knot will make an artificial fly stick out at right angles from the leader and swim across the current.

Riffle fly A buoyant fly used in a riffle-hitch, it moves across the stream creating disturbance on the surface.

Rim control Pressure applied by the finger to the rim of the reel spool to regulate line as it runs out while playing a fish on the exposed edge of a fly-reel spool.

Ring The line passes through rod guides or rings. These take the form of snakes – hard chrome or tungsten, silicon carbides or single leg Puji (lined) P.T.F.E.

Rise Term used variously to describe the action of a single trout coming to the surface to take a fly or another insect; the ripples produced in this way; or a large insect hatch on which trout feed, particularly in the evening, hence the term "evening rise."

Rolled wings Wings in an artificial fly (generally sedge patterns) that are made from a roll of feather fiber obtained from a tail or wing.

Run A group of steelhead or sea trout fording a river to spawn; or the initial flight of the quarry.

Search pattern A general artificial which resembles a variety of naturals.

Shank The straight portion of a hook between the bend and the eye.

Shooting head A fly-line normally between 9m. (30ft.) and 12m. (40ft.) long, which is attached to a nylon running line, to effect long casts.

Shooting line A technique used to increase casting distance and to assist the smooth fall of the line and the fly on the water. Line is stripped from the reel in coils and held in the hand (or left on the water surface or ground) until it is released as the cast fly approaches the water.

Shooting taper See shooting head.

Short lining Traditional loch-style fishing. A team of three or four flies is repeatedly roll cast out over the water and teased back by the action of the long rod. Seldom is there more than 3-5m. (10-15ft.) of fly-line outside the rip ring.

Sink and draw Movement addressed to a fly (natural or artificial) when moving toward the water surface in a zigzag progression, interspersed with pauses.

Sinking line A fly-line designed through various high densities to sink at various speeds – low, medium, and fast. Some very fast sinking varieties are referred to as lead-core.

Sink-tip A floating fly-line in which the last 3m. (10ft.) or so is designed to sink so that a fly can be presented just below the surface.

Smutting A rise form or a trout feeding on tiny insects, generally during extremely hot days.

Spent wings Artificial fly wings made from hackle-feather (or polypropylene) points and tied horizontally at right angles to the body to imitate a spent (dead) fly.

Spider An artificial fly incorporating hackles that are long in relation to the hook, causing it to land very lightly on the water, or a wet fly of North of England origin.

Spinner A mature upwing fly, also known as an imago. The female is described as a spent spinner, since she lies inert on the water surface after egg laying. Used familiarly, this term refers to a flashing imitation bait.

Spinner fall A specific period, generally in the evening, when egg-laying females in large groups fall on to the water to oviposit and ultimately die (spent spinners).

Split wings Artificial wings tied in a V-shape, as in a natural insect, either upright or leaning backward or forward. Most commonly used when tying split wing-quills (mallard/teal primary and secondary).

Stalking Keeping out of sight of the quarry when river fishing, but also in small clear stillwater. Stalking embraces the ability to blend with the background without striking any discordant note on the river bank.

Stonefly Common name for the many species of large aquatic flies that form the *Plecoptae* family.

Straight plane movement Action of a fly or fly-line continually moving along on one plane.

Streamer fly An artificial wet fly or lure with long wings of hair or feather that extend beyond the bend of the hook. It suggests a prawn, shrimp, minnow fry, or other small fish.

Strip To pull line from the reel in coils in preparation for casting or to pull the line smartly back on the retrieve with attractor patterns.

Strip and hang An alternative to "nymph and hang." Rather than employing an imitative system, a "traffic-light" set-up is used (orange lure, black lure, yellow/white etc. Sl0 std – 14 std.) then retrieved on Hi-D (extra fast) being allowed to sink then long quick pulls – a pause (the "hang") – then repeating until the fly line nears the surface where another hang is affected.

Strip back Rapid retrieval of a streamer or lure when fished on stillwater, getting the line back at the angler's feet in order to re-cast.

Sub-imago See Dun.

Tail fly The bottom fly in a team of flies. Also known as the point fly.

Tandem lure A lure with two hooks facing in the same direction joined together by monofilaments to create an extra-long pattern.

Target fishing A method of spotting, stalking, and casting to individual fish, selecting one specimen rather than another.

Team of flies Two, three, or four wet flies attached to the same leader by short lengths of nylon mono-filament known as droppers. The bottom fly is known as the point or tail fly, the middle fly (in a team of three) as the middle dropper, and the top fly, which bounces on the surface, as the bob fly or top dropper.

Through action The action of a rod that responds to the strain of a fish or strain of casting by bending gradually from the tip down to the handle. Also known as progressive action.

Tip action The action of a rod that responds to the strain of a fish or strain of casting by bending only in the tip section.

Tippet The thin terminal section of a leader, often knotted to it and usually about 30-45cm. (12-18in.) long, to which the fly is tied. Also known as a point.

Trolling Trailing a large wet fly or lure on a sinking line behind a moving boat. No retrieve is made, and the speed of the boat dictates the speed of the fly. A technique often used to cover a large area of water when no contact has been made with fish by more conventional methods. This practice is outlawed in most waters except large lochs and lakes.

Turn over Action of the leader and fly prior to landing on water.

Upright wings Wings in an artificial fly that are tied so that their points are separated.

Wake fly A dry fly that creates a disturbance when it is pulled across or through the water's surface.

Weight-forward A fly-line in which weight is concentrated in the forward section. Also known as a forward-taper.

Wet fly An artificial fly designed to be fished below the surface. Sometimes referred to as a sunken fly.

Whipping Method of binding a hackle to a hook's shank with repeated turns of silk or fine wire.

Window Trout's area of vision as it looks upward to the water's surface.

INDEX

A

Adams 120, 232, 260
  Loop-Wing Adams 120, 260
  nymph version (Adams Flashback) 131, 264
  parachute version (Gulper Adams) 120, 233, 260
Adams Irresistible 128, 263
Adams Midge 123, 261
Admiral 85, 244
Adult chaser (*Libellula* sp.) 45
Aelianus, Claudius 10, 13
AFTM rating 51, 53, 66
Agile darter (mayfly nymph) 38
Alaska Alexander 85, 244
Alder 128, 263
Alder Larva 105, 253
  natural form 47
Alevin 28
Alpine trout 31
Alwen (River) 149
Amadou 69
Amber Longhorn Pupa (Emergent) 130, 264
Amber Nymph 88, 245
America *see* North America; United States
American Black Gnat 112, 256
Anatomy, of trout 20-1
Anchoring 208-9
Angler's Curse 123, 261
Annabelle 102, 252
Anthripsodes (caddis fly) 41
Antique artificial flies 10, 78
  chalk/limestone rivers 110-11
  freestone streams 126-7
  reservoirs 86-7
Antique equipment 10-15, 60
Antron 94, 241
Antron Dry Emerger 143, 270
Ants 48
  artificial fly pattern 124, 125, 262
Antunez, Luis 145
Appetizer 89, 100
  fly dressing 245, 251
Arctic char (*Salvelinus alpinus*) 36
Arctic grayling (*Thymallus arcticus*) 37, 220
Asellus (hoglouse) 46
ATH Rio Orbigo (reel) 63
ATH Traun F1 (reel) 61
Attractors *see* Lures
August Brown 127
Australia
  fly patterns 140-1, 269
Austria, fly patterns 142-3, 270

B

BA Pretty 151, 274
Babine Special 85, 244
Baby Doll 89, 245
Badger Hackle 126, 137, 267
Baetis Nymph 143, 270
Baetis Spinner 123, 261
Baetis spinners (mayflies) 39, 180
Baikal (Lake) 147
Bait-fish 48, 49
  artificial fly pattern 101
Balinderry Olive 155, 276
Balloon Caddis 142, 270
Bank-fishing (reservoir) 198-203

Barrie Welham Nymph 108, 255
Bartellini Spider 144, 271
Beacon Beige 120, 260
Bead-Eyed Montana 90, 246
Bear-Hair Bugger 82, 243
Beetles 48
  artificial fly pattern 124, 125, 262
  coch-y-bondhu 48
  great diving 46
Belgian Sculpin 134, 266
Bell, Dr. Howard 88, 89, 99
Belly-boating 204-5
Bewick's Booby 90, 246
Bewl Green 99, 250
Bibio 154, 276
Bitch Creek 139, 268
Black, Howard 114
Black Ant 124, 262
Black Beetle 124, 262
Black Bob 97, 249
Black Chenille 100, 251
Black Emerger 125, 262
Black Ghost 81, 242
Black Gnat 128, 263
Black gnats 42, 43
Black Ke-He 152, 275
Black Matuka 140, 269
Black Midge 125, 262
Black Pennell 153, 275
Black River 35
Black Spider 88, 124, 129
  antique fly 127
  fly dressing 245, 262, 263
Black Stone 139, 268
Black Zonker 135, 266
Black-&-Orange Marabou 89, 245
Black-&-Peacock Spider 88, 245
Blackie (Waddington) 150, 274
Blae & Black 86
Blagdon Reservoir 88, 97, 148
Bloodworm (midge larva) 42, 43
Bloody Butcher 151, 174
Bloody Doctor (Yorke's Favorite) 149, 273
Blue Damsel 105, 253
Blue Dun
  antique fly 127
  Paraleptophlebia Nymph 147, 272
Blue Quill (Paraleptophlebia Nymph) 147, 272
Blue-Tag Red Palmer 153, 275
Blue-Winged Olive
  artificial flies 113, 116, 256
  natural insect 39
  Nymph fly dressing 258
Bluebottles 43
Boat fishing 197, 206-7
  anchoring 208-9
  rudder fishing 208-9
  versus bank fishing 196
  fluorescent 69
Bobbin-holder 226
Bob's Bits 96, 249
Bomber (Finland) 82, 243
Boots
  chest-high waders 73
  thigh waders 75
  wading 72, 204, 212
  wellington boots 73
Bottom-Scratcher 133, 265
Buoyancy waistcoat 73
Bow-Tie Buzzer 117, 258
Box Canyon Stone 133, 265
BP Buzzer 93, 247
Braided butt 67

Brass Multiplier 60
Brassy Pheasant Tail 108, 255
Bread Crust 132, 265
Breeding cycle of trout 25, 28
Bristol Emerger 95, 248
Bristol Hopper 96, 249
Broadoaks Creek, Pennsylvania, 137
Brobst, Hiram 137
Brook fly rod 13
Brook trout (*Salvelinus fontinalis*) 19, 32, 36
Brooks' Stonefly 157, 277
Brown Ant 125, 262
Brown Damsel 108
Brown Emerger 95, 248
Brown Midge 125, 262
Brown Miller 122, 261
Brown Nobbler 106, 254
Brown silverhorn (caddis fly) 41
Brown trout (*Salmo trutta*) 29-31
  diet versus rainbow trout 33
  European subspecies 31
  evolution/distribution 18, 19
  from the sea 31
  in rivers and lakes 30
  varieties 30
Brown Wool 108
Bullhead 49
Burlap 80, 242
Burleigh 153, 275
Bustard & Orange 87
Butcher Nymph 92, 247
Butterflies, artificial fly pattern 125
Buzzer 89, 245
BW Nymph 108, 255

C

Caddis flies 40-1
Caenis Fallen Spinner 123, 261
Cahill, Don 113, 157
Cahill 129, 137
Canada
  brook trout 36
  brown trout 29
  lake trout 36
Cane rods 14, 53
Caperer (caddis fly) 41
  Carey Special 157, 277
Carnhill, Bob
  Carnhill Adult Buzzer 95, 119
    fly dressing 248, 259
  Carnhill Nobbler 98, 250
  Carnhill Poly-Rib Buzzer 93, 247
Casting 7, 159-69
  false casting 159, 164-5
  keeping a low profile 182, 192
  long cast 199
  overhead cast 159, 160-1
  parachute cast 178-9
  precise delivery 216
  roll cast 159, 168-9
  Sawyer nymphing method 184-5
  shooting line 159, 162-3
  single and double haul 159, 166-7
  slack-line (parachute) cast 178-9
  switch cast 177, 220
  tuck cast 212
Casual Dress 133, 265
Catch-and-Release conservation policy 26, 27, 223
  grayling 220, 221
  rainbow trout 174, 212, 220
  steelhead 219

when float-tubing 205
  wild brown trout 216
Caterpillar (artificial fly) 139, 268
Caterpillars 48
Cat's Whisker 98, 250
Chalk streams 171, 180
  artificial flies 110-25, 256-62
  dry flies 190-1, 216
  fishing tactics 180-91
  brown trout 216-17
Chaoborus species (phantom pupa) 42
Chars (*Salvelinus* sp.) 19, 32, 36
Chest pack 70
Chew Reservoir 96, 148
Chile
  brook trout 36
  brown trout 29
  rainbow trout 32
China, history of angling 9
Chironomid Pupa 95, 143
  fly dressing 248, 270
Chironomids 42, 43
Cholmondley-Pennell 153
Chomper (Series) 89, 245
  Appetizer 89, 245
  Black Chenille 100, 251
  Brown Emerger 95, 248
  fishing rods 56, 58
  Goldie 100, 251
  Jack Frost 101, 251
  Mini Appetizer 103, 252
Clan Chief 152, 275
Claret Bumble 154, 276
Clarke, Brian 88, 120
Clothing 7, 72-5, 194
  camouflage 182-3, 222
  life-jacket 197, 204
  see also Footwear
Coachman 129, 137
  fly dressing 263, 267
Coat, Goretex 74
  see also Jackets
Cocchetto Nymph 144, 271
Coch-Y-Bondhu 128, 149
  fly dressing 263, 273
  natural beetle 48
Cock Robin 87
Cockwill's Hare's-Ear Shrimp 107, 254
  fishing rod 56
Collyer Deer-Hair Midge Pupa 119, 259
Collyer's Brown Nymph 89, 245
Colorado cutthroat 34
Colorado Gold Muddlerbou 134, 266
Color sensitivity of trout 22
Coloration of trout 20, 21
  brook trout 36
  brown trout 29, 30
  cutthroat 34
  grayling 37
  rainbow trout 32
Competition marinas 214-15
Concrete Bowl 98, 250
Connemara & Black 155, 276
Conservation 7, 26-7, 217
  artificial fly dressings and 241
  see also Catch-and-Release
Conway Red 148, 273
Conway (River) 148
Copper Nymph 131, 264
Coregonididae (Whitefish) 18, 19

Corixa 91, 246
Corixae (water boatmen) 47
Corsica 31
  Green Drake 111
  Grey Drake 110
Cove, Arthur
  Black Spider 88
  Cove's Pheasant Tail 89, 245
  Cove's Sedge Pupa 93, 247
  Red Diddy/Rubber-Band Fly 108, 255
Cove knot 278
Cranefly 42, 43
  artificial fly patterns 96, 138
Cream Crawler 133, 265
Cream Suspender 118, 259
Creel, antique 10
Creeper (stonefly) 44
Crickets 48
Crowe Beetle 125, 262
Cul-de-Canard oil 69
Cut-Wing Dun 157, 277
Cutter 68
  tweezers/cutter 69
Cutthroat trout (*Oncorhynchus clarki*) 18-19, 34-5
  coastal 35

D

Daddy-Longlegs 96, 138, 249
  fly dressing 268
Daddy-longlegs 42, 43
Dai Ben 149, 273
Daiwl Bach 148, 273
Damerham Reservoir 108
Damp Crane-Fly 107, 254
Damsel nymphs 45
Damselflies 44-5
Danube basin 18, 19
Daphnia (water flea) 46
Dark Caddis 142, 270
Dark Cahill 113
Dark Hendrickson 156, 277
Datchet Razzler 98, 250
Dave's Chamois Leech 156, 277
Dave's Hopper 138, 267
Dave's Stonefly Nymph 133, 265
Davies, David Benjamin Glynn 149
De Animalium Natura (Aelianus) 10
Deane, Peter 115, 120, 122
Dee (River) 149
Deep Olive Pupa 130, 264
Deep Pupa 91, 246
Deer-Hair Emerger 92, 142
  fly dressing 248, 270
Deer-Hair Hatching Buzzer 95, 248
Deer-Hair Midge 93, 247
Degreasing agent 68
  Orvis Mud 69
Dennis, Jack 128, 139
Denver Springs (Hampshire) 107
Depositing Caddis 122, 261
Derg (Lough) 30
Diawl Bach 92, 247
Diptera 42-3
Dispenser (tippet) 69
Ditch Dun (Paraleptophlebia Nymph) 147, 272
Dobson fly 47
Dog's Body 148, 273
Dolly Varden 36
Doobry 152, 275
Dormouse Nymph, the 144, 271

ACKNOWLEDGMENTS

I am aware that the cover of a book does not reflect the industry and *esprit de corps* of those who compile the contents. They are the unsung heroes without whom no book, especially this one, would have been possible. I cannot express my thanks enough.

The History Alan Clout and his collection of antique tackle.
The Quarry Jon Beer, who helped immeasurably, and the fishery managements that allowed Peter Gathercole and myself full reign.
Equipment Hardy Bros. of Pall Mall, in particular John Gibson; The Orvis Co. Inc., in particular John Russell and Richard Banbury for putting up with quaint requests at short notice; Sage Rods, in particular Partridge and Alan Bramley for their assistance; Barry Welham of Leeda Tackle and Air Cel and Wet Cel and Philip Parkinson of Airflo Lines, for their generous support; Paul Vekemans, Belgian reel manufacturer *extraordinaire*.
The Fly Barry Unwin of Fulling Mill Flies, for help far beyond reason; Stan Headley for the Scottish patterns; Juha Pusa, Veli Autti and all others who helped with Finland; Tony Deacon, who researched and tied the antique flies; John Hatherell for his painstaking research.
Waters and Tactics Roger Thom of Rutland, England; Chris Klee and staff at Chew Valley; the staff of Bewl Water and Bewl Bridge on the Kentish Stour Benson and Hedges Fly Fishing Competition, in particular John Ketley; Brian Leadbetter, Angus Warhouse and all other folk who allowed Peter and I to disrupt normal routine and play about with cameras and fly rods.
The Catch Jim Teeny especially, steelheader *par excellence*, whose contributions have been invaluable. Also Roman Moser, fly-fisher of the Traun, who made Austria the high spot of the book; and Harold at the Wirt am Bach, Gumunden, who put up with the combined chaos of Jardine and Gathercole; and Peter Cockwill, trout-hunter supreme.

Particular thanks are due to my dear friend Peter Gathercole, whose expertise with the camera is astonishing. Also to Sandy Leventon who suggested the project and David Lamb who commissioned it; to Nick Harris and Carolyn King for their guidance; and, for their professional and uplifting support, Corinne Hall, Caroline Murray and Liza Bruml, all of whom worked tirelessly on the project.

Words are not enough to thank the patient typist of this work, my wife Carole, whose encouragement has made the black days better and the good ones excellent. And finally the trout, without which everything else would be superfluous anyway.

Dorling Kindersley would like to acknowledge the following contributors: Kevin Marks and Deborah Skinner for the illustrations; Karin Woodruff for the index; and Richard Dawes and Helen Douglas-Cooper for their editorial assistance.

PICTURE CREDITS